The Reverb series looks at the connections between music, artists and performers, musical cultures and places. It explores how our cultural and historical understanding of times and places may help us to appreciate a wide variety of music, and vice versa.

reverb-series.co.uk
Series editor: John Scanlan

*Already published*

The Beatles in Hamburg
Ian Inglis

Brazilian Jive: From Samba to Bossa and Rap
David Treece

Easy Riders, Rolling Stones: On the Road in America, from Delta Blues to '70s Rock
John Scanlan

Heroes: David Bowie and Berlin
Tobias Rüther

Jimi Hendrix: Soundscapes
Marie-Paule Macdonald

Neil Young: American Traveller
Martin Halliwell

Nick Drake: Dreaming England
Nathan Wiseman-Trowse

Remixology: Tracing the Dub Diaspora
Paul Sullivan

Tango: Sex and Rhythm of the City
Mike Gonzalez and Marianella Yanes

Van Halen: Exuberant California, Zen Rock'n'roll
John Scanlan

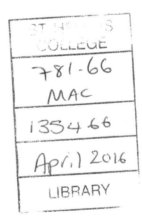

# JIMI HENDRIX

# SOUNDSCAPES

## MARIE-PAULE MACDONALD

REAKTION BOOKS

*To Thérèse Ruest Lévesque and M. C. Bernadette Macdonald*

Published by Reaktion Books Ltd
Unit 32, Waterside
44–48 Wharf Road
London N1 7UX, UK
www.reaktionbooks.co.uk

First published 2016

Printed and bound in Great Britain by Bell & Bain, Glasgow

A catalogue record for this book is available from the British Library

ISBN 978 1 78023 530 1

# CONTENTS

# INTRODUCTION: EXTRATERRESTRIAL BLUES

I want a big band . . . I mean a big band full of
competent musicians that I can conduct and write for. And
with the music we will paint pictures of earth and space,
so that the listener can be taken somewhere.

Jimi Hendrix, London, 5 September 1970[1]


If an alien were to come down to study the American, European
and African cities and landscapes that Hendrix frequented, what
kind of impression would they make? What roles do urban and
architectural locations play in musical experience, in collective
meaning? The Vancouver-based science fiction writer William
Gibson said: 'The future is already here – it's just not very
evenly distributed.'[2] Is the future embedded in sound and its
environments? That seems to be the case for the Hendrix sound,
which is so often described as a sound of the future.

Out of nowhere, and traversing boundaries, Hendrix was a
virtuoso guitarist who avidly refined his craft, and his influence
lives on in recordings, texts and imagery. There is consensus in
the collective perception that his legacy remains culturally fresh
and relevant. At first there was criticism that the mass reception
of his band's music was primarily by a targeted white youth
market, but in 2010 the *Pop Matters* journalist Mark Reynolds
stated: 'Hendrix has been claimed by the black mainstream as a
cultural innovator of the highest order.'[3] With recent reworkings
of disciplinary barriers, classical musicians, as well as blues, rock,
rap and folk artists, admire and draw inspiration from Hendrix's
sonic innovation and composition.

Just as there are many diverse audiences, so there are many
possible approaches to the work and legacy of Jimi Hendrix,

from biographical and historical to musicological or sociological, to this contemporary perspective, informed by current, shifting ideas about music, sound and media communication in our technological society. This approach reflects on the particular resonance of Hendrix and his influential performing and recording career in terms of soundscape, environment, landscape, place, geography and built form. It relates issues of location to perceptions of digitally produced placeless sound and the repercussions, in the Obama era, of an extended reception by a mass audience listening for innovative sound.

The notion of soundscape, which varies with place and climate, presents a frame for perceiving the aural textures that Hendrix heard, invented, composed, edited and incorporated into his guitar and recording vocabulary. In his formative years, Hendrix lived in Seattle and Vancouver. His acoustic environment was a moist soundscape whose keynote sound is the sound of wood, in the words of the composer R. Murray Schafer, who coined the term 'soundscape'. The forested ocean-side climate of the Pacific Northwest endures as a dampened, rained-on mountainous landscape, often with a horizon of heavy cloud, punctuated by a linear, continuous sound of running water. Humour about the rainforest often invokes Noah.

Along with the environment-based notion of soundscape, the conceptual framework for the history of the blues, no longer constrained by state lines, has overflowed into bioregions. Blues historians emphasize that the migration that defined the lives of blues musicians was more sympathetic to geography: lowlands; bottomlands; deltas or watersheds, like that of the vast Mississippi River; smaller towns; crossroads; migration hubs along rivers, railways or highways.[4] William Gibson's quip about the distribution of the future could launch a riff on the places of a particular time, in the manner of the literary theorist Mikhail

Bakhtin, whose notion of chronotope fused a cultural moment and its location.[5] The idea of long duration, or *longue durée*, in the terminology of the historian Fernand Braudel, marks a parallel approach to rooting events to specific locations.[6] In the case of Hendrix, the intensity of his migratory life introduced a new paradigm, a meteoric, moveable geography of sound.

Hendrix emerged from a specific coastal environment, and within that from a disparate set of homes. In his brief adult life he moved constantly, from many different houses in the early years in Seattle to many anonymous hotel rooms, then on to slightly more personal recording studios and several apartments on two continents. At the beginning of the twentieth century the German architect Paul Scheerbart wrote: 'We live for the most part within enclosed spaces. These form the environment from which our culture grows.'[7] Hendrix roamed city streets. When he did check into a lodging, he tended to stay inside the rooms, practising guitar riffs, recording and dreaming sounds. With the intense, sensual perception of a musical being, he digested his world of sound, that is, of corporeal vibrations bouncing off immediate surroundings, mingled with smells, humidity and illumination.

Hendrix's body of work has been expanding continuously, as its own particular universe. He was born at the very start of the Second World War baby boom and was part of a generation that gave rise to numerous youth movements and cultural phenomena. The influence of his generation has begun to fade even as his audience continues to grow. There is a continuing lively business aspect: the album *Valleys of Neptune* charted at number four in the United States in 2010, and that year Hendrix sold more than a million albums altogether.[8]

In search of places to play music, Hendrix began performing wherever he could, and as his notoriety grew he began to be booked in both conventional and unconventional venues. Part of the reason for this was the effect of the youth movement on culture and the explosive growth in rock music. As sales of records and tickets soared, promoters jumped into the game. Young entrepreneurs, moved by the new music, tried out new kinds of gathering, in open-air venues or in inexpensive, underused music halls, in dilapidated psychedelic ballrooms, in acoustically absorbent or reverberant spaces in any available building. The hippy movement was fascinated by innovative, ad hoc performance spaces. Hendrix himself developed discerning opinions on venues based on playing gigs in many kinds of performance circuit. He preferred to play tiny clubs or open-air venues, and he enjoyed relating to an audience that was moving and milling around in the ambience of the sound.

This book considers the environments, territories and landscapes Hendrix encountered, as well as investigating what Hendrix called '3D sound'. The three-dimensionality of sound relates to urban geography, urbanism and architecture, topography, ideas of place, bioregion and ordinary spaces. Noises, radio, dissonant and ambient sound, and specific conditions, such as the rush of air past the ears on a parachute jump, were all ingredients in Hendrix's musical soundscape.

'I had these dreams that something was gonna happen, seeing the numbers 1966 in my sleep, so I was just passing time till then.'[9] In 1966, the year when Hendrix broke through, or at least dreamed that he would break out of the underground into mass media, the Canadian media theorist and public speaker Marshall McLuhan made a series of remarks in a speech to publishers and writers at a lunch at the Shoreham Hotel in New York. In between jokes about miniskirts, he talked about the significance of sound – what he called echo-land – in the electric age:

> We live in an electric age . . . interval resonance . . . the bond . . . that holds the world together is sound, resonance.

> We live in echo-land now, in a simultaneous, instantaneous, all-at-once electric world that is echo-land, and that is auditory space, [which] has a very peculiar property. It is a perfect sphere whose centre is everywhere and whose margin is nowhere.[10]

These remarks relate to Schafer's discussion of aural awareness as spherical and centred, compared to the frontal nature of vision.[11] McLuhan's influence was far-reaching and pervasive. He judged the effect of television on popular culture to be inescapable, writing: 'It permeates nearly every home in the country, extending the central nervous system of every viewer.'[12] Privately he wrote to his son to suggest that he not allow his children to watch television, calling it 'vile'. Perhaps because of his six children, McLuhan observed and heard youthquake, counterculture and underground society coalesce through sounds (experimental and conventional) and through music and televisual media. He remarked: 'The young today live mythically and in depth.'[13] McLuhan, an analyst, kept his distance from short-lived pop phenomena, rather holding his finger on a pulse, the shared sound that was bringing the youthquake generation together. His echo-land, an abstract sonic space, paralleled the cosmic soundscapes of The Jimi Hendrix Experience.

Hendrix emerged as an innovator in the realm of sound, music, performance and recording, integrating ambiences and situations. A walking sound locator, a slender young man with large appendages, oversized ears, hands and fingers and weak eyesight, Hendrix lived with sound flowing through his mind, an inventive guitarist and manipulator of spatialized sound equipment. He came from an impoverished family, but in a prosperous city, so that his working-class community had the resources to help out informally and spontaneously. He frequented the ordinary districts of the inner city, on streets, on pavements, in back gardens and on porches, haunting basement dives and jukes.

Hendrix leapt from the regional to the international stage, and moved across cityscapes in an accelerating spiral of American and European tours. In intimate clubs he set off an interplay of loud sound with tight quarters, then he explored mass audiences in arenas and at festivals. In this book we track Hendrix geographically as he jumped sonic platforms, from local to regional, from west to south to east, and finally across oceans.

# 1 WEST: VANCOUVER, SEATTLE, MONTEREY, SAN FRANCISCO, LOS ANGELES

## THE PACIFIC NORTHWEST SOUNDSCAPE

The Pacific Northwest ecosystem is a coastal ecology dominated by pristine mountains and ocean, its surface a dense tapestry of rainforest. Seattle and Vancouver occupy adjacent positions in the bioregion that some romantics call Cascadia, and others Ecotopia. The cities correspond loosely in scale. Cities of the ocean and mountains, they are surrounded by water, islands, peninsulae, lakes and temperate rainforest, with the Pacific Ocean an immense space to the west. Both are western grid cities, laid out in rational rectangular blocks. Plain, traditional patterns of detached wooden houses characterize the urbanized hillside landscape beyond the masonry architecture of the downtown area. Both cities are former gold-rush towns and sit at the end of the road for migrants and nomads.

During the 1960s the Canadian composer, acoustic ecologist and music theorist R. Murray Schafer worked on an environmental sound-recording project with the Vancouver-based musicological research group the World Soundscapes Project. In 1968 he published an essay, 'The New Soundscape', in which he coined the term, and in 1977 he published *The Tuning of the World*, a manifesto connecting the perception of sound to landscape. The title was derived from the engraving *Utriusque cosmi historia* (History of the Two Worlds) of 1617 by the cosmologist and mathematician Robert Fludd, 'in which the earth forms the body of an instrument across which strings are stretched and are tuned by a divine hand'.[1] It could be seen in parallel to the artist Piero Manzoni's declarative sculpture *Base of the World* of 1961, which placed the planet on an upside-down pedestal.[2] The sonority of the landscape gained a specific status, one that would 'treat the world as a macrocosmic musical composition'.[3] Schafer discussed the primal, instinctive connection of hearing to the senses and consciousness, in comparison with the visual – for example, the lack of ear lids links to the unconscious. Hearing, he argued, was a primary means of auto-protection. He also discussed the connection of loud noise with power and authority.[4]

Schafer proposed terminology that introduced such ideas as keynote sound, archetypal sounds and soundmark (parallel to landmark). He defined soundscape as 'events *heard* not objects *seen*'.[5] One example is the sound of a train whistle in the landscape and its bending through the Doppler effect; the event is further differentiated by the fact that such a whistle is a single tone in the USA but a triad in Canada. The keynote sounds of a landscape are those created by its geography, fauna and climate: water, wind, forests, plains, birds, insects and animals.[6] Schafer defined signals as foreground sounds.[7] He proposed another term related to recording: schizophonia, or the removal of sound from its natural origin. He differentiated aggregate sound, such as that of a swarm, from the singular, and he used the visual analogy of figure and ground for sound relationships. His musicological analysis led to a career of composition and performance. His term 'soundscape', integrated into a contemporary musical sensibility, remains effective, especially in the context of contemporary ecological perspectives (such as biomimetics) and the work of contemporary composers such as the Pulitzer prize-winner John Luther Adams, whose work addresses place, landscape and the acoustics of situation.

Schafer experimented with ear-training exercises during musical workshops. He asked students to exchange notes while moving, to awaken an awareness of spatial sound. Volunteers would stand at diagonally opposite corners of the room, walk forward while singing a note and trade notes as they walked past one another. When he asked participants to hold a note, typically 'the tone produced by the majority of individuals is a B, the resonant frequency of electrical devices ranging from fluorescent lights to amplifiers to generators, operating on an alternating current of 60 Hz. In Europe, the same experiment yields a tone of G#, which approximates the resonant electrical frequency of 50 Hz used throughout the continent.'[8] This suggests that hearing internalizes the frequencies that are bound up in surrounding spaces. The registration of a certain frequency on bodily senses and habits underscores contemporary critiques of McLuhan's idea of media as bodily extension. For example, the philologist and media theorist Friedrich Kittler's critique proposed, rather than extensions, an influence of technological logic on human capacity and sensation, generating new hybrids.[9]

In Schafer's terminology of soundscape, the keynote sounds of the coastline would be those of the ocean, of rain falling and of forests and wood; of wooden things, from logs and branches to the lumber of wall and roof structures, to refined instruments made of wood. A soundmark trinity would be the aggregate sound of rain drumming on a wooden roof by the coast. Hendrix could achieve sound with liquid clarity and a fluid crystalline quality, echoed in his lyrical aquatic themes, such as walking under water, or his many allusions to weather, storm and sky. An early environmentalist, he referred to the ecology of the Pacific Northwest, from seasonal jellyfish and dragonflies to wind, thunder and weather noise, to ordinary dust.[10] Current discussions on forest networks, developed by writers such as Michael Pollan, report on debates among scientists over the extent to which forests communicate (by releasing certain chemicals in response to phenomena). The contemporary artist Ryuichi Sakamoto has made a sound work, *Forest Symphony* (2013–14), using sensors.[11]

The Pacific Northwest nurtures a coniferous rainforest with a tall forest canopy, the habitat of Sitka spruce, red cedar and Douglas hemlock, species that have no tolerance for pollution and need moisture, rain and a temperate climate. A key feature of this forest is silence. The British Columbian painter and writer Emily Carr (1871–1945), who captured a Western rootedness, wrote with great intensity about the acoustic and visual experience of the coastal wilderness: 'So still were the big woods where I sat, sound might not yet have been born.' The forest infiltrated her dreams:

> One night I had a dream of greenery. I never attacked the painting of foliage quite the same after that dream I think; growing green had become something different to me.[12]

Accompanied by a sister and Native American guide, Carr visited the Tlingit settlement of Sitka, Alaska, in 1907. She painted forests, trees, landscapes and totem poles, presenting the work of aboriginal culture to the West. Anthropologists also showed interest in West Coast native rituals of the Haida, Kwakiutl, Nootka, Tlingit and Coast Salish, in particular, the rite of *potlatch*, a collective redistribution and destruction of wealth and precious material goods. From the French sociologist Marcel Mauss' essay on 'The Gift', Georges Bataille derived an essay, 'The Notion of Expenditure', which identified excess and reckless, extravagant loss as an advanced cultural practice.[13]

Carr identified the importance of the aspect, direction and framing of landscape by simple buildings:

> In my dream I saw a wooded hillside, an ordinary slope such as one might see . . . in the roof peak of the apartment house . . . In its west-end wall the room had two large windows which appeared to be narrow because they were

so high, beginning at the floor and ending right at the point of the gable. These windows let in an extensive view, a view of housetops, trees, sea, purple mountains and sky.[14]

In counterpoint is an image conjured by Hendrix's cover, made in 1969 but not released until after his death, of the Ray Charles hit 'Lonely Avenue', written in 1956 by Jerome 'Doc' Pomus. The lyric depicts a sombre, bleak room with two windows, where the sun never shone, suggesting gloomy scenes of a clouded childhood.

## VANCOUVER: MIGRATING AMERICAN FAMILIES

Vaudeville figured in the Hendrix family history. Zenora Rose Hendrix, née Moore (1883–1984), was a dancer who performed with her sister Belle Lamar in an African American travelling vaudeville troupe, Lacy's Dixieland Band. With its six musicians and seventeen vaudeville actors and dancers, the band performed in a 'Great Dixieland Spectacle' at the Alaska Yukon Pacific Exposition in Seattle from 1 June to 16 October 1909.[15] Zenora's husband, Bertram Philander Ross Hendrix (1866–1934), was a stagehand. After the end of the Exposition, the troupe travelled between Portland and Seattle; by 1912 it had disbanded and the couple settled in Vancouver.

Zenora Moore, born in Georgia and raised in Tennessee, was the daughter of Fanny Moore, who was half Cherokee. In Vancouver Zenora and Ross Hendrix raised a family together until the death of Ross in 1934. Zenora Hendrix lived at 827 East Georgia Street, near Hogan's Alley. 'Nora' co-founded and remained involved with the African Methodist Episcopal Church. Her son James Allen Hendrix (1919–2002) was the youngest of four: there was also Leon, who died young, Patricia and Frank. James ('Al') was born with six fingers on each hand, and his mother tried tying a string around each extra finger to remove it.

As a young adult, Jimmy Hendrix visited his Grandmother Nora in Vancouver in late 1962, probably staying with her at East Georgia Street, and remained until early 1963. Vancouver had some 400,000 inhabitants in the early 1960s, with extensive suburbs; the population of the greater metropolitan area was 800,000. Grandmother Nora cooked in a restaurant known as Vie's Chicken and Steak House, at 207 Union Street, from 1950 until 1976.[16] Hendrix mentioned her in March 1969 in an *International Times* interview: 'She lives in a groovy apartment building. She has a television and a radio and stuff like that. She still has her long silver hair though.'[17] Nora attended a Jimi Hendrix Experience concert at the Vancouver Pacific Coliseum in 1968 and was subsequently interviewed, complaining about the loudness in a Northwest-Canadian accent similar to her grandson's. She said: 'I knew he had music in him . . . but I didn't know he had that much music in him.'[18]

Zenora Hendrix, Jimi Hendrix's grandmother, interviewed after the Jimi Hendrix Experience concert, Vancouver Pacific Coliseum, 7 September 1968.

Hendrix played Vancouver with the Experience on 7
September 1968. When a Canadian music journalist interviewed
the band members, Hendrix asked, with a quizzical expression,
whether there was still a 'Dawson Annex School'. He had begun
first grade there, in 1949.[19]

## SEATTLE: AN AMERICAN CITY NAMED AFTER ITS NATIVE LEADER

This looks like Brussels, all built on hills. Beautiful. But
no city I've ever seen is as pretty as Seattle, all that water
and mountains. I couldn't live there, but it was beautiful.

Jimi Hendrix, arriving by air in San Francisco[20]

Lucille Jeter Mitchell (1925–1958), Jimi Hendrix's mother, was born in
Seattle, the youngest of eight children of Preston Jeter and his wife,
Clarice. Preston, born in 1875 in Richmond, Virginia, had come to
Seattle from the small mining town of Roslyn in Washington state,
where he worked in the Roslyn mines. Clarice Lawson was born in
Little Rock Arkansas in 1894. She contracted tuberculosis when her
children were young, and for a time they lived with a foster family.

Al Hendrix moved to Seattle in 1940 and began a long struggle to
find skilled blue-collar work. He wrote of living on skid row when he
first arrived in the city: 'I used to tell him [Jimi], when I first come to
Seattle I used to sleep in boxcars and open fields, and one thing and
another. Eat my meals around skid row with the bowl of beans.'[21]

Lucille and Al met at Washington Hall on 14th Avenue in
November 1941, at a dance where Fats Waller was headlining. They
courted and, after learning Lucille was pregnant, married on 31
March 1942. Al Hendrix was drafted that same week. They partied
at the Rocking Chair Club the night before he shipped out. Private
Al Hendrix, stationed at Fort Rucker, Alabama, was denied furlough
when James Marshall Hendrix, first named Johnny Allen, was

born, on 27 November 1942 in Seattle King County Hospital, now
Harborview Medical Center, at 325 Ninth Avenue. Lucille's mother,
Clarice Jeter, was a family friend of Minnie Gautier and her daughter
Freddie Mae Gautier. They were all members of the same church
and Clarice did house-cleaning work for the Gautiers. Freddie Mae
described in interviews how her family took in the child while Lucille
was involved with a man named John Page. At one point the baby
was hospitalized with pneumonia. Clarice and Lucille's older sister
Delores Hall Hamm arranged through their Pentecostal church for
him to be taken in by the Champs, a family in Berkeley.

Al Hendrix returned to Seattle in September 1945, and the
following month he travelled by train to fetch the child from
Berkeley.[22] He changed his child's name from Johnny Allen to
James Marshall in 1946. Until the boy was eight years old he went
by the nickname Buster.

Seattle's Central District was an animated community spread
over several blocks along Jackson Street, anchored by the railway
station. The music historian Charles Cross described Seattle's black
community as having 'its own newspapers, restaurants, shops and . . .
entertainment district, centered on Jackson Street. There, nightclubs
and gambling dens featured nationally known jazz and blues acts.'[23]

The typical detached wooden houses of the district varied in
size from small bungalows to larger two- or three-storey houses,
often with front or back porches, grassed yards and gardens at the
back and side, and a tree canopy overall. The houses were close
enough together that people would get to know one another.
Seattleite Xenobia Bailey emphasized the cooperation among
residents, who often came from the Southwest and were ushered
into the Central District or Rainier View District to the south to
join existing black and Asian populations:

When Black folks were investigating the home buyer's
market, the white realtors mostly showed them homes in the

Central District . . . In the projects in Seattle you had a yard and a fence. In the neighborhood almost all the adults worked at the Boeing plant, the Bethlehem Steel Yards, the shipyards, the hospitals, or on the military bases . . . They didn't let Black folk work in the department store too much back then unless it was sweeping the floors.

Bailey described how basements turned into hubs for regular musical gatherings:

My family didn't own a piano . . . The Freeman family, who lived behind us, had one of the two pianos in the neighbourhood . . . John Freeman, Sr. used to leave the door unlocked so my sister and I could practice our music . . . musicians would rehearse in his basement and when they were finished they would leave all of their instruments set up.

In just about every household there was a musical instrument that was connected in some kind of way to a band. In the Freeman's basement he had this whole setup, this mirrored red leather bar with red leather bar stools and space for the musicians to set up with the piano on the side. It could almost be considered an after-hours joint. The guys would finish their gigs downtown or in other parts of the city and come down there and play until daybreak almost. I could hear them all night long from my bedroom window that faced their house.[24]

In the early years of the party-filled home of Lucille and Al and their young family, Seattle's music scene was happening on the Main Stem, peaking by 1951. Ray Charles, who travelled by bus from Florida and arrived in 1948, found the city worth his long move. He wrote in his autobiography:

It was cool when I got to Seattle. The first gig was cool and
the weather was cool. Had to be around March of 1948. The
town was still wide open. And the entertainment business was
something of a boom. Competition was fierce . . . Seattle was
different than any place I had seen. It rained continually, it
was cold and frosty much of the time and, most amazing
of all, it snowed . . . Yes, by 1948 and 1949, I had my program
together . . . I could see that in a city like Seattle – a place which
was more sophisticated and open than what I was used to – my
act was going to pay off.[25]

Quincy Jones, who at the age of fourteen asked sixteen-year-old
Ray Charles Robinson (as he was then) to teach him how to arrange
music, remembered clubs that got going at midnight: 'When I was
13, I used to play hooky from school and go down the Palomar
Theatre every day because that's the only way we could get contact
with musicians, the real deal. We'd talk to them, listen to them.'[26]
The family had moved from Chicago to Washington state for better
opportunities, as Jones explained: 'Living in Bremerton we had just
one bedroom[,] a living space and a kitchen. Ten people lived in two
rooms.'[27] In 1946–7 they moved to 22nd Street, a block from Garfield
High School. Jones played in bands, one of which was the Bumps
Blackwell Junior Band. Blackwell became Little Richard's producer.
A highlight for Jones was playing behind Billie Holiday and Billy
Eckstine.[28] He described the Seattle nightlife of his early days:

Ten thirty, we would go to the Get Down Club, with a small
orchestra. Black and Tan Club, the Rockin' Chair, where we'd
meet up with Ray Charles. It was a jumpin' town. A lot of clubs
didn't open up until 12 and 1 at night . . . Two in the morning,
after the Get Down Club, we'd go to the Elks Club, where we
played for ourselves, all be-bop. We played everything in Seattle.
I remember Ray said one time, 'Every music has its soul.'[29]

Ray Charles said: 'Quincy wanted to know how to write jazz. [He said,] "I would like to take some lessons from you." He asked me to show [him] . . . He asked me to write this, to write that. We just sort of clicked as they say . . . and he'd come over to my house about 9 o'clock in the morning, wake me up.'[30] According to Jones, 'I asked him, "How in the hell do eight brass players play at the same time and not play the same notes?" And he said "Easy," and bang! he hit a Bb7 in prime position and a C7. That was the bebop sound. That opened the door.'[31]

The Hendrix family, meanwhile, moved in with Lucille's sister Delores at the Yesler Terrace housing project east of downtown Seattle. Built in 1941–3, the project is said to be the first racially integrated social housing in the United States. To build it, the site was razed, and in an example of modern urban renewal the existing housing pattern was erased and a diagonal site plan established, restructuring the traditional city blocks. Yesler Way – formerly Mill Street – was the original Skid Row, and Seattle the city where the term was invented.[32]

Al Hendrix found work as a merchant seaman, settling with his family in a room in the Golden Hotel on Jackson Street before he left. When he returned, he discovered that they had been evicted. In the spring of 1947 the couple rented the family's first apartment, at 3121 Oregon Street in the Rainier Vista Projects, social housing occupied for the most part by black and Jewish families, in former military accommodation. Lucille had lived temporarily with a Filipino man, possibly the father of Leon, born on 13 January 1948. The family moved to a two-bedroom apartment on 3022 Genesee Street in Rainier Vista Projects. Joseph Allen was born, with several disabilities, in 1948. The three boys spent the summer of 1949 in Vancouver living with their aunt and uncle and their grandmother Nora. That September Jimmy Hendrix began first grade at Sir William Dawson School in the city. The children were back in Seattle in October, where Jimmy was enrolled at Rainier Vista School.

Yesler Terrace, aerial view in 2012, by Seattle photographer John Stamets.

In 1949, while Hendrix was in second grade and living with his aunt Delores, his sister Kathy Ira was born, blind. In 1951 Pamela was born. That autumn Lucille left again. Lucille and Al Hendrix divorced on 17 December 1951. Al retained custody of the three boys. In the summer of 1952 Joe was given up for adoption. As a single father, Al relied on the boys' grandmothers, Clarice and Nora, and on Delores and a close family friend, Dorothy Harding, for help raising the children while he worked at a variety of jobs.

Lucille and Al had a tumultuous relationship of break-ups and reunions. After the divorce they would run into each other at neighbourhood taverns and they continued their relationship intermittently. While living apart, they had several children, with various disabilities, whose medical care they could not afford. Faced with these domestic crises, four of the children were adopted: Joseph, Kathy Ira, Pamela and Alfred. Later Al denied fathering most of the children.

The Hendrix family – Al, Jimmy and sometimes Leon – lived in many detached houses, apartments and rooms in the Central District of Seattle. At times they shared a 46-sq.-m (500-sq.-ft) house with another couple, took a room in a rooming house or occupied a backyard garage.

With all the moves from home to home, the young Hendrix attended several elementary schools, including Horace Mann Elementary School at 2410 Cherry Street and Leschi Elementary School at 135 32nd Avenue, where he met friends – including Pernell Alexander, Jimmy Williams and Terry Johnson – with whom he remained in lifelong contact.

Leon described how eagerly the brothers visited their mother. In 1952 when Jimmy was ten years old and Leon six, Lucille lived apart from her sons. Divorced, she moved in with her mother in an apartment over the Rainier Brewery, some thirteen blocks away. In 1953 she moved to 13th Street and Yesler and started working at the Far West Café. Early in 1953 she had Alfred, who also had disabilities and was also given up for adoption.

In 1953 Al Hendrix was able to make a down payment on a house at 2603 South Washington Street, at 26th Street and Washington. The house was about 84 sq. m (900 sq. ft), and was shared with Al's niece Grace and her husband, Frank Hatcher. The Hatchers later moved out and Ernestine and Cornell Benson shared the house. That year Hendrix spent time with his aunt Pat and uncle Frank on Drake Street in Vancouver. Back in Seattle, beginning fourth grade at Leschi Elementary School in the autumn, he met Jimmy Williams.[33] They became childhood friends.

In 1954 Leon was sent to live temporarily with foster parents, Arthur and Urville Wheeler, who had six children, including a son, Doug, and four other foster children. The Wheeler home was only six blocks away, and so Jimmy visited his brother and regularly slept over and ate there. Eventually Leon moved to a series of foster homes, spending weekends with Al and Jimmy.

In 1955 Jimmy Hendrix was twelve years old and living with Dorothy Harding, who had nine children and worked at Boeing on the day shift as well as as a domestic. Her children included Melvin, Ebony and Shirley. Jimmy was quiet boy. He did make friends at school; a photograph from 1955 shows him in sixth grade with his friend Jimmy Williams.[34] Al was working as a landscaper and garden designer, first with his brother-in-law Pat (Patricia Hendrix's second husband), and then on his own. He shared the house with Cornell and Ernestine Benson, while Jimmy lived for a time with Al's brother Frank, who also worked for Boeing, and his wife, Pearl, and children Bob and Diane. He kept in touch by telephone with Diane.

The young Jimmy Hendrix spent the summer of 1956 in Vancouver. That year Frank and Pearl Hendrix split up, and Jimmy was sent back to Al. Al's house was repossessed. The Bensons moved out. Al and Jimmy moved to a boarding house on 29th Avenue run by a Mrs McKay. Leon noted that when he was home all three slept in the same bed.[35] Jimmy moved school frequently, to Meany Junior High School in 1955, then Asa Mercer Junior High School, then in December 1958 to Washington Junior High School, at 2101 South Jackson Street, where he repeated ninth grade.[36]

After the boarding house Al and Jimmy lived with a cousin, Gracie, and her husband, Buddy, at 1434 Pike Street at 29th Street. In the spring of 1958 father and son moved to a two-bedroom home, less than 46 sq. m (500 sq. ft), on College Street in Beacon Hill, which they shared again with friends Cornell and Ernestine Benson. Al and Jimmy lived in the garage behind the house. Leon recalled listening to Ernestine's collection of 78 rpm blues records, which included Muddy Waters, Lightnin' Hopkins, Robert Johnson, Bessie Smith and Howlin' Wolf.[37]

The Hendrix family was poor, and Al was often out working and at times drinking and gambling. There were friends and neighbours, an extended family and Al's brother Frank, who helped out. The neighbourhood was close to Lake Washington, where, with friends, the boys would watch hydroplanes land on the water. Leon described their afternoons after school: they explored downtown Seattle, past Pioneer Square, the centre of Skid Row, populated by the down-and-out and marked by a Tlingit totem pole. They discovered underground Seattle and the layered urban archaeology of its downtown:

> No point in rushing back to the house because nobody was going to be there waiting . . . our dad didn't get off his shift until midnight . . . We ran around in nearby Leschi Park . . . to play cowboys and Indians, or made our way down to the docks and . . . the train yard . . . downtown . . . we found exactly what we were always looking for . . . watching the Flash Gordon serials . . . another world exists beneath the sidewalks and streets of Seattle. Subterranean passageways are under the city covered by First Avenue. Originally, the streets of Seattle were built at sea level, so they . . . flooded after a heavy rain . . . The city's central business district . . . sixty blocks, burned to the ground in 1889 . . . The city decided to rebuild the streets above the floodplain . . . a city was built over a hidden city on the waterfront. Buster found the passageway down by the ocean. A crack that looked to be about eight inches [20 cm] or so was between two dilapidated buildings . . . We'd . . . slipped through a portal into a forgotten world. There was an old, boarded-up barbershop, a general store, and a hotel . . . sidewalks were made out of withered planks . . . above, the city had built glass blocks into the new sidewalks . . . sun streamed through and illuminated our way.[38]

In the summer of 1956, when he was eight and Jimmy thirteen, Leon recalled picking berries and butter beans in the fields and swimming in Green River:

> There wasn't much, if anything at all, to eat for breakfast, so my brother and I began getting up at 4:30 a.m. to catch the bus out into the bean, carrot, cucumber, or strawberry fields to work with some of our friends.[39]

The Hendrix family led an unstable existence, moving frequently. The decline and death of Lucille added the circumstances that caused Jimmy to perform poorly in school. He was obliged to repeat ninth grade. His mother had been hospitalized for cirrhosis of the liver the previous autumn and for hepatitis in January 1958. She had remarried, to William Mitchell, a longshoreman decades her senior. On 1 February she was found unconscious in an alley near a tavern. She was taken to hospital, but her injury was not diagnosed or treated in time. She died a day later. After her death it was determined that she had died as a result of an injury that had caused a ruptured spleen.[40] Al Hendrix attended her visitation, but he, Jimmy and Leon did not go to the funeral.

Hendrix understood his wayward mother. In an interview in 1967 he explained, shaving a few years from his age: 'My mother used to like having a good time and dressing up. She used to drink a lot and didn't take care of herself. She died when I was about ten [he was actually sixteen]. But she was a groovy mother.'[41] He recounted a delicately colourful reverie of his mother:

> My mother . . . was going underneath these trees. You could see the shade . . . the leaf patterns across her face while she was going under . . . these were in green and yellow shadows.

He wrote a number of songs to her. In early interviews he said he wished to see her again.[42]

After the loss of his mother, Jimmy Hendrix withdrew in grief and became more introverted. He had had a ukulele since 1955, and in about 1957 he obtained a second-hand acoustic guitar for five dollars. Leon remembered it as an old Kay hollow-body. Various stories circulate as to how it was acquired, whether from a stoned man playing cards or from a disabled boy living in the same boarding house as the Hendrixes.[43] A Lacanian psychoanalytical view would suggest a case of transference to the object of the guitar, as Jimmy kept it with him, constantly practising, teaching himself to play by ear.

In the late summer of 1957 Little Richard (Richard Wayne Penniman) visited Seattle and Leon learned of his arrival in the neighbourhood. He spotted Little Richard's black limo while gathering mustard greens from the garden of a neighbour, Mrs Magwood, to take to a Mrs Penniman two blocks away, where, Leon found out, Little Richard was visiting family. The brothers heard him preach at the Goodwill Baptist Church at 14th and Spring streets. This was one of a series of circumstances presaging both performers' futures.[44] (Little Richard left performing to preach for a time, then returned to music. Hendrix eventually joined his backing band and briefly became bandleader.) On 1 September that year, when Hendrix was fourteen and in ninth grade, he saw Elvis Presley play in front of 15,000 spectators at Sick's Stadium, possibly from a hillside. Often drawing, colouring and cartooning, he made sketches of a Presley figure performing onstage.

In the autumn of 1958 the family moved again to live briefly in a house shared once more with Grace and Frank Hatcher. The next year the fifteen-year-old Hendrix began tenth grade at Garfield High School, at 400 23rd Avenue. The school was much larger in scale, with 1,688 pupils, and was integrated, with 20 per cent Asian students, 30 per cent African American and the rest white. That autumn Al and Jimmy moved to a second-floor studio apartment on 1314 East Terrace Street on First Hill, opposite

DEC • 65

SICKS SEATTLE STADIUM

Sick's Stadium, Seattle, 1965.

the juvenile court, a sketchy neighbourhood where prostitutes worked the streets. Al called it 'scrumdum'.

Hendrix acquired his first electric guitar after they moved to First Hill. Al bought him a pale Champagne-coloured Supro Ozark for $15, on sale at Myers Music Shop at 1214 First Avenue in downtown Seattle, and rented a C-melody saxophone for himself. Jimmy restrung the right-handed guitar to play left-handed. His father did not allow him to play left-handed, so Hendrix taught himself to play both ways. He could flip it to play with his right hand, whether or not the guitar was restrung. The Supro Ozark was stolen from the stage at Birdland in 1960. He borrowed right-handed guitars to play without restringing them, until he was able to replace it.

Hendrix recalled some of his influences in an interview for KMPX FM radio in 1968: 'I was diggin' everything like Billy Butler, he used to play with Bill Doggett . . . all the way up to Muddy Waters and Eddie Cochran.'[45] In interviews his friend Jimmy Williams recounted that Hendrix would stop by the house with a guitar. His mother would request old rhythm and blues songs, asking: 'You play "Bad, Bad Whiskey" so well . . . will you play that for me?' Williams recalled that they were listening to Louis Jordan, B. B. King and Albert King.[46] Another guitar-playing Seattleite from the neighbourhood, Sammy Drain, mentioned that Hendrix loved playing country. Various earwitnesses recalled his favourite or first tune. For some, the first tune he played was 'Peter Gunn', the TV series theme tune by Henry Mancini. A girlfriend, Carmen Goudy, said it was 'Tall Cool One' by the Tacoma band the Fabulous Wailers. Others recalled him playing the rockabilly of Duane Eddy. Hendrix mentioned his preferences:

> I liked Buddy Holly, Eddie Cochran, Muddy Waters, Elmore James, B. B. King. The first guitarist I was aware of was Muddy Waters. I heard one of his old records when I was a little boy and it scared me to death because I heard all these *sounds*. The *Grand Old Opry* would come on, and I would watch that.[47]

In the neighbourhood there was a guitarist, Randy 'Butch' Snipes, who could play behind his back like T-Bone Walker and do the Chuck Berry duck walk. Another local musical presence was the Lewis family, Dave Lewis Sr and Dave Lewis Jr. The first gig Hendrix played may have been with an unnamed band in the basement of a synagogue, Temple De Hirsch Sinai at 1511 East Pike Street. Hendrix, however, mentioned another night, at the Washington National Guard Armoury in Kent, in June or July 1959: 'I remember my first gig was at an armoury, National Guard type of thing, and we earned 35 cents apiece.'[48] He recalled playing the bassline on a regular six-string guitar, with James Woodberry on vocals, Webb Lofton and Walter Harris on saxophone, the guitarist Ulysses Heath Jr and the drummer Lester Exkano.[49]

Hendrix's first band was the Velvetones, which was formed by the pianist Robert Green and Luther Rabb on tenor saxophone, and included Pernell Alexander and Anthony Atherton. On weeknights the band had a regular gig at Birdland, at 2203 East Madison. On Friday nights they played Yesler Terrace Field House. The Velvetones played one of their own compositions, 'Jimmy's Blues'. Another tune Hendrix played was Bill Doggett's 'Honky Tonk'.[50]

The Velvetones evolved into the Rocking Teens in late 1958. Some time the following year the band became the Rocking Kings; they continued to play Birdland, and the line-up now included Heath on guitar, Exkano on drums, Harris and Lofton on saxophone, pianists James Woodberry and Terry Williams and manager James Thomas. Their repertoire included tunes by B.B. King, Duane Eddy and Chuck Berry. The Rocking Kings played the Polish Hall at 1714 18th Street South in 1959 and the Spanish Castle in Kent in 1960.

Hendrix replaced the Supro Ozark, stolen in 1960, with a white Danelectro Silvertone and matching amplifier, bought at Sears for $49.95. The band chipped in. Bill Eisiminger, a school friend, and Hendrix both had a Danelectro. Eisiminger described his bass as the 'bottom of the line' and said that Hendrix kept his with him always: 'He would always carry that with him slung over his back – no case.' Danelectro instruments were made of Masonite-covered poplar, Formica and vinyl. Jimmy painted his red and named it after his girlfriend Betty Jean.[51] Sammy Drain talked about their musical practice: 'My brother played keyboards and I played guitar and we would write songs, jam together, exchange licks. Just gathered stuff around the neighbourhood.'[52]

The Seattle historian Peter Blecha listed local bands around town: The Sharps, The Dynamics, The Frantics, Little Bill & the Blue Notes, and The Dave Lewis Combo. He mentioned summer matinees in 1957, at which touring artists such as Little Richard, Bill Doggett and Hank Ballard & the Midnighters performed. Blecha also mentioned the local guitarist Bud Brown of the Dave Lewis Combo, who played at Birdland, as well as Butch Snipes.[53] The definitive regional Northwest dirty rock sound could be heard in the Fabulous Wailers' song 'Tall Cool One' and the Kingsmen's rock anthem 'Louie Louie', while surf virtuosity was represented by the Ventures of Tacoma.

Seattle musician Ronald Buford mentioned the many local venues in Hendrix's neighbourhood: 'Within walking distance there was at least thirty different places that you could walk to and play.'[54] A photograph shows the Rocking Kings posing on 20 February 1960, when they played Washington Hall, where Hendrix's parents had first met and danced. The venue remains, a large, wood-framed, brick-faced edifice at 14th and East Fir streets, near one of the places where Lucille worked. Washington Hall was designed by Victor Voorhees and built in 1908 by Hans Pederson as a fraternal lodge for the Danish Brotherhood. It was a place of assembly for many communities; a Grand Benefit Ball took place there for the National Association for the Advancement of Colored People in 1918, with Lillian Smith's Jazz Band, and Billie Holiday performed there in 1951.[55] Other Central District clubs in Seattle included the Encore Ballroom, the Black and Tan at 1207 South Jackson Street, the American Legion Hall at 620 University Street, the 410 Supper Club, the Rocking Chair on 14th Avenue and Birdland at Madison and 22nd Street. Another popular venue, the Spanish Castle, was on Pacific Highway in Kent, on the way to Tacoma.

In 1960 the Hendrix family moved to 2606 East Yesler Way, two blocks from Garfield High School.[56] By this time the population of Seattle was 600,000, and over 1 million in the wider metropolitan area. By 1960 Hendrix was in a band called Tommy, or Thomas & the Tomcats, and playing various gigs in Washington state. James Thomas, having managed the Rocking Kings, continued to hone his managing skills and added vocals. He lived on 21st Avenue, and had a 1949 Studebaker to ferry them further afield. The band played the u.s. Naval Reservation at Pier 91 in Seattle, Paine Field in Everett and an army base in Fort Lewis. The line-up fluctuated, typical for young bands. At first it consisted of the drummer

Washington Hall, Seattle, 1914.

Exkano, the pianist Perry Thomas, Roland Green on bass, saxophonists Lofton and Harris and guitarist Heath. In April 1961 Leroy Toots, Bill Rinnick and Richard Gayswood replaced Green, Lofton and Exkano, respectively.[57] The band's repertoire included Earl King's 'Come On'. A photo of the Tomcats in 1961 shows the band playing the Bors Brumo Club.[58]

Xenobia Bailey heard a collective musicianship in the guitarists' practising:

> I think Jimi was more the one that gave the guitar a voice, and
> made it articulate, and made it speak in vowels and syllables.
> He took that aspect further than anyone else. He was part
> of a pack of guitar players that was always practicing. The
> music was always being created. They were either rehearsing,
> practicing, or performing.[59]

Leon related the story of a radio that Jimmy Hendrix dismantled, curious about sound, looking for the source of the radio's disembodied voices. Later, Hendrix bought a pickup and secretly rewired his father's stereo to use as a guitar amp.[60]

Some of the lyrical imagery of Hendrix's songs derived from local houses and landscape. The roadside venue the Spanish Castle became a mythic destination arrived at by dragonfly. The Red House was a real house of another colour, on 29th and Yesler, the home of Betty Jean Morgan and her younger sister Maddy. Maddy went out with Leon, who called her Mattie B.

After dropping out of high school in October 1960, Hendrix worked reluctantly with Al as a landscape labourer. While working on her property, he talked to the jazz pianist Melody Jones (Derniece Harris), who had performed with Fats Waller in Harlem.[61] Jones remembered talking to Hendrix about playing in Harlem, and emphasized the practice of competitive 'cutting', a term for duelling solos:

> He knew I was originally from New York and he was very curious about it. He was too young as a high school student to go in the places they'd call 'after-hours' so Jimmy would like me to tell him about the gangsters in New York and how they would shoot up the clubs. He had a way of playing guitar that would almost talk to you. I wanted him to study music, but he didn't want to. He had those ideas in his mind of what he wanted to do and he was successful with them. I tried to explain to him about basic chord structure, but he'd rather take a shortcut and get there in a great big hurry.[62]

Much later, on 23 May 1969, The Jimi Hendrix Experience played the Coliseum in Seattle. Hendrix flew in from New York with his girlfriend Carmen Borrero. They stayed at the Sherwood Inn, a university district hotel far from the old neighbourhood. In the rain after the concert, Hendrix asked a fan with a run-down Volkswagen Beetle to drive them around Seattle, directing him past his former addresses and haunts – houses, burger joints: 'Over the course of the next two hours he pointed out the ramshackle homes he'd lived in, the clubs he'd played in. [Borrero] was surprised at the sheer number of different homes, apartments, hotels, and boardinghouses he had lived in. [Borrero realized,] "On every block there was someplace he had stayed."'[63]

In May 1961 Hendrix was caught joyriding twice in one week. He enlisted in the United States Army after a week in juvenile detention at the Rainier Vista 4H Center, across the street from the apartment on East Terrace where he had once lived.[64] The army was a way out of a jail term. It shifted his prospects to a life in music and constantly in motion. He zigzagged from the west to the south, then east, absorbing the soundscapes of a travelling life structured by touring. In the early anonymous years, postcards he sent home to his father tracked his peregrinations. They lost touch while he made the radical move to London in 1966, until the Experience broke into mass distribution.

## WEST: MONTEREY, SAN FRANCISCO AND LOS ANGELES

It didn't even rain. No buttons to push.

Jimi Hendrix[65]

The futuristic Seattle Space Needle, an exclamatory icon in the skyline for the Seattle World's Fair of 1962, was under construction in 1961 when Hendrix left the hometown drizzle for a new life in the army. He was stationed for basic training in the Monterey Peninsula south of San Francisco, at the out-of-town base Fort Ord (then some 10,000 ha / 25,000 acres, now decommissioned), from 31 May until 8 November 1961. The Monterey Jazz Festival had been held since 1958 at the local county fairground at 200 Fairground Road, at the state-owned arena built

in 1939 by the Works Public Administration, one of the largest
New Deal agencies. The 2,600-sq.-m (28,000-sq.-ft) structure was
adaptable for use by horse shows and rodeos. Hendrix's army
posting was another coincidence in his career: six years later he
would be back, performing at the Monterey Pop Festival of 1967.

A series of festivals led up to the cultural shift signalled by
Monterey Pop. The Oregon writer Ken Kesey hosted intermittent
Acid Test parties. His experiments with mind-altering drugs as
a volunteer in 1960 led to a series of proto-happenings at his log
cabin home in a redwood forest in La Honda. The Grateful Dead,
at first called the Warlocks, played at Merry Prankster parties
in La Honda. Kesey, with a manic Neal Cassady driving the bus
eastward, rode in a Merry Prankster road trip across America to
New York and back. The bus was wired and rigged, a travelling
feedback loop, and the film of the cross-continental trip was
projected during the Acid Test parties.[66] A waning beat subculture
merged with the rise of counterculture.

Counterculture organization expanded to promote more
open public events in San Francisco. The Trips Festival of 21–22
January 1966 was held at the Longshoreman's Hall, a reverberant
octagonal union auditorium at 400 North Point. Augustus Owsley
Stanley III, the underground chemist who manufactured pure
LSD in large quantities, handed out free tabs to accompany the
Grateful Dead. Acid Test events took parties to public places.
Performers at the Whatever It Is Festival of 30 September–
2 October 1966 at San Francisco State College included Mimi
Farina and the San Francisco Mime Troupe, as well as the Merry
Pranksters, Ken Kesey and the Grateful Dead.

Marty Balin, a folk artist who electrified his sound, ran a San
Francisco club, the Matrix, with his business partner Matthew
Katz. The Matrix opened on 13 August 1965 in a renovated pizza
shop at 3138 Fillmore Street in the Marina District. It was a venue
for The Doors, the Grateful Dead and Big Brother & the Holding

Company, and Balin was in the house band, Jefferson Airplane. Another San Francisco folk venue, the Hungry I, was influential when it was at 599 Jackson Street. It was sold and moved to 546 Broadway, becoming just another strip club.

On 14 January 1967, in the run-up to that year's Summer of Love, converging on the Haight-Ashbury district of San Francisco – 'Hashbury' – a Human Be-in was held at Golden Gate Park. The political rhetoric criticized the legislation that made LSD illegal. The name 'Be-in' referred to the civil rights sit-ins of Greensboro and Nashville. The Be-in featured speakers known from the beat era and a rock-music bill including Jefferson Airplane, the Grateful Dead, Big Brother & the Holding Company, and Quicksilver Messenger Service, and drew some 20,000 spectators.

Barry Jenkins, drummer for the New Animals, described looking over at Hendrix on the plane arriving at San Francisco International Airport for the Monterey Pop Festival:

Human Be-in, 14 January 1967, Seattle, poster by Michael Bowan.

We were on the same flight, and I'll never forget seeing Hendrix sitting in his seat with his ear pushed up against the side wall of the plane. I asked him what he was doing and he said, 'I'm getting inspiration for the next album, man.' He was listening to the sounds of the engine vibrating inside the walls.[67]

The Jimi Hendrix Experience made its American debut at the Monterey Pop Festival on 18 June 1967, on grassy fairgrounds dotted with mature oak and pine trees over 8 ha (20 acres). The weather had been misty, grey and cool on the Friday, but the fog lifted, the weather warmed and it became sunny over the three days. The small, 5,800-seat, U-shaped arena was well sited, its perimeter partially roofed by a modern, light structure of folded plates with good sight lines. The central oval of the rodeo was set up with rows of folding chairs to boost seating to some 7,500. Abe Jacob handled the sound professionally, raising the standard for outdoor festivals. The journalist Keith Altham recalled a moist, humid atmosphere, the scent of marijuana and incense, and occasional warm drizzle.[68]

The festival had begun that year when its founder, Alan Pariser, and a promoter, Ben Shapiro, contacted Derek Taylor, formerly The Beatles' publicist. Lou Adler, who was between labels and working with The Mamas & the Papas, spread the word to band members John and Michelle Phillips. Ultimately Adler and John Phillips received credit as producers of the festival, which turned into a not-for-profit venture. Adler, Phillips, Terry Melcher, Johnny Rivers and Paul Simon each put up $10,000 to make $50,000 to buy the dates at Monterey. In April Paul McCartney visited Los Angeles for ten days, en route to Boulder, Colorado, to meet Jane Asher. He, Adler and the Phillipses met at the house of Cass Elliot (of The Mamas & the Papas) on Woodrow Wilson Drive in Laurel Canyon to discuss the festival. The music of Bob Dylan figured in a discussion of rock as art form, and the group identified a shared desire to validate rock music in relation to contemporary culture.[69]

A board of governors was established for the festival, including British singer-songwriter Donovan, Mick Jagger, Paul McCartney, Jim McGuinn (who later changed his name to Roger McGuinn), Melcher, Andrew Loog Oldham, Pariser, Rivers, Smokey Robinson, Brian Wilson, John Phillips and Adler. Adler and the Phillipses worked on the project over four months to develop its philosophy and aims. John Phillips's autobiography recounted their ambitions, as well as the detail involved in preparing a festival. Adler and Phillips attended local meetings about municipal issues to allay concerns from the citizens of Monterey about security, accommodation, sewage and noise. Phillips wrote: 'The only people who voiced resistance and trepidation were the citizens of Monterey. Their serene Peninsula of Paradise was facing an invasion of rockers and druggies.'[70] He described negotiating while stoned: 'I had to present an image of straight efficiency, and tripping on acid during most of these speeches definitely helped.'[71]

Monterey Pop Festival was a first in scale, its acts carefully selected for quality, relevance, even solidarity. Brian Jones, the founder and original guitarist of The Rolling Stones, said that a community had come together, and that was particularly true for the musicians, who met in a makeshift green room underneath the stage. In their plans for the festival, Adler and the Phillipses aimed to produce a musical event, at an international scale, that would be cutting edge, peaceful and harmonious, channelling McLuhan, who wrote: 'We now live in a global village . . . a simultaneous happening. We are back in acoustic space.'[72] The organizing team established a bill of 32 acts in five shows, setting a relaxed pace for staging, instruments, lighting and sound. They selected three headliners: Simon & Garfunkel, The Mamas & the Papas and Otis Redding. With music from India, Britain, Memphis, San Francisco and South Africa, the acts included Mike Bloomfield, Paul Butterfield, The Byrds, The Electric Flag, Janis Joplin, Jefferson Airplane, Hugh Masekela, Buffalo Springfield (without Neil Young) and Ravi Shankar (the only performer to receive a fee). Some financing – in the order of $200,000 – came from a proposed ABC television special.

McCartney and Jones, echoed by Oldham, recommended The Who and The Jimi Hendrix Experience. Phillips called Chas Chandler, the Experience's manager, in London to invite them. By chance, Brian Jones picked up the phone. He agreed to attend and introduce the band. Los Angeles bands The Byrds and Buffalo Springfield signed up quickly. No one invited The Doors.

The festival's production offices were in Los Angeles, at the Renaissance Jazz Club, an old building on Sunset Boulevard in West Hollywood. To minimize friction with the San Francisco bands, the organizers contacted the Grateful Dead and sent Simon & Garfunkel to the Dead House.[73] John Phillips explained the negotiations between the San Francisco and Los Angeles factions:

> Then we turned to the emerging Bay Area music scene. So many groups were coming out of the San Francisco area that we had to open the weekend up to some of them. There were the Dead, the Airplane, Janis Joplin with Big Brother and the Holding Company, Country Joe McDonald and the Fish, Quicksilver Messenger Service, Canned Heat, Electric Flag, a dozen others. There was a definite rivalry and antagonism between the LA and San Francisco camps. We had trouble getting them to even talk to us. To the suspicious Bay Area rockers, LA was Star City – slick, moneyed, plastic, and elitist. Haight-Ashbury was becoming the universal hippie mecca for both the drug and rock cultures. Musicians saw themselves as organic post-capitalist advocates for 'power to the people' . . . The Dead had been giving free concerts for a while and we respected what they were doing . . . Paul [Simon] and Artie [Garfunkel] went up to San Francisco and visited the 'Dead House', the band's Victorian commune and base of operations on Haight Street. 'It's the spookiest place I've

ever seen and these people are the strangest people I have ever encountered in my life,' Paul reported . . . 'I'm sure they're all stoned. They sit around and riff all day. The girls do the chores and the guys work on the music.'[74]

Numerous journalists attended the Monterey Pop Festival. Hype hit new highs. There were reports that over 1,000 journalists requested press passes. In addition to dozens of photographers, there were American and European television and film crews, including an ABC television crew covering the festival in order to produce a television special. This was never to be aired, however: 'Not on my network,' said the television executive and Southern gentleman Tom Moore after screening clips of Hendrix humping the Marshall amps.[75] D. A. Pennebaker, the filmmaker recognized for his Bob Dylan documentary *Don't Look Back*, was hired by the television company CBS and filmed the entire Experience set. For him it was far more than a television show – it was a major rock-concert film. His documentary, featuring standout performers Otis Redding and Jimi Hendrix, was released in 1970.

The festival became famous as the epitome of mellow. Unticketed youth roamed and camped the fairground while an estimated 20,000 people attended the festival shows over the three days. The crowd wandered the fairground smoking dope and tripping on LSD, with no danger from traffic or trouble from police. There was some rain, but no mud. Public order prevailed; lavatories were in place. Private security and medical staff worked effectively. Organizers had arranged with the municipal board of education to allow the festival crowd to camp on the football field of a nearby school, setting up portable lavatories. The Monterey organizers even set up a bummer tent for bad trips, with volunteers to care for audience members on psychedelic drugs. The existing facilities had provided the cues for festival infrastructure.

The Experience's management and its label, Track Records, paid to air-freight the equipment – Marshall stacks for volume – there, giving them the freedom to bash their gear during the act. Since the festival line-up was fluid, Pete Townshend of The Who confronted Hendrix over who would follow whom. Both bands had planned guitar acrobatics, but The Who had not brought their Marshalls, making do with Vox amps sourced locally. Having followed the Experience on the same bill at the Saville Theatre in London, and without their own equipment, Townshend was loath to follow Hendrix onstage. Phillips intervened with a coin toss; Townshend won and The Who played first. They performed in front of the throbbing, pulsating blobs of a light show, wearing dandy finery of ruffles, flowered fabrics and fringed scarves. They played 'Substitute' and Eddie Cochran's 'Summertime Blues' with verve. Keith Moon began tossing about bits of drum kit. Townshend smashed his guitar, smoke bombs exploded behind the amps and concert staff scuttled to rescue high-end microphones. Finally Moon kicked over his drum kit as the band left the stage.

In between The Who and The Jimi Hendrix Experience, the Grateful Dead played a set. Jerry Garcia summed up the band's performance: 'We blew Monterey *and* Woodstock.'[76] Hendrix wondered whether the Grateful Dead and the audience, all supposedly tripping on acid, would be peaking in unison; supposedly Hendrix timed his Purple Owsley trip to peak during his own set.

Hendrix opened with his show-stopping, uptempo version of Howlin' Wolf's 'Killing Floor'. The set included B.B. King's rhythm and blues hit 'Rock Me Baby' of 1964, also played fast, and the slow 'Hey Joe'. A charged version of Bob Dylan's 'Like a Rolling Stone' must have caught the attention of the musicians from Dylan's band who were there: Mike Bloomfield, Dylan's guitarist, and Al Kooper, the organist on the song. The journalist Charles Shaar Murray commented: '"Like a Rolling Stone" was an inspired six-minute monument that inter-played with

The Jimi Hendrix Experience, Monterey Pop Festival, 18 June 1967.

the final number, since it used the same nominal chords as The Troggs' cover of "Wild Thing".[77] Last was Hendrix's resounding arrangement of The Troggs' hit. The set ended with a sacrifice, as Hendrix performed a guitar burn onstage. He knelt over a guitar – one he had painted that afternoon – squirted lighter fluid over it, set it alight, fanned the flames and then smashed it into pieces. While its electrical guts squealed, he tossed the scraps to the crowd.

The audience, in an arena filled to capacity at 6,000, can be seen in Pennebaker's documentary, rapt, listening to fluid, psychedelic, orchestral rock sound and uninhibited, innovative, virtuoso guitar. For those with no tickets or no access to the arena, there were promotional performances including spontaneous jam sessions at the Monterey Peninsula Community College sports stadium across the highway interchange, where Hendrix, Jorma Kaukonen of Jefferson Airplane and John Cipollina of Quicksilver Messenger Service played free for the young crowd. Gary Duncan, Quicksilver's guitarist, described how LSD fuelled Hendrix:

Hendrix walked in, looked over at me and said, 'Hey,' . . . Then he reached in his pocket, took out this little candy tin, popped the lid and offered me some acid. He had about 20 hits in there: I took about five and he took the rest.[78]

Later that year, Eric Burdon and his band The Animals released a song about Monterey and its insider ambience. A camera followed Burdon as he roamed the empty fairground and arena, listing the performers – The Byrds, Ravi Shankar, The Who, Hugh Masekela, Jimi Hendrix – and Rolling Stone Brian Jones's appearance strolling the midway dressed as a wizard. The lyric crowned him 'His Majesty Prince Jones'.[79]

Mike Bloomfield offered a critical opinion a year later. Of the San Francisco scene, he said:

I don't dig San Francisco groups. I love San Francisco and I love the guys in the groups, and I love the people here, I love this nice cheap house that I live in in a groovy neighborhood. I like it here. But I think San Francisco music isn't good music. Not good bands. They're amateur cats; . . . it's a fraudulent scene. I don't think that many good bands have come out of San Francisco.[80]

Monterey was where the Experience engaged the sound engineer Abe Jacob, who was to work with the touring team for the rest of the band's career. He said:

I was doing sound hired by the Mamas and [the] Papas . . . We had a very simple system. I went back to work for McCune sound in San Francisco. And Jimi opened for the Monkees on the Dick Clark Caravan of Stars. While he was out with the Dick Clark, I got a call from Gerry Stickells who was his tour manager. They wanted somebody to do their sound. I stayed with the Experience from then on. I was there for almost all of the . . . Experience gigs. He came out and just destroyed the audience with this musical ability that we had just not had before, and then the showmanship was just the topper to all of that.[81]

On 21 February 1965 Hendrix had played the influential Fillmore (the top underground live venue, at 1805 Geary Street from 1965 to 1968) as a backing musician for Little Richard. In June 1967 Hendrix was back there in his own right: the promoter Bill Graham, who ran the venue, had booked the Experience to play five nights. What began as the Experience supporting Jefferson Airplane lasted only for the first night. The Hungarian guitarist Gábor Szabó remained on the bill, and Big Brother & the Holding Company with Janis Joplin replaced Jefferson Airplane, who had become unavailable. The Experience ended their first Fillmore run topping the bill.

The Experience's drummer, Mitch Mitchell, was agog at the band's quick ascent:

The reaction happened so fast . . . I think the best thing that happened within those eight months before America, even right after Monterey . . . Bill Graham took us on as a risk. We played the original Fillmore with the Airplane, Janis Joplin, Gábor Szabó.[82]

Abe Jacob contrasted the peaceful vibe of Monterey with the militant antagonism of the Berkeley crowd in 1970, when the Experience played there on Saturday 30 May:

Berkeley Community Theater was [a] 3,500-seat school auditorium at one point. But a lot of shows travelled there, lots of other concerts played there. They decided that, after the concert was booked, that we might as well record it. Mike Neil, who took over doing sound, mixed the sound . . . Between there and the University of California, and the student riots, and because the Berkeley Community Theater was such a small space, there were a lot of people trying to get in. So one of the things we did with the truck that was parked out in back of the theatre was, I said, let's just open the back doors, and we had maybe 300 or 400 people listening

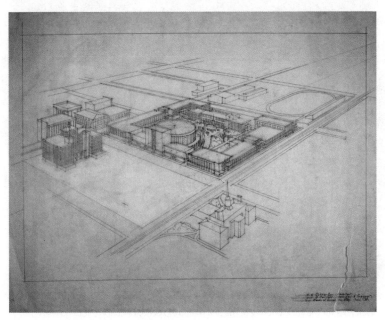

Berkeley Community Theater, drawing by architect Henry Gutterson, 1937.

to the monitors in the truck so that precluded having a little bit more of a riot than what might have happened.

Jimi was as good right from the beginning. There's no logical explanation for what he was able to do on that guitar that gave him that stature. It was amazing. Just his fingers, the strings and a few pedals created an entire vocabulary of guitar music that is still being emulated today.[83]

'Watchout for the Fuzz' bootleg of the Jimi Hendrix Experience concert at Berkeley Community Theater, 30 May 1970; photograph by Robert Altman.

Another perspective on the radical audience came from a spectator, Craig Street, who emphasized the chaos at 'Bezerkeley':

Berkeley was basically in a state of war. The National Guard was there, and there had been riots going on for weeks. In an effort to defuse things they were letting a lot of people into this show, even though it was sold out. I remember being at the back door and somebody associated with the band letting a lot of people in. I remember going to the front of the stage, the pit, just as Hendrix was coming out . . . The power of the music was insane . . . What he did have . . . were two incredibly supportive and sympathetic musicians backing him up. He got the solid rhythmic foundation he needed from [bassist] Billy Cox and he got that over-the-edge sonic thing he needed from Mitch Mitchell. He was able to fill in the space between because he had a profound understanding of how to make a three-piece sound incredibly huge.[84]

## WEST: LOS ANGELES

That's western sky music.
Hendrix on the music of Crosby, Stills & Nash[85]

Along with its international cinema profile, the metropolis of Los Angeles was the regional music business capital and nerve centre for music creation. Before the New York-based pull of Atlantic Records, a critical mass of artists, musicians and rhythm and blues labels were working in Los Angeles. Early hubs of African American nightlife were the Dunbar Hotel on Central Avenue at 41st Street and, next door on Central Avenue, the Club Alabam. Record labels were scattered over the metropolitan region. The Specialty label, owned by Art Rupe (born Arthur Goldberg), moved from 2719 West Seventh Street to 311 Venice Boulevard in 1947, then in

1949 to a long-held address, 8508 Sunset Boulevard, Hollywood.
Its well-known producers included Robert 'Bumps' Blackwell and
J. W. Alexander, and its artists included Guitar Slim (Eddie Jones),
John Lee Hooker and Little Richard, the label's most commercially
successful artist, recorded by Blackwell in 1955. Guitar Slim recorded
'The Things I Used to Do' on Specialty in 1953. Other Los Angeles
labels included Imperial Records, founded by Lewis Chudd, which
released New Orleans rhythm and blues; and Aladdin Records, for
which Louis Jordan, Clarence 'Gatemouth' Brown, Billie Holiday
and Lightnin' Hopkins, among others, recorded.[86]

The rock music journalist Harvey Kubernik, a native of Los
Angeles, listed a culture of regional rhythm and blues record
labels and their local footprints:

> Los Angeles-based record labels included Specialty, Capitol,
> Dootone. Modern, where Elmore James, John Lee Hooker,
> Howlin' Wolf, Richard Berry and Johnny 'Guitar' Watson did
> records, was actually in Culver City. B. B. King was on Kent.
> Aladdin Records was located in Beverly Hills; they put out
> discs by Amos Milburn, Louis Jordan, Floyd Dixon, Lowell
> Fulson, Lester Young, Charles Brown, Helen Humes and
> Maxwell Davis, a mentor to [Jerry] Leiber and [Mike] Stoller.
> LA always had mind-blowing R'n'B radio stations.[87]

Wild, rollicking guitar sounds emerged from Los Angeles-based
artists such as Johnny 'Guitar' Watson, influenced by T-Bone
Walker and Clarence 'Gatemouth' Brown. Watson's 'Space
Guitar', recorded in 1954, was atonal, dissonant and fractured with
reverb, distortion and shredding. Frank Zappa said that listening
to Watson's 'Three Hours past Midnight' (1956) inspired him
to play the guitar. Stevie Ray Vaughan suggested other obscure,
possibly Californian influences for Hendrix: 'Boot Hill' and
'I Believe in a Woman' by Sly Williams.[88]

Ray Charles built his music industry headquarters in Los Angeles. His empire included a recording studio, the two-storey RPM International building, which he had built in 1963–4 in the Harvard Height district of central LA. With his move to the Atlantic label, he had learned that it was most lucrative to retain ownership of his masters. He held firm creative control and retained command of his recording studio. Charles wrote in his autobiography:

Ray Charles's RPM Studios, 2107 West Washington Boulevard, Los Angeles.

I began my own record company in the early sixties . . . But back in 1962, most of my business dealings were still in New York. That was a drag. It was difficult living in California and having all my main people on the other coast, so I decided to build a small office building in LA and centralize the operation in one spot . . . I bought the property and helped design the place. I was more interested in low costs than high prestige, so I put up the building in a normal, black, working-class neighborhood of LA. It ain't Beverly Hills . . . We began in 1963 with a three-track machine.[89]

After Hendrix began using psychotropic drugs in the summer of 1966, musicians and their entourages speculated on the effect of LSD on his playing. David Crosby marvelled at it; he said the strings melted when he tried to play while tripping. A synaesthetic altering of the user's perception of reality is common with the use of LSD. Some early scientific research on psychedelics took place on the West Coast; Dr Oscar Janiger conducted promising experiments with LSD, supervising about 900 patients, using a house in the mid-Wilshire district of Los Angeles as his office. Many LA artists tested the drug under his care from 1954 to 1962. The writer and diarist Anaïs Nin documented the intellectual and sensual impressions in her doctor-supervised experience in the autumn of 1955. Dr Janiger had invited her to participate as a writer, along with a painter and a biologist. Nin's text captured a sensual feel of synaesthesia, while her interest in dreams and eroticism lent empathy to her perception of the experience. She called the twelve-hour trip a 'reverie', and found the sensation of turning into gold erotic, comparable to lovemaking:

The rug . . . had become a field of stirring and undulating hairs . . . like the movement of the sea anemone or a field of wheat in the wind . . . doors, walls, and windows were liquefying . . . as if I had been plunged to the bottom of the sea, and everything

had become undulating and wavering. The door knobs . . .
melted and undulated like living serpents. Every object in the
room became a living, mobile breathing world . . . The dazzle
of the sun was blinding, every speck of gold multiplied and
magnified. Trees, clouds, lawns heaved and undulated too, the
clouds flying at tremendous speed . . . now appeared the most
delicate Persian designs, flowers, mandalas, patterns in perfect
symmetry. As I designed them they produced their matching
music. When I drew a long orange line, it emitted its own
orange tone. My body was both swimming and flying. I felt gay
and at ease and playful . . . the colours in the designs gave me
pleasure, as well as the music. The singing of mocking birds
was multiplied, and became a whole forest of singing birds. My
senses were multiplied as if I had a hundred eyes, a hundred
ears, a hundred fingertips . . . music vibrated through my body
as if I were one of the instruments and I felt myself becoming
a full percussion orchestra, becoming green, blue, orange. The
waves of the sounds ran through my hair like a caress. The
music ran down my back and came out of my fingertips. I
was a cascade of red-blue rainfall, a rainbow. I was small, light,
mobile . . . I could dissolve, melt, float, soar. Wavelets of
light touched the rim of my clothes, phosphorescent radiations
. . . As each design was born and arranged itself, it dissolved
and the next one followed . . . Each form, each line emitted
its equivalent in music in perfect accord with the design. An
undulating line emitted a sustaining undulating melody, a circle
had corresponding musical notations, diaphanous colours,
diaphanous sounds, a pyramid created a pyramid of ascending
notes, and vanishing ones left only an echo. These designs were
preparatory sketches for entire Oriental cities.[90]

Hendrix first arrived in Los Angeles in 1965. In January he sent
a postcard home with news of his forthcoming address at 6500

Selma Avenue, Hollywood. While touring with Little Richard for
five months in 1965, he used the stage name Maurice James. In LA
he stayed at the Wilcox Hotel on Selma. From 5 to 13 March 1965
he played second guitar with Ike & Tina Turner's backing band,
the Kings of Rhythm, at Ciro's Le Disc, 8433 Sunset Boulevard in
West Hollywood. The Byrds were their support act.[91]

Hendrix met the singer Rosa Lee Brooks in February 1965 at an
Ike & Tina Turner revue performance at the California Club. They
became involved, spending time at Brooks's mother's house in the
Crenshaw district of the city. They organized a recording session
together, a rare Hendrix collaboration with a female musician.
The recording studio for Revis Records was a converted garage
behind Billy Revis's house on Western Avenue, near 54th. The band
assembled two performers from Major Lance's band from Ciro's:
the drummer 'Big' Francis and a bassist called Alvin. Hendrix played
guitar for Brooks on a single, 'My Diary', co-written by Arthur Lee
(Arthur Taylor Porter), with an improvised number, 'Utee', on the
B-side. The meeting of Hendrix and Lee was another fortuitous
event, as their trajectories ran in parallel. At the time Lee was in the
California Club's house band, but that year he formed the influential
psychedelic, integrated band Love with (among others) his fellow
band member Johnny Echols on guitar.[92] He said of Hendrix:

> Jimi Hendrix was one of the first long-haired black cats I'd
> ever seen . . . He liked the way I wrote, I needed a guitar
> player who could play like Curtis Mayfield.[93]

Little Richard played Ciro's with Hendrix in the backing band on
9 and 10 April 1965. Brooks's single was released in June.[94] Hendrix
returned east with Little Richard's backing band for a mid-April
booking in New York.[95]

Hendrix was not in Los Angeles at the time of the Watts Riots,
the uprising on 11–17 August 1965 that destroyed a swathe of the

inner city. According to Velvert Turner, the lyric to 'House Burning Down' referred to the event, a pivotal week when African Americans in the Watts district lashed out over local injustice, devastating their own neighbourhood. Watts residents complained about race-related problems ranging from limited job opportunities and police brutality to exploitative merchandisers: local supermarkets selling overpriced, low-quality goods and price-gouging furniture shops. According to the political geographer Edward W. Soja, 'the Watts Riots burned down the core of African American Los Angeles and had an even larger, worldwide impact.'[96]

Frank Zappa influenced the rock and pop music of Los Angeles with his subversive attitude. His musical education and the influence

On the third day of the Watts rebellion, 11–17 August 1965, 103rd Street burned and was called 'Charcoal Alley'.

of the composer Edgard Varèse led him to integrate noise into
musical conventions. His lyrical themes and contrarian ideas were
inspired by social margins. For a while his log cabin at 2401 Laurel
Canyon Boulevard, on the northwest corner of Laurel Canyon and
Lookout Mountain, was home to a dozen and the headquarters of
a freak society, in counterpoint to the mellow, druggy middle-class
hippy culture of Laurel Canyon. He observed and gave a platform
to the bizarre street life of marginalized Sunset Strip characters. The
bands in his stable included the GTOS (Girls Together Outrageously),
whose auto-critique addressed the oddities of groupie culture
and the collective eroticism of female music fans. Zappa parodied
unorthodox behaviour, in the shadow of hippies, the beach crowd
and surf sound. When a Hendrix lyric crowed about waving his
freak flag high, it saluted Los Angeles freaks, among others.[97]

The transition from folk to electric, heard in the sounds of
The Byrds and Buffalo Springfield, was taking off as part of a
Los Angeles phenomenon, evolving out of The Beatles' sound
and expanding. Joni Mitchell arrived in Los Angeles in late 1967,
moving to a house at 8217 Lookout Mountain. Her prodigious
songwriting talent and innovative musicianship marked the music
scene that she joined in the fragrant, dry forest of Laurel Canyon.
A clique gathered weekly to share new compositions in a song
circle, as Howard Kaylan of The Turtles recalled:

> On any given Friday night, Stephen Stills, David Crosby,
> Jackson Browne, Mark [Volman], and whoever would sit
> around Joni's living room in a circle and someone would play
> his newest heartbreaker. Everyone would comment on it and
> the guitar would be passed to the next writer.[98]

Hendrix was invigorated in the wake of Monterey. Stills recalled
a marathon jam with Hendrix and Buddy Miles in Malibu, on
Thursday 27 June 1967:

It was a pretty eclectic bunch . . . Hugh Masekela, Buddy
Miles and Bruce Palmer . . . [Palmer was] around my house all
the time because he was the bass player in Buffalo Springfield,
and Hughie would show up now and then. We went through
two sets of players that night, me and Jimi, because we kept
going. We played to one dawn, through the morning and next
day, all the way into the next dawn.[99]

Doug Hastings of Buffalo Springfield gave an account of part of
the occasion:

I did a jam one afternoon at the Malibu house with Jimi Hendrix,
Buddy Miles, David Crosby and Stephen Stills. I think Stephen
played bass. It was the four of us playing in one part of the room,
and Jimi playing about 15 feet away from us, off in a corner with
his back to us. We probably played for a couple of hours. Buddy
sang and Jimi sat, off in the corner, playing his wah-wah pedal.[100]

In another interview, Stills said:

I could never get him to sit down with a good rhythm section,
but one time we did out at my beach house in Malibu. We played
fifteen hours straight, we didn't stop, and I think we must have
made up twenty rock 'n roll songs. Bruce Palmer was there and
Buddy Miles and me. Bruce got tired and I played bass.[101]

When Buddy Miles told the story, he mentioned that Neil Young
participated, and the length of the session stretched to '36 hours,
non-stop'.[102]

After Monterey the Experience picked up a festival booking
in Santa Barbara on 1 July 1967. The guitar player for Strawberry
Alarm Clock, Ed King, shared a dressing room with them, and
commented on the spare organization backing Hendrix:

Hendrix had just finished playing the infamous Monterey Pop Festival a month earlier, so he was big news. We finished playing our set . . . I . . . sat [in the dressing room] watching Jimi change the strings on his white Stratocaster . . . This one guy set up the drums, the amps, drove the equipment truck and collected the money . . . He walks in with a case of Snickers bars . . . 24 to the box . . . and starts unwrapping them and handing them to Hendrix, who was downing them in two bites each while turning the tuning keys on his guitar. He probably ate three quarters of the box in about 10 minutes. Energy. That was the only time I ever heard Hendrix play. His amp buzzed and crackled the whole show. I guess what that roadie could *not* do was fix amplifiers. I had never seen a Marshall amp up close before, but these were the most beat-up pieces of furniture I had ever seen.[103]

Whisky a Go Go, 8901 Sunset Boulevard, West Hollywood.

Hendrix appeared elated with the warm West Coast vibe. In an interview that year he said: 'We had a great time in LA, where Dave Crosby and a group called the Electric Flag came round to see us at the Whisky a Go Go. I love the West Coast, all those beautiful people.'[104]

Hendrix reportedly connected with Devon Wilson, who became an intermittent, long-time girlfriend, on 17 August that year. At the time, Wilson lived at Willow Glen Road. They met up at the Psychedelic Temple, a hippy gathering place run by a local biker gang, the Barons, at 1039 South Ardmore. It was the location for an Experience promotional film; the building and its garden featured in Roger Corman's low-budget movie about LSD, *The Trip* (1967), written by Jack Nicholson and starring Peter Fonda. Nicholson's script explored his psychedelic experience in 1962, under Dr Janiger. The geometric spaces of the Psychedelic Temple translated the kaleidoscopic patterned sensations of a trip.

At the end of the summer the Experience played the Hollywood Bowl in Los Angeles, on a bill with Scott McKenzie, headlined by The Mamas & the Papas. The Hollywood Bowl, a fabled venue, dates back to 1920; with almost 18,000 seats it is one of the largest natural amphitheatres. In 1967 the Experience was poorly received by a gentle flower-power audience; Noel Redding quipped, 'We died a death at the Hollywood Bowl.'[105] The Experience returned to headline on 14 September 1968, when the audience jumped into the reflecting pool, with onlookers reporting that 'even a security guard fell in the reflection pool after it filled with dancers who'd climbed or jumped from the stage.' Hendrix criticized the water feature that separated the stage from the crowd: 'I like to play anywhere. So long as I can play close to people. Not where I'm playing a hundred feet away like we did in the Hollywood Bowl. That was a drag, standing so far away from people.'[106]

Hendrix invited his brother Leon to stay with the band at a rented house at 2850 Benedict Canyon Drive, Beverly Hills, in September and October 1968. Hendrix was driving a Corvette,

possibly without a driver's licence and his spectacles, although his vehicle registration did arrive in the post.[107] The brothers and their entourage frequented Sunset Strip clubs such as the Whisky a Go Go when not recording at TTG Studios.

Leon described the decadent neighbourhood pool and party life, emphasizing the piles of free cocaine.[108] He also depicted the alienating behaviour of young women who gathered at parties, by pools, backstage and in hotel lobbies and corridors, recording studios and clubs, waiting to connect with anyone who was linked to a band. He described staying in one wing of the Benedict Canyon house with Hendrix and Buddy Miles, while the English crowd occupied another wing. When he wandered by there to visit Mitchell and Redding, they would be watching cartoons on television.[109] Paul Caruso remembered an octagonal, fully mirrored dressing room in Hendrix's quarters that may have led to the lyrics of the song 'Room Full of Mirrors'.

Hendrix was in Los Angeles in October 1968 to record, as well as to produce Eire Apparent, a Northern Irish band managed by Mike Jeffery, who opened for the Experience during summer touring. They used sixteen-track tapes at TTG Studios, at 1441 North McCadden Place, Hollywood. Recording in Los Angeles for around two weeks in late October attracted numerous visitors, all of them welcomed by the band. During the session, from 14 to 17 October, TTG (one of the first sixteen-track facilities) attracted a range of musicians, from Billy Preston and Ike Turner to Lou Reed. This was also the occasion for Hendrix and the producer Bumps Blackwell to share tales of Little Richard's temperamental antics.

There were opportunities to jam with Stephen Stills, Lee Michaels, Buddy Miles and the bassist Carol Kaye, and at some point Vic Briggs sat in with the Experience.[110] An engineer at TTG, Angel Balestier, became aware of Hendrix's sensitivity to reflected

Hollywood Bowl, Los Angeles.

vibrations. He described the process of capturing a particular
quality of sound reverberating in the recording studio during
a session on 24 October 1968:

> While recording 'Peace in Mississippi' – What Jimi had been
> hearing was the sound bouncing off the glass separating
> the studio from the control room. I put up a microphone to
> capture that, which gave me three positions to mix and put on
> tape. He came inside, listened, and said, 'I'd like to get a little
> more of *that* here.' That's how Hendrix was . . . I went back
> out, put three Manhasset music stands in a corner to bounce
> more of his sound, changed my microphone positions slightly,
> and he said, 'Yeah. *That's* what I'm looking for.'[111]

While on tour in Los Angeles that year, Hendrix had met Sharon
Lawrence, a writer for United Press International, backstage when
the Experience played Anaheim on 9 February. They had remained
in touch and she visited him while the Experience was recording at
TTG in the autumn. She was assigned to interview him for UPI at the
Beverly Rodeo Hotel on 1 May 1969 and observed the hippy girl who
tossed a pill bottle at Hendrix. She included detailed observations in
her interview notes and became a key witness for the defence during
Hendrix's trial in Toronto in December 1969 (see Chapter Six).[112]

According to Lawrence, Hendrix spoke of building a
headquarters or ranch retreat in Los Angeles. She wrote about
meeting Hendrix while he was staying at the Beverly Rodeo Hyatt
House, 360 North Rodeo Drive, Beverly Hills, and recounted his
proposal for Skychurch, a place to which he would invite musicians
including Roland Kirk and Steve Winwood. Hendrix sketched out for
her a site with two stages – one outside, one inside – and a U-shaped
bunkhouse. With Lawrence, he later inspected a three-storey
property owned by Phil Spector on the southeast corner of Sunset
Boulevard and Carol Street, with Skychurch in mind.[113]

## 2 SOUTH: NASHVILLE, MEMPHIS, ATLANTA, NEW ORLEANS

Jimi Hendrix landed in Nashville in 1962 and used the city first as a base, then as a launch pad. He began bouncing from Nashville on local and then longer-haul tours, understanding how the system of TOBA (Theater Owners' Booking Association) clubs in Southern cities – a network of mainly white-owned venues for black vaudeville, which overlapped with the Chitlin' Circuit, the venues that were geared towards music by and for African Americans – interacted and were connected in a network. Nashville was a working-class centre for country music; Memphis a centre for rhythm and blues; New Orleans the authentic home of traditional live performance and of the J&M Recording Studio on Rampart Street; and Atlanta the base for the Rev. Dr Martin Luther King Jr and an emerging music hub. Venues on the Chitlin' Circuit ranged from large, metropolitan-scale music halls of the vaudeville era, such as the Madam C. J. Walker Theater on Indiana Street, Indianapolis, to smaller clubs, such as the Royal Peacock in Atlanta. The crowds could be rough. The Animals' bassist Chas Chandler summed up what might happen beyond booing: 'If they didn't like it they would throw things at you.'[1]

Nona Hendryx, a cousin of Hendrix and a vocalist and songwriter, performed with Patti LaBelle on the Chitlin' Circuit and later became well known as part of the trio Labelle. She gave an unvarnished account of the circuit, which she toured with leading artists James Brown, Otis Redding, Joe Tex, Sam Cooke, the Staple Singers and Curtis Mayfield & the Impressions:

> Going on the road at that time meant the Chitlin' Circuit, so-called for the low budget, bus riding, station wagon, fried fish, chicken in a box, sardine and soda cracker eating, rooming house-type hotel staying, mostly southern route taking, playing mostly clubs on the wrong side of the tracks. Maybe you'll get paid or maybe you won't, or maybe you'll be cancelled without notice. In the South in the early 60s, during the civil rights movement, things were escalating. Desegregation, bussing, early black militancy, the murder of JFK, Malcom X, Dr King, Medgar Evers and those four little girls killed by a bomb in the 16th Street Baptist Church [in Birmingham, Alabama]. We were on the Chitlin' Circuit so our encounters with white southerners were far less destructive. We were met with No Room in the Inn (if you were a certain colour), white and coloured bathrooms and drinking fountains. So we stayed in coloured hotels or rooming houses and coloured-friendly motels when we could. Being refused service at a rest stop restaurant was common and sometimes it ended with a threat to send us to our maker.[2]

Nona Hendryx performed with Patti LaBelle & the Bluebelles, who shared a backing band with The Vibrations. Hendryx described how they worked with House bands, and listed the major metropolitan venues of the Chitlin' Circuit, from the Apollo in New York to the Fox in Detroit:

> Only artists like James Brown, Otis Redding, Sam Cooke, Joe Tex, Little Richard, Bo Diddley, B. B. King and other big stars had their own bands. When we played the Uptown Theatre

in Philly, . . . the Howard in Washington, DC, the Regal in Baltimore, the Royal in Chicago, the Brooklyn Fox . . . or the Peachtree nightclub in Atlanta, it was with the house band. We had charts – musical arrangements – and would rehearse with the band the day before if we were lucky or the afternoon before the show at night. In our case it was usually anywhere between two or four shows so you couldn't depend on your hit or semi-hit; you had to have a deep musical well to draw from and for most of those places you had to be really good. Theatre gigs were welcomed because it meant we were in one city, one hotel for a week to ten days. Moving from city to city doing one-nighters was an exhausting way of life even for teenagers.[3]

Jimi Hendrix, meanwhile, was meeting Southern African American musicians, experiencing and hearing about stunning performances that happened in small-town, unpretentious venues as musicians came together with audiences on the Chitlin' Circuit. Guitar Slim (Eddie Jones) was a musician with a reputation for upstaging all the others on the bill, as Earl King described, referring to a gig of around 1954:

> [Clarence] Gatemouth Brown, T-Bone Walker, Lowell Fulson and Guitar Slim were all performing one night at the White Eagle in Opelousas, Louisiana. Slim was headlining because 'The Things I Used to Do' [his hit of 1954] was a scorcher. They were all sitting in the dressing room and Guitar Slim walked up to 'em and said, 'Gentlemen, we got the greatest guitar players in the country assembled right here. But when I leave tonight, ain't nobody gonna realize you even been here.' We all laughed, but that's exactly what happened. Slim come out with his hair dyed blue, blue suit, blue pair of shoes. He had 350 feet [over 100 m] of mike wire connected to his guitar, and a valet carrying him on his shoulders all through the

crowd and out into the parking lot. Man, he was stopping cars driving down the highway. No one could outperform Slim. He was about the performingest man I've ever seen.[4]

Stories about stellar blues showmanship ranged from the ribald theatrics of Muddy Waters to unexpected acrobatics by the heavyset Howlin' Wolf, who, at age 55, climbed a stage curtain to close a set during a Memphis blues package bill in 1965. Robert Palmer described the event:

The MC announced Wolf, and the curtains opened to reveal his band pumping out a decidedly homegrown shuffle . . . Suddenly he sprang out onto the stage from the wings. He was a huge hulk of a man, but he advanced across the stage in sudden bursts of speed, his head pivoting from side to side . . . He seemed to be having an epileptic seizure, but no, he suddenly lunged for the microphone, blew a chorus of raw, heavily rhythmic harmonica, and began moaning. He had the hugest voice I have ever heard – it seemed to fill the hall and get right inside your ears, and when he hummed and moaned in falsetto, every hair on your neck crackled with electricity. The thirty-minute set went by like an express train, with Wolf switching from harp to guitar (which he played while rolling around on his back and, at one point, doing somersaults) and leaping up to prowl the lip of the stage . . . Finally, an impatient signal from the wings let him know that his portion of the show was over. Defiantly, Wolf counted off a bone-crushing rocker, began singing rhythmically, feigned an exit, and suddenly made a flying leap for the curtain at the side of the stage. Holding the microphone under his beefy right arm and singing into it all the while, he began climbing up the curtain, going higher and higher until he was perched far above the stage, the thick curtain threatening to rip, the audience screaming with delight.

Then he loosened his grip and, in a single easy motion, slid
right down the curtain, hit the stage, cut off the tune, and
stalked away, to the most ecstatic cheers of the evening.[5]

Muddy Waters had a beer-bottle routine that he used when
playing 'Mannish Boy'. His harmonica player Paul Oscher
described the scene when they played at the Moonlight Lounge in
St Louis in 1965:

We played 'Mannish Boy' for our last number, and Muddy
had a longneck Budweiser bottle concealed in his pants before
the song. He really worked the crowd on that song, shouting
like a preacher possessed, and when he got the crowd hot
enough, he'd shout out, 'I'm gonna show you a man,' then
he'd move that bottle in his pants like he had a huge hard-on.
The audience screamed.[6]

During his quasi-anonymous early touring on the Chitlin'
Circuit, as a sideman calling himself Maurice James, Hendrix
absorbed the ordinary and the extraordinary in local musicianship
and showmanship. He gathered performance experience
travelling the United States, Canada and Bermuda, and grabbed
every opportunity to jam in obscure after-hours dives and jukes,
both urban and rural, wherever he landed. His immersion in
regional blues and rhythm and blues traditions provided tools
for composing, structuring and embellishing songs. Hendrix was
fascinated by the techniques and equipment involved in making
loud, funky, greasy sound. Layered on the various regional sonic
environments were the evolving technology of amplified sound
and the drones of the motorized modern world.

From Fort Ord, Hendrix was sent for paratrooper training. He
arrived at Fort Campbell, Kentucky, on 8 November 1961. The

base was fenced terrain, over 40 ha (100,000 acres) fully equipped for training military personnel. There, in 1961 in Service Club Number One, Hendrix met Billy Cox, a fellow member of the elite 101st Airborne Division. Hendrix earned his Screaming Eagle patch on 11 January 1962 in about eight months, for 25 parachute jumps, including jumps in Hawaii. He recreated the sonic experience, the whoosh of a parachute jump, in his letters home.

Hendrix refocused his attention on playing the guitar in bands. His family sent his Danelectro from Seattle. Hendrix, Cox, the drummer Gary Ferguson, Jimmy Darden and (briefly) Major Charles Washington played local service clubs as the Kasuals. According to Washington, Hendrix had a habit of pawning his guitar and then insisting he had to get it back when a gig came up.[7]

That season, Hendrix and Cox drove to Indianapolis to participate in a talent competition in a bar named George's. There they met the guitarist Alphonso 'Baby Boo' Young, whom they invited to join them gigging in Nashville. The weekend activities meant that Hendrix was occasionally unable to make bed check; he lost rank for sleeping on duty, for inattention and for masturbation. He was able to obtain a discharge by July 1962, after eleven months in the army.[8]

### CLARKSVILLE AND NASHVILLE, 1961–2

The closest town to the Fort Campbell army base was Clarksville, a town with a population of 22,000, and segregated, as were Southern and many other American towns at the time. Hendrix told of spending his army earnings the day he was discharged at a single bar. He stayed in Clarksville to wait for Billy Cox, renting a room at 411 Glenn Street, then 610 Ford Street, and played regularly at the Pink Poodle club on College Street. When Cox was discharged in October they reformed as The King Kasuals with Young, Tee Howard Williams on saxophone, the drummer

Freeman Brown and the vocalist Harry Bachelor, and played the American Legion in Clarksville.[9]

Hendrix attended regular Tuesday-night gigs by the Imperials to watch the leading guitarist Johnny Jones. During the autumn of 1962, according to biographer Charles Cross, through Jones, Hendrix met B.B. King and the left-handed, Flying V-playing guitarist Albert King, musicians who played what the writer Charlie Gillett called 'city' blues as opposed to 'country' blues.[10] B.B. King recalled first meeting Hendrix at a later date, at the Harlem Duke Social Club in Prichard, Alabama, in January 1965. King remembered getting to know him backstage, while they were on a travelling package tour when Hendrix was playing in Little Richard's band. Cox and Hendrix auditioned and were hired for the house band at the Del Morocco Club at 2417 Jefferson Street in Nashville, which had opened in 1935.

Nashville, or 'Music City USA', was the capital of country, bluegrass and rockabilly music songwriting, publishing and performing, where half of American recordings were made. Elvis Presley recorded over 200 records at the RCA Victor Studio B. Blue-collar Nashville had plenty of clubs where a band could play, and several rhythm and blues record labels, including Bullet, Calvert, Cherokee, Tennessee and Republic. One was Excello Records, known for recording Slim Harpo's 'I'm a King Bee' (1957), and specializing in Louisiana swamp blues. Nashville had an urban population of some 200,000 in the early 1960s and overall a suburban population in its metropolitan area of 400,000. A significant proportion – 43 per cent – was African American. For Hendrix, Nashville became a stopover, a crossroads on the Chitlin' Circuit club network. Later, in autumn 1964, he would use an Atlanta address while touring the South.

In Nashville, there were clusters of clubs along Jefferson Street, including the Del Morocco Club, Club Baron, Maceo's Club, Sugar Hill, Club Revillot, Deborah's Casino Royale, Ebony

Circle and Pee Wee's. According to Hendrix's biographer Steven
Roby, Nashville's African American clubs of 1962–4 included,
dispersed at the city edges, the Top Hat and John's Barbecue Stand
and, near Jefferson Street, the Three Stooges, the Viaduct, the
Wigwam and the Stealaway.[11] The New Era, a club with about
100 seats located at first on Fourth Avenue (near the clubs Gradys
and the Bijou Theater), built a reputation for regularly booking
rhythm and blues artists. By 1955 urban renewal had erased the
Fourth Avenue North block from Cedar to Gay, taking out the
New Era and the Bijou Theater as well as tram and taxi stands,
and so the New Era moved to 1114 Charlotte Avenue. The 25-year-
old Etta James recorded her live album *Etta James Rocks the House*
there, in shows on 27 and 28 September 1963.[12] The New Era
booked such acts as Jerry Butler, Aretha Franklin, B.B. King and
Joe Tex. American urban renewal of the 1960s was notorious for
demolishing African American districts: in 1968 construction of
the I-40 highway disconnected Jefferson Street from the rest of the
city and eliminated the Del Morocco and other significant venues
on the street.[13] A few venues survived. The Elks Lodge, at 2614
Jefferson Street, was formerly the Club Baron, where Larry Lee
listened and looked on as young Hendrix lost a guitar duel with
Johnny Jones.

Another kind of urban performance put Nashville in the
media spotlight in the early 1960s: the work of civil rights activists
linked to Fisk University. They conceived of a strategy of non-
violent resistance action, targeting public and privately managed
semi-public inner-city places. The sit-ins worked to desegregate
downtown places such as lunch counters, sitting rooms and rest
rooms, and became recognized as innovative and effective. From
February to May 1960, activists occupied eleven lunch counters
in downtown Nashville. Walgreens, Woolworths, S. H. Kress and
McLellans on Fifth Avenue North, Grant and Harvey's on Church
Street, and the Moon-McGrath Drug Store on Union Street

were targeted, as well as the Greyhound Bus Station on Sixth
Avenue and Commerce Avenue, and the Trailways bus centre on
Sixth Avenue. The occupiers were met with hostility, and some
temporary desegregation. In December 1962 integrated groups
of activists continued the protests, attempting to be served at
another series of restaurants: Herschel's Tic Toc Restaurant, the
Krystal and the B&W Cafeteria on Church Street. As documented
in newspaper photographs, demonstrators were thrown out on to
the street and arrested.[14]

Hendrix and Cox conducted their own dual sit-in, ignoring
a 'white only' sign in a Nashville diner in December 1962. As
a result, local police booked them. Their employer, Theodore
'Uncle Teddy' Acklen, bailed them out. Cox noted: 'When we
first came into Nashville in the 101st Airborne, we sat where we
wanted to.'[15]

Protest marches and sit-ins continued throughout 1963 and 1964.
A riot followed a march by 200 civil rights protesters in downtown
Nashville on 27 April 1964.[16] Some urban lunch counters and
public places were desegregated, and protesters appeared at public
places where they were excluded – cinemas, libraries, museums,
beaches and swimming pools – for sit-in actions. Eventually Civil
Rights Movement activists refocused on the Voter Registration
Campaign. The Civil Rights Act of 1964 ended legally sanctioned
segregation in America.

The Civil Rights Movement organized what would be
hailed ultimately as a historic sequence of events of non-violent
resistance to protest against racial injustice and segregation in the
South, eventually moving the nation to enact political legislation.
Leaders included James Lawson, John Lewis, Diane Nash, Bob
Moses, Ralph Abernathy and Rev. Dr Martin Luther King Jr.
Long-term actions were orchestrated, such as the Montgomery
bus boycott of 1955–6, a protest against bus segregation that lasted
for a year. News media covered the dramatic confrontation of

young Freedom Riders in 1964. Photographs of youths attacked
in the street by police and dogs and pummelled by water hoses
held by firemen appeared in televised news and print media
in 1963 and 1964. *Life* magazine published a photo series of the
violence against peaceful young protesters in Birmingham in
1963. Warhol appropriated a photograph of police dogs attacking
peaceful protesters for his disaster series of silkscreen images in
1964. The violence of a bomb that killed four black girls at the
16th Street Baptist Church earned Birmingham a name of shame:
Bombingham. The March on Washington for Jobs and Freedom
of 1963 was a successful assembly of over 250,000, possibly 300,000
people, led by King, and the occasion of his moving 'I have a
dream' speech, for which occasion the sound system was repaired
by the army after an overnight sabotage.

The dramatic height of the movement was the series of three
marches from Selma to Montgomery, Alabama, in the spring of
1965. After the first, on 7 March 1965, 'Bloody Sunday', television
broadcast the violence and police brutality encountered by the
peaceful protesters. The third march left on 16 March, arriving
on 24 March. Entertainers gathered for the march on the State
Capitol in Montgomery on 24 March, to arrive the next day, and
held a concert where Nina Simone's rendition of 'Mississippi
Goddam' inspired and captured the determined collective mood
of the crowd.[17]

When Hendrix arrived in Nashville, his temporary lodging
consisted of camping at a construction site. He said in an
interview:

> I went to Nashville where I lived in a big housing estate they
> were building. Every Sunday afternoon we used to go downtown
> to watch the race riot. We'd take a picnic basket because they
> wouldn't serve us in the restaurants. One group would stand on

one side of the street, and the rest on the other side. They'd shout names and talk about each other's mothers, and every once in a while stab each other. Sometimes if there was a good movie on that Sunday, there wouldn't be any race riots.[18]

Humour aside, Hendrix struggled to get by, as he later explained: 'I lived in very miserable circumstances. I played in cafés, clubs and in the streets. That's where I really learned to play.'[19] It is possible that he relied on his girlfriend Joyce Lucas, who may have moved with him from Clarksville to Nashville.

Hendrix credited the Nashville scene with motivating him to advance to an expert level on the guitar:

In the bars I used to play in you really had to play, 'cause those people were really hard to please. It was one of the hardest audiences in the South; they hear it all the time. Everybody knows how to play guitar. You went down the street and people are sitting on their porch playing more guitar. That's where I learned to play, really, in Nashville.[20]

While in the house band at the Del Morocco on Jefferson Street, Hendrix stayed next door, in one of the upstairs rooms at Joyce's House of Glamour, which Acklen owned as well as the Del Morocco. The Del had a capacity of some 200 people, in a hall 46 by 15 m (150 by 50 ft). Upstairs was the Blue Room, with access to private gambling. According to the band guitarist Larry Lee, they played four nights a week for eleven dollars a night.[21] Billy Cox listed The King Kasuals' house band repertoire, including 'Blue Suede Shoes', 'Green Onions', 'Let the Good Times Roll', 'Poison Ivy', 'Hey Bo Diddley', 'Tutti Frutti', 'Stand by Me', 'Twist and Shout', 'I'm a Man' and 'What'd I Say'.[22] To work out techniques of performing in a crowd, Cox purchased a long guitar cord, which, as he explained, enabled Hendrix to

'leap off the stage and take his theatrics into the audience . . .
Jimi wanted to play outside the front door of clubs.'[23] When he
was not performing, Hendrix gained a reputation as spaced out –
and the nickname Marbles. Larry Perigo, saxophone player with
The Continentals, said:

> The last time I saw him, he was walking down Jefferson Street
> with his guitar in his hands, not in a case, and an amp cord was
> still plugged in. The other end was bouncing on the sidewalk.[24]

In March 1963, looking for opportunities to travel, Hendrix met the
MC Gorgeous George (Theophilus Odell George), who was known
for his tailoring, the stage costumes he made for his act and other
R&B Bands, improvised stage patter and acrobatics, and a blond
or silver wig. Hendrix found a precarious job backing him as he
introduced the acts. They joined a tour with Aretha Franklin and
Hank Ballard & the Midnighters. Hendrix sent a postcard home
from Columbia, South Carolina, saying he had played Charleston.
Hank Ballard & the Midnighters left him stranded in Knoxville,
Tennessee, in April 1963.

Hendrix was back in Nashville in May 1963, and with Cox
reformed the King Kasuals, spending time with a group of
musicians around Marion James. James declared: 'Jimmy Hendrix
was never on time for any of our gigs! I helped Jimmy get bands
together to back him when he came to Nashville from Clarksville.'[25]
Cox mentioned that some of the King Kasuals became the horn
section at Muscle Shoals recording studio in Alabama.[26]

Hendrix toured with Solomon Burke that year. The acts on the
tour included Otis Redding, Sugar Pie DeSanto and Joe Tex, along
with the comic Pigmeat Markham. The tour left Hendrix stranded
again.[27] He toured in September and October with Bob Fisher &
the Bonnevilles, who had a rhythm and blues hit, 'Cherokee Twist',
from 1962. Tennessee was part of the Cherokee Nation, though

it is impossible to say whether Hendrix was reminded of this heritage, his Cherokee ancestry, when he later sketched out his song 'Cherokee Mist'.[28]

For a month in November The Bonnevilles backed The Marvelettes – vocalists with the first Motown hit, 'Please Mr Postman' – and Curtis Mayfield & the Impressions. The smooth sound of Mayfield combined with a positive activist message made a lasting musical impact on Hendrix. The Bonnevilles line-up included the rhythm guitarist Larry Lee, Fisher on trumpet and vocals, Willy Young on bass guitar, Sammy Higginbottom on saxophone and the drummer Isaac McKay.[29] Cox also mentioned playing with Mayfield:

> Jimi, Larry and myself toured as the backup band for Curtis Mayfield and the Impressions back in the early Sixties for about a dozen gigs within 150 mile radius of Nashville.[30]

Bobby Womack, playing with The Valentinos and backing Sam Cooke in 1964, recalled Hendrix from this tour:

> I first saw Jimi Hendrix playing with the MC Gorgeous George Odell . . . There was no one like him – the way he dressed, the way he played, the way he heard music. He was always saying, I've got to find my corner, because he wasn't even accepted for his own race . . . Jimi made music like an abstract painting.[31]

Hendrix practised incessantly, as Womack recalled:

> I met Jimi on the road with the Valentinos during the mid-'60s at the time Jimi was backing Gorgeous George Odell. Those were lean times as Hendrix would cut his sandwich in half and wrap the other half . . . A week later, he'd open that sandwich back up and chow down. The main thing I

remember about Jimi is that he constantly played his guitar all the time when we were on the bus, and I do mean non-stop. You could hear that scratching sound. I learned to accept him. I took a liking to him and vice-versa.[32]

Cox mentioned that Hendrix reappeared in Nashville periodically, and in about September 1964 he stopped back in town. That autumn he left The Isley Brothers and their back-up band, the I. B. Specials (see Chapter Three). In an interview Hendrix vaguely jumbled some of the acts: 'So then I quit, I quit them in Nashville somewhere . . . this guy, he was on a tour with B. B. King, Jackie Wilson and Sam Cooke, and all these people, Chuck Jackson . . . I was playing guitar behind a lot of the acts on the tour.'[33] Also in September, Hendrix played with a rhythm and blues band in Atlanta, the Tams, who wore matching berets, all they could afford when the band had started out in 1962.[34] According to band member Charles Pope,

We always had to buy food for Jim. He never had any money. And when we were on tour, Jimi and Gorgeous George would sometimes fight on the bus. We really didn't care too much for his playing. He played more of a rock style.[35]

On 28 September Hendrix sent home a postcard from Columbus, Ohio, writing: 'I'm on a tour which lasts about 35 days. We're about half way through it now. We've been to all the cities in the mid-west, east and south.'[36]

In October and November, Hendrix travelled on a tour headlined by B.B. King, Sam Cooke and Jackie Wilson. He may have played with them in a grandly scaled music hall with a vast proscenium stage in Richmond, Virginia. The Cooke and Wilson tour played two sold-out shows at the 3,200-seat venue The Mosque in Richmond. Hendrix mentioned how much he learned in those 35 days, particularly from

Cooke, who was unexpectedly shot and killed in Los Angeles in December of that year.[37]

Sam Cooke's biographer Peter Guralnick emphasized the specific role Gorgeous George played on tour, running the after show and bussing the bands to a large local club after the concerts to perform, eat and unwind, charging the club's owner a fee of about $100. On the Cooke and Wilson tour, at the 1,500-capacity Carlotta Club in Greensboro, North Carolina, Hendrix backed Gorgeous George in the late-night jam and show.[38]

Hendrix had an Atlanta address in October 1964. On 8 October, on a postcard with a photo of Jacksonville, Florida, he wrote to his father from Cincinnati:

> Dear Dad. Here we are in Florida, we're going to play in Tampa tomorrow – then Miami, we're playing all through the south. We'll end up in Dallas Texas. My home address is Atlanta. I hope everyone's ok. Tell Grama in Canada hi for me. Tell Leon to be kool and go to school. I must run now – take it easy – My address is 318 Fort St. apt. 3 Atlanta Ga. Jimmy.[39]

In January 1965 Hendrix joined Little Richard's band as guitarist, possibly meeting or auditioning at the Royal Peacock in Atlanta. Hendrix, then still using his stage name, Maurice James, toured for five months with Little Richard, who refused to be upstaged by Hendrix playing show-stealing guitar. Hendrix complained about Richard's rants: 'Little Richard wouldn't let us wear frilly shirts on stage. Once, me and Glyn Wildings [sic; the guitarist Glenn Willings] got some fancy shirts because we were tired of wearing the uniform.'[40] Hendrix went on to explain how Richard called a meeting:

> 'I am Little Richard, I am Little Richard, the King, the King of Rock and rhythm. I am the only one allowed to be pretty.

Take off those shirts.' Man, it was like that. Bad pay, lousy
living, and getting burned.[41]

Later Hendrix said he wanted to do with the guitar what
Little Richard did with his voice. Little Richard pushed social
boundaries, claiming: 'My music made your liver quiver, your
bladder spatter and your knees freeze.'[42]

In 1965 an early performance of Hendrix playing back-up
was broadcast on a local Nashville television programme, *Night
Train*. The Nashville studio was WLAC-TV studios in the Life
and Casualty (L&C) Tower, which, at 30 storeys, was the tallest
building in Tennessee for seven years after it was built in 1957.
Designed by Edwin Keeble, and with structural engineering
by Ross Bryan Associates, it was Nashville's first skyscraper. In
that prestigious location, at 401 Church Street and 159 Fourth
Avenue North, in June or July 1965, Hendrix performed 'Shotgun'
in a bank of guitarists, saxophonists and trombonists in Little
Richard's backing band, the Royal Company, behind the singers
Buddy and Stacy.[43]

In 1965 Hendrix stopped in Memphis long enough to meet
guitarist, songwriter and producer Steve Cropper, who played in
the Stax Records session band, Booker T. & the MG's. Hendrix and
Cropper ate in a soul food restaurant together, and he showed
Cropper how he played 'Mercy, Mercy' on the Don Covay release
in 1964. Hendrix said:

Steve Cropper turned me on millions of years ago, and I
turned him on millions of years ago too, but because of
different songs. Like we went into the studio and we started
teaching each other. I found him at the soul restaurant eating
all this stuff right across from the studio in Memphis. I was
playing this top 40 R&B Soul Hit Parade package with the
patent leather shoe and hair-do's combined.[44]

Memphis was home to Stax Records, which operated from a converted cinema on McLemore Avenue. The asymmetry of the studio, with its sloping floor, the seats removed, may have contributed to its distinctive sound. Stax was famous for its early success with a casually colour-blind sound. Stax's recording artists and bands were integrated Southern musicians working together. The city was home to blues and rhythm and blues musicians, ranging from B.B. King in his early career to Al Green. The urban blues axis, Beale Street, was neglected until the demise of Elvis Presley, when a flood of music fans prompted city officials to attempt to cash in as tourists flocked to Graceland. Beale Street was reassembled, if not put together backwards, repurposed for visitors.

In the city the photographer Ernest Withers created a series of posters documenting the 'I Am a Man!' campaign of 1968. It may be coincidence that these images, of the striking Memphis Sanitation workers with their 'I Am a Man' posters, appear to connect to the Hendrix lyric 'I'm a man'.[45]

Memphis remains one of the poorest cities in the United States. In the early 1960s its population was centralized in the city, with 497,524 inhabitants, while the population of its metropolitan area was 627,000. Sam Phillips created Sun Records at his Memphis recording studio. Memphis was where, in 1954, Elvis Presley recorded his first hit, 'That's All Right', written by Arthur 'Big Boy' Crudup. Presley recorded 'Mystery Train', leaning on a rendition recorded and released by Junior Parker in 1953, releasing his version on 20 August 1955. The Presley cover also appropriated a guitar riff from Junior Parker's 'Love My Baby' of 1953.[46] Presley's version of the song might be called a mash-up. Ike Turner saw methodical exploitation. Turner wrote 'Rocket 88', one of several songs recognized as among the earliest rock tunes, along with such New Orleans recordings as Roy Brown's 'Good Rockin' Tonight', 'The Fat Man' by Fats Domino (1948), 'Shake,

Rattle and Roll' by Big Joe Turner and Little Richard's early
releases. In a 2003 interview Ike Turner was sceptical about rock
history:

> I'm not sure, but I think in those days Sam Phillips was more
> used to recording commercials . . . I don't think he was really
> into recording bands . . . I don't think that 'Rocket 88' is rock
> and roll. I think that 'Rocket 88' is really R&B, but I think
> 'Rocket 88' is the *cause* of rock and roll existing. Back in those
> days, white radio stations didn't play black music: they called it
> race music . . . Sam Phillips got Dewey Phillips to play 'Rocket
> 88' on his program – and this is like the first black record to
> be played on a white radio station – and, man, all the white
> kids broke out to the record shops to buy it. So that's when
> Sam Phillips got the idea, 'Well, man, if I get me a white boy
> to sound like a black boy, then I got me a gold mine', which
> is the truth. So, that's when he got Elvis and he got Jerry Lee
> Lewis and a bunch of other guys and so they named it rock
> and roll rather than R&B and so this is the reason I think rock
> and roll exists – not that 'Rocket 88' was the first one, but that
> was what caused the first one.[47]

Hendrix appreciated the intimate scale, the atmosphere,
the climate and the sensation of performing on the Chitlin'
Circuit:

> It's fun to play in little funky clubs, because that's like a
> work house. It's nice to sweat. I remember we used to play
> sometimes, even the amplifiers and guitars actually were
> sweating, everything is sweating. It seemed like the more it
> got sweaty, the funkier it got and the groovier. Everybody
> melted together, I guess! And the sound was kickin' em all in
> the chest. I dig that! Water and electricity![48]

He reacted to the geography and atmosphere of touring, savouring the skyline of a night in a new town:

> I love to play in Texas – Texas and Florida. I don't know why. Maybe it's the weather, and the feeling of it, you know . . . I dig the South a little more than playing in the North. It's more of a pressure playing in the mid-West, you know, like Cleveland or Chicago. It's . . . like being in a pressure cooker, waiting for the top to blow off. The people there are groovy, but it's just the atmosphere or something, you know. Down South is great. New Orleans? That's great . . . Arizona is fantastic. It's great playing in Utah, you know, the colleges and all those places . . . the people . . . once we're off stage it's another world, but like the people are great . . . But like when we play at the gigs, they was really listening, they was really tuned in some kind of way or another. I think it was the air. People make sounds when they clap, so we make sound back. I like electric sounds, feedback and so forth, static.[49]

The Chitlin' Circuit shaped a taste for a funkier, greasier Southern sound. The anarchic interplay of groups contrasted with the catchy Motown recording techniques, where the same band, the Funk Brothers, played underneath different distinctive vocalists, and where an innovative bassline from an inventive bassist such as James Jamerson was revered. Hendrix was acute in his critique of Motown technique:

> It's artificial in a very, very commercial and very, very electronic made, very . . . synthetic soul sound. It isn't a real sound of any . . . Negro artist singing, you know, it's so commercial, and it's so put together, you know so beautifully that . . . I don't feel anything from it, except maybe the Isley brothers . . . and maybe the Four Tops, but as far as the rest . . .

all they do is they put a very, very hard beat to it . . . a very good beat; they put about a thousand people on tambourines and these bells . . . and they gotta thousand horns, a thousand violins, and then a singer, he overdubs his voice millions of times, or he'll sing in an echo chamber . . . it comes out . . . so artificial . . . but . . . it has a good beat and it sounds very good . . . it's very commercial for the younger people.[50]

# 3 EAST: HARLEM, NEW YORK, NEW JERSEY

Hendrix moved to New York from Nashville by bus in late 1963 or early 1964, with a coat borrowed from the guitarist Larry Lee. He travelled with Carl Fisher, concert promoter for Henry Wynn's Supersonic Attractions.[1] En route Hendrix may have stopped in Philadelphia for a recording session with the saxophonist Lonnie Youngblood (Lonnie Thomas; also known as the Prince of Harlem). A single by Youngblood and his band, including session man Hendrix, 'Go Go Shoes' (backed by 'Go Go Place'), was released in 1966 on Fairmount Records, with the misleading date '1963' printed on the label.[2]

Hendrix made it to Harlem's Hotel Theresa and crashed with a music crowd: he stayed first with Fisher, then moved to share a room with Dean Courtney and James Oscar 'Pushay' Thomas, a valet to Little Richard, whose business paid for the room. Early in 1964 he won the $25 prize at the Apollo Theater's Wednesday Amateur Night. The Apollo at 253 West 125th Street, designed by the architect Charles Keister, was built in 1913 by Jules Hurtig and Harry Seamon as a white burlesque theatre. It became a black theatre in 1934, and remains a monument to live music, with an audience that maintains its reputation as engaged, expressive and raucous.[3]

Down the street at the Palm Café, Hendrix met Lithofayne Pridgon, known as Apollo Faye, a discerning meta-groupie and

a friend of Etta James. Pridgon called a set of musicians her
repertoire: Brook Benton, William Edward 'Little Willie' John,
David 'Fathead' Newman, Otis Redding, Jackie Wilson, Johnny
'Guitar' Watson and Wilson Pickett. In particular she was known
as an ex-girlfriend of Sam Cooke. She brought Hendrix to meet
Cooke backstage.[4]

Pridgon became a girlfriend of Hendrix, and supported him
as he entered the Harlem scene. They stayed together first at the
Hotel Seifer and then at a variety of hotels, including room 213 in
the then shabby Hotel Cecil over Minton's Playhouse – famous for
bebop – at 210 West 118 Street and Saint Nicholas Avenue.[5] They
also stayed at Pridgon's mother's apartment on West 98th Street.
Pridgon mentioned that they sometimes arrived home after her
mother had left for the day, and that they listened to her blues
record collection:

> [Hendrix] got all excited about her blues records. She had the
> low-down stuff . . . Ruth Brown, and beyond that. She had
> Muddy Waters, Lightnin' Hopkins, Judy King, Junior Parker,
> and folks like that and Jimi loved those people. He got out his
> guitar and played along with some of the records.[6]

After her mother lost patience with Hendrix, they slept where
they could, including the floor of Etta James's hotel dressing
room.[7] They stayed with a friend, Bootsie, at 210 West 118th
Street, and shared an apartment with the Allen twins, Albert and
Arthur, the vocalists known as the Ghetto Fighters, who changed
their names to Tundera and Taharqua Aleem. Pridgon eventually
married Tundera.[8]

Hendrix made the rounds to clubs such as the Palm Café at
209 West 125th Street and Smalls Paradise, a large basement club
at 2294½ Seventh Avenue at 135th Street that held a crowd
of 1,500. A musician friend, Jimmy Norman, said of roaming

the streets and hanging out in Harlem clubs: 'Small's Paradise, at 135th Street and Seventh Avenue, Count Basie's, Sugar Ray's, the Baby Grand – sometimes I run into him four or five times a night.'[9] Hendrix was hoping to sit in, but met with little success, even on jam nights. A guitarist with Curtis Knight witnessed Hendrix trying to sit in, only to be rebuffed: 'These were supposed to be jam sessions. Anybody could come up, but they'd always give him some excuse . . . Most of the guys then had their hair conked and Marcels [hairstyles] and not in a do-rag like Jimi would wear.'[10]

Pridgon described Hendrix's eventual acceptance in Harlem clubs: 'He did "Walking the Dog" by Rufus Thomas all by himself and he really killed them. Then from then on, there was a certain crowd that looked forward to him . . . they knew what Jimi was all about.' Hendrix and Pridgon shared a taste for blues music, as she explained:

> There was a time when he was heavy, heavy . . . into blues. Blues was it. He would play a little rock every now and then, a little rhythm and blues . . . It was stomp down, funky blues. Elmore James was his favorite. He would take a little glass and put it on the strings and get that sound that Elmore got. 'The Sky Is Crying' was his favourite, 'It Hurts Me Too', 'Bleeding Heart' . . . He was just going crazy about Bob Dylan, telling me all about it.[11]

In March or April 1964, Hendrix connected with The Isley Brothers, who had a hit in 1962 with a cover of a song written by the Brill Building composers Phil Medley and Bert Berns (Bert Russell), 'Twist and Shout'. The song was covered by The Beatles in 1964 and turned into a British rock anthem. Various people have recounted The Isley Brothers' meeting with Hendrix. In one version, a singer and friend of The Isley Brothers, Tony Rice,

heard Hendrix play at the Palm Café and let him know that The
Isley Brothers were looking for a guitarist as theirs had moved to
California. In a melodramatic version, O'Kelly 'Kelly' Isley ran
into a homeless Hendrix in a record shop in 1964 and brought
him to live with the family in Englewood, Bergen County, New
Jersey. With the Isley family in New Jersey, they watched the CBS
television broadcast of The Beatles' first appearance on *The Ed
Sullivan Show*, on 9 February 1964, along with an estimated 70
million viewers. On 23 February the show broadcast The Beatles'
version of 'Twist and Shout'. Pop, rock, rhythm and blues and
soul rolled into the mainstream media.

Ernie Isley was asked in an interview about tracking down
Hendrix. He described how hiring Hendrix involved dealing with
his pawned guitar and his lack of strings, as well as his lack of a
place to stay. According to Ernie, 'Before he came to the house
for the first time, Kelly got him a brand-new guitar. We went to
Manney's . . . and got a brand-new white Strat (Stratocaster) at his
request. His very first one.'[12] At their house he watched television:
'Super Chicken, Bean and Cecil, Bonanza, Mutual of Omaha's
Wild Kingdom.'[13] And he practised:

> We had a full-length mirror near the front door of the house,
> and he would be playing the guitar and looking at himself in
> the mirror to see how he looked. He would flip it behind his
> back, or under his leg. You never saw anybody interact with
> an instrument like that. Like it was a yo-yo.[14]

Marvin Isley described how Hendrix 'would practice phrases over
and over again, turn them inside out, break them in half, break
them in quarters, play them fast'.[15]

Hendrix resumed touring as a member of the I. B. Specials,
The Isley Brothers' backing band, with a horn section – trumpet
and saxophone. They toured in March and April, playing a concert

in a baseball stadium in Bermuda, and they played Montreal, where Hendrix met Buddy Miles, playing with Ruby & the Romantics at the Upton Club (although Miles remembered the name of the club as the Grand National).[16] Hendrix toured with the brothers for nine months, recording 'Testify' on their label, T-Neck Records. On release it did not chart.

After a gig in Seattle Hendrix stayed on an extra day to see Betty Jean Morgan. Oblivious of the tour schedule, he ended up missing several dates on the tour. On his return to New York he found an opportunity to record. On 13 and 18 May 1964 he played the guitar on Don Covay & the Goodtimers' recordings 'Can't Stay Away' and 'Mercy, Mercy'. The latter was released as a single, backed with 'Can't Stay Away', in early August.[17]

Race issues and police brutality continued making headlines, not only in the South. In New York on 18 July 1964, with the temperature at 33°C (92°F), violent demonstrations racked Harlem and Bedford-Stuyvesant. On 16 July 1964, in Harlem, a 1.8-m-tall (6-ft) white off-duty police officer, Thomas Gilligan, shot and killed a fifteen-year-old, 54-kg (122-lb) African American teenager named James Powell in front of friends and other witnesses. Over six days several thousand people demonstrated, smashing windows, lighting fires and looting local businesses. The Harlem Race Riot of 1964 foreshadowed inner-city riots in July and August in Philadelphia, Rochester, Chicago and Jersey City.[18] The seven-day Watts Rebellion of August 1965 in Los Angeles (see Chapter One) and the Detroit 12th Street riots of July 1967 were on the horizon.

In April 1965 Hendrix returned to New York, where he stayed at the Hotel Theresa at 2090 Seventh Avenue. On 16 April he played with Little Richard's backing band, billed as the Royal Company, at the Paramount Theatre, a 3,664-seat movie palace at 43rd Street and Broadway. Designed by the Chicago firm of Rapp and Rapp, it opened in 1926. Graham Nash of The Hollies was impressed with the venue, marvelling at 'marble columns, a crystal chandelier, a grand staircase, and balconies layered one on top of the other like a New York skyscraper'.[19] The headliner for 'Soupy Sales' Easter Show' was the children's comedian Soupy Sales (Milton Supman) at the height of his televisual popularity. The line-up also included The Detergents, The Hullaballoos from Hull in the UK, the Hullabaloo Dancers from the American TV series of the same name, The Exciters, Little Richard with The Royal Company, The Hollies, Sandie Shaw, The Vibrations, Shirley Ellis, Dee Dee Warwick, King Curtis & the Kingpins, The Uniques and a film screening. The infamous mobster Morris Levy of Roulette Records promoted the show.[20]

Graham Nash sang with The Hollies, performing two songs five times a day on a twelve-band bill. He raved about rock on New York radio, and recounted his fascination with Times Square and particularly with Little Richard and his band. Nash witnessed Little Richard and Hendrix up close, backstage:

> We were thrilled to be there, especially watching the master, Little Richard, five times a day. The guy was unreal. An incredible showman. He'd pound that piano as if it were a tough piece of meat and throw his head back and wail. And that band of his kicked ass, especially his guitar player, a young, skinny kid with fingers out to there . . . One night I was standing in the wings as Richard came off stage and he was livid, his eyes bugging out like a madman, screaming . . . at that poor kid. 'Don't you ever do that again! Don't you ever upstage Little Richard!' They got in the elevator, slammed the gate, and I could still hear him ten floors above . . . '– playing your guitar with your teeth!' [Hendrix] was called Jimmy James then.[21]

In May 1965 Little Richard played Long Pond Inn, Greenwood Lake, New York, adding the comic Jackie 'Moms' Mabley. She

wore a suit backstage and was called Mr Moms. The duo Don and
Dewey (Don 'Sugarcane' Harris and Dewey Terry) was also added
to the bill. Terry, a guitarist, confirmed that Hendrix was annoying
Little Richard with guitar feedback onstage:

> Jimi would let the guitar feed back some nights . . . it covered
> Richard's vocals. Little Richard put him with us because he
> wanted that rock-and-roll sound. Hendrix looked like a hippie.
> He talked about 'playing in space'.[22]

The tour also played the New Era club in Nashville. The tour
manager, Robert Penniman, said he fired Hendrix in July 1965
after playing a week at the Apollo, for missing the tour bus to
Washington, DC.[23] Hendrix said he left over monetary issues.

Hendrix made an impression playing guitar with The
Isley Brothers, during a performance with Booker T. & the
MG's at DePauw University's Bowman Gymnasium in
Greencastle, Indiana, on 9 October 1965. Local musicians
Rod Kersey and Steve Michael, then in high school, were at
the show and described how the bands were set up one at
each end of the gymnasium, with alternating sets. Hendrix
performed his stunts – playing behind his back and with his
teeth – and watched guitarist Steve Cropper's technique during
the MGS' set. According to Michael, 'Hendrix studied his every
move on the guitar. He seemed to be making Cropper kind of
nervous.'[24]

That same month Hendrix auditioned for Joey Dee &
the Starliters in Lodi, New Jersey, and toured with them. The
Starliters was the house band at the Peppermint Lounge, 128 45th
Street, during a prolonged dance craze for the Twist in about
1961, set off by a rhythm and blues hit of 1958 by Hank Ballard
& the Midnighters. Dee had a hit with 'Peppermint Twist' in 1962.
The Ronettes made their debut at the venue. A front for mob

loan-sharking and gambling, the 'Pep' lost its licence in December
1965. Joey Dee & the Starliters signed with Roulette Records.
The band, originally from Passaic, New Jersey, played the
northeast: Boston, Buffalo and Connecticut. It was an integrated
band, its line-up including Charles Neville (of New Orleans 'first
family of funk', The Neville Brothers) for a time, and several
of its members later formed The Young Rascals. The band
was booked in large venues, playing to crowds of up to 10,000
people. But the twist fad wound down. Hendrix was dissatisfied
with a dated scene:

> I quit Little Richard because of a money misunderstanding
> and to rest. But who can rest in New York? I got a job with
> another band. I had all these ideas and sounds in my brain and
> playing this 'other people's music' all the time was hurting
> me. I jumped from the frying pan into the fire when I joined
> up with Joey Dee and the Starliters. Mind you, this is an out
> of sight group, but . . . after sucking on a peppermint twist
> salary, I had to quit and began playing with a jukebox band,
> and finally quit that, too.[25]

In mid-January 1966 Hendrix was back in New York, playing with
respected musicians, such as King Curtis & the Kingpins at
Smalls Paradise. He and Pridgon attended Apollo Blues Revue,
featuring T-Bone Walker, Muddy Waters and Bo Diddley.[26] In
February he toured with King Curtis & the Kingpins. On 5 May,
at the Prelude Club, Hendrix played with a band wearing tuxedos,
assembled for an Atlantic Records release party for the Percy
Sledge album *When a Man Loves a Woman*, with King Curtis and
the guitarist Cornell Dupree backing Sledge and Wilson Pickett.
In the rhythm and blues world, Hendrix had arrived. Photographs
by William 'PoPsie' Randolph showed him looking sophisticated
and elated.[27]

## MUSICAL NEIGHBOURHOODS

Music divided New York City into districts: the rhythm and blues of Harlem; commercial music in the predominantly white Midtown, where recording studios such as ABKCO and music-industry hubs such as the Brill Building at 49th and Broadway were clustered; and the Greenwich Village folk scene, where Bob Dylan was the leading songwriter. Hendrix was listening intently to Dylan, whose lyrical social criticism he admired and related to. Hendrix was scruffy, too non-conformist for Harlem clubs, and was brushed off when he tried to sit in with rhythm and blues musicians at Smalls, the Palm Café and 125th Street clubs.

The Village offered many small, street-orientated clubs and an eclectic range of music. Folk was popular, and pop and rock were evolving. Besides Dylan, Greenwich Village was a place to hear American pop, New York jazz – Ornette Coleman, John Coltrane and Miles Davis – and British sound The Who, Eric Clapton, Jeff Beck, The Yardbirds. The Troggs' hit of summer 1966, 'Wild Thing', written by Chip Taylor, became a key tune in the Hendrix repertoire.

Miles Davis had written about the dynamism of small, vibrant Midtown clubs on 52nd Street two decades earlier, in the post-war era, pointing out their scale, quantity, intensity and proximity, and connecting the context with a shift in discerning musicianship:

Around 1945 a lot of black musicians were playing down on 52nd Street, for the money and the media exposure. It was around this time that the clubs on 52nd – like the Three Deuces, the Onyx, the Downbeat Club, Kelly's Stable and others – started being more important for musicians than clubs uptown in Harlem . . . To have experienced 52nd Street between 1945 and 1949 was like reading a textbook on the future of music. You had Coleman Hawkins and Hank Jones at one club . . . 52nd Street was something else when it was happening. It would be crowded with people, and the clubs were no bigger than apartment living rooms. They were so small and jam-packed. The clubs were right next to each other and across the street from each other. The Three Deuces was across from the Onyx and then across from there was a Dixieland club. Man[,] going in there was like going to Tupelo Mississippi. It was full of white racists.[28]

Davis linked the intimacy of the brownstone living-room-sized clubs with the nimble intensity of the music:

That part of 52nd Street was nothing but a row of three- or four storied brownstones . . . Those clubs were too small to hold big bands. The bandstand couldn't hardly hold a five-piece combo let alone one with ten or twelve people. So this kind of club created a new kind of musician, who was comfortable in a small band setting. That's the kind of musical atmosphere I came into when I started playing on The Street.[29]

By the mid-1960s, Midtown clubs were expanding into larger spaces on the large-scale Cheetah discotheque model. In the West and East Village, a hybrid multimedia club scene was developing from the youthquake collision of pop art and pop music, rock and folk.

The Greenwich Village folk idea equated community with political power. Jazz was focused on musical sophistication, exclusivity and 'chops' (technical ability), while folkies were participatory activists, their musicianship plain and homespun. When Nina Simone, whose work transcended categories, sang 'House of the Rising Sun', recording her first version on *Nina at the Village Gate* in 1962, her sound was saturated with social relevance. The song was appropriated by Dylan from Dave Van Ronk's original arrangement; Dylan's lyrical ambiguity muted the social meaning. A cover of the song became a commercial hit for The Animals in 1964;[30] The Animals' white soul version had a wider, crossover appeal to a more commerical audience, its lyrics heard as another night of Eric Burdon over-partying. Van Ronk had a last remark, as he later noticed that the Rising Sun was a stone frieze over the doorway to the New Orleans' Women's Prison.[31]

The number and array of small clubs in Greenwich Village in the 1960s made the scene lively and intense. There was the Cafe Wha? at 115 Macdougal Street, on the corner of Minetta Lane, with a capacity of 325 people; the basement Cafe au Go Go at 152 Bleecker Street, with a capacity of about 200 people; the street-level Garrick Theatre directly above it, with 300 seats; the basement Gaslight, the smallest – a shoebox – at 116 Macdougal Street. The Purple Onion was at 135 West Third Street, The Bitter End at 147 Bleecker Street, the Tin Angel and Charlie Washburn's Third Side Coffeehouse on Bleecker, the Kettle of Fish on Macdougal Street, Gerdes Folk City at 11 West Fourth Street and the Night Owl Café at 118 West Third Street. Café Bizarre was at 106 West Third Street. The Commons was at 11–13 Minetta Street. The Village Gate was in a building designed in the Chicago School style of architecture by Ernest Flagg in 1896, at Thomson and Bleecker Streets, its sign still visible above the chain pharmacy that now occupies the corner.[32]

Joni Mitchell used the metaphor of a puddle to describe the spatial qualities of the urban soundscape of street-side folk clubs in the Yorkville blocks of Toronto, resembling those of Greenwich Village, in an impromptu song introduction while touring:

While I'm still here I'd like to play a little song called 'Night in the City'. It's about a night in any city where you go out and wander around listening to music. I wrote it about a place in Toronto, Ontario, called Yorkville Avenue, it's a little village there, there are clubs along several blocks you can just walk along and stand in what I think of as music puddles, where music sort of hangs from here to here, and if you step too far over in the other direction [you're] into a new music belt or a music puddle. And it's dedicated to all those people who took much too long to get ready, you know who you are.[33]

The Brooklyn-born musician Richie Havens described the young people arriving in the Village as on an indeterminate quest: 'In the early 60s people were searching for something. They didn't know what it was . . . they were running away from something.'[34] The folk singer Eric Andersen connected social experimentation with lyrical subjects: 'All these things influenced the material. There was a reaction to events happening around us . . . There was a drug revolution, a sexual revolution, a whole bunch of stuff was going on.'[35] The folk singer Melanie spoke of the guitar as a visible badge for the folk crowd:

> People walked around with guitars hanging on their backs. People didn't have guitar cases. That was unthinkable. You just didn't have a guitar case. Nobody had a guitar case. A guitar case was for people who graduated Juilliard.[36]

Andersen reflected on the duration of songs, defining folk songwriting as criticism by virtue of its form. For his peers, lengthy songs constituted a protest against the pop culture product:

> When I was writing 'Violets of Dawn' . . . before anyone had heard it, I was . . . on Macdougal Street . . . reciting the lyrics to Phil [most likely Phil Ochs] – this was the thing that happened a lot, where people would recite their lyrics to each other. I was walking down the street reciting 'Violets of Dawn'. He said, 'Well it's really great, but it's not long enough.' And this is . . . rebellion to Top Forty radio, like the Brill Building songs had to be two minutes long. Where we were operating, three minutes long was like an incomplete

song. It was not, how could that, what kind of song could that be? it's only three minutes . . . I stayed overnight in some hotel in New York, and I dreamt up the third verse for the song. It just came to me in a dream and I wrote it down and it was finished and I eventually recorded it.[37]

In October 1965 Hendrix joined the New York rhythm and blues band Curtis Knight & the Squires, after he ran into Knight in the lobby of the Hotel America, at 145 West 47th Street, near Times Square. Knight had taken note of a small recording studio in the Hotel America lobby, and Hendrix was staying in the hotel with Pridgon.[38] Knight, a middling musician whose day job was pimping, provided Hendrix with a guitar and promised to feature him. Hendrix objected that his amp was turned down: 'I got a cheap guitar, and a small amp. Curtis can't play good, and he turns his big amp up, and my little amp down.'[39] Hendrix was playing in other bands as well, with the saxophone virtuoso King Curtis, touring from January to April, in Texas (Houston and Dallas) as well as Oklahoma, Louisiana and California.[40]

Hendrix played with Curtis Knight & the Squires at the Lighthouse on 76th and Broadway, and a New Jersey club called George's. The Knight connection led to a Midtown record label and what would be a persistently troublesome record-label owner, Ed Chalpin of PPX at 300 West 55th Street. On 15 October 1965 Hendrix signed a three-year contract with Chalpin, who would go on to launch volleys of lawsuits, based on an absurd agreement that claimed the totality of Hendrix's artistic production for three years in exchange for one dollar. On 27 July that year Hendrix had signed a contract with Henry 'Juggy' Murray of Sue Records on West 54th Street.[41]

The Cheetah Club opened on 28 April 1966. This Midtown venue, at 1686 Broadway and 53rd Street, was a sizeable ballroom, formerly the Riviera Terrace and before that the Arcadia

Ballroom. The critic Alastair Gordon wrote of this rebranded psychedelic dance and live music venue: 'It was another of a string of "total environment" clubs with devices like a suspended wheel of colour-coded lights.'[42] The Cheetah had a three-storey space, a stage 15 m (50 ft) wide, a capacity of 1,800 on a large dance floor of 740 sq. m (8,000 sq. ft), a light show, dancers and extras such as a boutique and a Scopitone, a now-obsolete film-viewing jukebox. The club advertised continuous live music by three bands. Neville Brother Charles, then a New York-based musician, described how a non-stop music system worked:

> There were three bands each night, and each band would get several forty-five minute sets. So when one band's time was up, the singers in the band would start leaving the stage. Their rhythm section kept playing while the new band took over. One drummer kept the cymbals going as the new drummer sat down and kept the same rhythm going. You went out of one song right into another.[43]

Hendrix played the Cheetah in 1966 with Curtis Knight & the Squires, from 12 May to 25 May. The following week he played there with another band, the Philadelphia-based Carl Holmes & the Commanders, until 3 June. Richie Havens was at the Cheetah and met Hendrix at one of the Commanders gigs. Havens overheard Hendrix saying: 'I don't play guitar, I play amplifier.'[44] Havens, a Village musician throughout the 1960s, urged Hendrix to try out Cafe Wha?, mentioning the owner.

The Cheetah was nearly empty when Linda Keith, Keith Richards's girlfriend, arrived with her friends Roberta Goldstein and Mark Kaufman. Seymour Stein, later the owner-founder of the Sire record label, had introduced Andrew Loog Oldham, the manager of The Rolling Stones, to Goldstein. Linda Keith was staying in Manhattan while The Rolling Stones toured the USA.

The house band wore cheetah-print shirts matching the club decor, but Keith spotted Hendrix, 'a backup guitarist who played his right-handed guitar left-handed, upside down and strung backwards'.[45] Keith was a fan of rhythm and blues, and her father was the BBC radio presenter Alan Keith. She invited Hendrix – Jimmy James – to listen to records at Goldstein and Kaufman's apartment on 63rd Street, and she introduced Hendrix to LSD as well as to choice insiders of the London rock scene. She played him a promotional copy of Tim Rose's slow version of 'Hey Joe'. Hendrix quit the jukebox band after the Cheetah, remarking of backing bands: 'I couldn't imagine myself for the rest of my life in a shiny Mohair suit with patent leather shoes and a patent leather hairdo to match.'[46]

In an interview, Linda Keith recalled: 'We got him a guitar . . . he dressed and looked like Dylan. We all dressed and looked like Dylan. We looked ridiculous walking down the street.'[47] She lent him Richards's white Stratocaster, and – with the East Village harmonica player Paul Caruso – she and Hendrix panhandled and played Greenwich Village street corners.[48]

Hendrix was still seeing Pridgon, who was staying on the Upper West Side, in Park West Village. She was not a fan of Dylan, and was not impressed when Hendrix bought *Blonde on Blonde* at Colony Records, the 24-hour record shop on Broadway at 49th Street:

I felt betrayed when he brought a Bob Dylan album home. Not only did his music change colour, but the colour of his friends did too. I remember when he brought me to meet John Hammond [Jr] and his parents, who were white. I found out John Hammond sang the blues, and I guess I showed a little too much interest. Every time I looked twice at John, I felt Jimi digging his long bony fingers into my thigh under the table. John Hammond and his parents were the first of a new order of social acquaintances I met through Jimi.[49]

At the Cheetah Hendrix met Carol 'Kim' Shiroky, an escort who became a girlfriend. He stayed at the Lennox Hotel and met Mike Quashie (the Limbo King), a performer at the African Room club across the road on 44th Street. Shiroky mentioned buying Hendrix a Stratocaster at Manny's Music shop, and witnessed his acid hallucination, when he said: 'I looked in a mirror and thought I was Marilyn Monroe.'[50]

Hendrix formed a band, Jimmy James & the Blue Flames, sometimes called The Rainflowers. Band member Randy Wolfe, known as Randy California, recalled them playing the Cafe Wha? five sets a night, six nights a week, to a crowd of about 75 people. The band developed new material and interpreted covers of 'Mercy, Mercy' and 'High Heel Sneakers'. According to California, 'He had a real knack for moving the whole band with him when he was on stage. He would do this by his presence and the way he moved to the rhythm of the song. On a lot of the songs he would teach us as were going along.'[51] In addition to afternoon jams at the Night Owl and the regular gigs at Cafe Wha, Hendrix was playing blues with John Hammond Jr at another Village basement club, Cafe au Go Go. Hammond was interviewed about playing with Hendrix in 1966:

> I was just awed that he'd be playing at the Cafe Wha? . . . I got a job at the Cafe au Go Go, and within a week we opened there. I didn't even play guitar . . . I sang. He played the guitar. There was a back-up guitar player, Randy Wolf, who later became Randy California. I got to know Jimi pretty well. We worked not more than two or three weeks there. It was really a sensation kind of thing. I had already established a name for myself in that area. But Jimi Hendrix was unbelievable. At that time he was Jimmy James and he called his little group the Blue Flame. You couldn't help but notice that this guy was unbelievable.[52]

In July 1966 Hendrix asked to play informally with Ellen McIlwaine at the Cafe au Go Go. She had seen him play in Atlanta with King Curtis. In that context, not knowing his name, she said they called him Dylan Black. McIlwaine welcomed the new performer, but other acts were dismissive. Once at the Cafe au Go Go, when Hendrix tried to sit in with the harmonica player Junior Wells, Wells left the stage.[53]

Hammond was convinced of the influence of Robbie Robertson's guitar playing on Hendrix.[54] The allure may have been a confluence of Robertson's Native American roots, songwriting and guitar skill, and the Dylan Connection. Jaime 'Robbie' Robertson's mother was of Mohawk descent, his father Jewish, and he took his stepfather's name, spending summers in his youth in the Mohawk land of the Six Nations. During 1966 he was lead guitarist and primary songwriter for The Hawks, the band backing Dylan on his controversial transition tour as a rock performer. After trying out band names like The Crackers, The Hawks mutated from a bar band into an uber-band called The Band. The Band worked with Dylan from May to November 1967 on the Basement tapes, released as an influential double album in 1975, copiously bootlegged, and released in a multiple-disc box-set in 2014. Robertson recalled hanging out with Hendrix. He discussed their songwriting aspirations in the context of the Village:

[We] used to hang out years ago in the Village . . . He was playing guitar for John Hammond Jr, and John Hammond was somebody that . . . at the time, I made two records with . . . I was living at the Chelsea Hotel in New York. He called and said, listen I got this new guitar player, you got to come down and hear this, he's really, really special. And that night Brian Jones from the Rolling Stones called me – he used to call me whenever he came to New York – I said, 'I told John I was gonna hear this guitar player.' He said, 'Oh great, I'll come with you.' He did all those things – played the guitar behind his head, with his teeth. I said, 'I know the guitar players where you got that from' and he said, 'I know you know.' And we kind of became friends. What Jimi Hendrix mostly wanted to talk to me about at the time was songwriting. He desperately wanted to learn how to write songs. Because I was playing with Bob Dylan, he thought I must know, so he was picking my brain. We were talking about ideas. I had been writing songs since I was very young. We had great times hanging out together . . . his name was Jimmie James.[55]

The Rolling Stones and their entourage saw Hendrix play the Midtown club Ondine's, 309 East 59th Street, on 2 July 1966. Ronnie Spector remembered performing with Hendrix in a house band that summer.

In the Village Hendrix encountered the hippy daily life of improvised, communal crash pads. He was known to stay at the Albert Hotel on Tenth Street, its basement a practice space and its twelfth floor a jam loft and musician hang-out. The science-fiction writer Samuel R. Delany mentioned the Hotel Albert, the drag performer Divine and Holly Woodlawn, the transgender Warhol Superstar, in *Flight from Nevèrÿon*:

The whole hotel, always colorful, for years a haven for rock groups, ragamuffins, and the generally outrageous, with invasions of Hell's Angels and admiring cross-dressers from several states – Divine's and Holly Woodlawn's visits were the talk of a month – and student leaders of Gay Liberation university groups from Jersey trooping through all day. . . again, I found myself sharing the elevator with one and another six-foot-two, football-shouldered, teak-black prostitutes in miniskirts, with mouths red as a Christmas ornament, some of whom, an operation or so ago, had been men, and some of who [sic] had not.[56]

Hotel Albert, East Tenth Street, New York, c. 1907.

Another friend, the drummer Danny Casey, reported that he and
Hendrix shared a basement apartment at 211 East Fifth Street,
and stayed for a short while on the third floor in a building
at Greenwich and Reade streets.[57] At times Hendrix shared a
room with Diana Carpenter, also known as Regina Jackson,
a teen runaway and prostitute. They had met at a coffee shop
called Ham and Eggs on Broadway at 52nd Street. She left town
pregnant, and he may have been the father of her child, Tamika.
Later his friend Sharon Lawrence said Bob Dylan's hit 'Like a
Rolling Stone' summed up his mood: 'It made me feel that I
wasn't the only one who'd ever felt so low.'[58]

Linda Keith brought her friend Sheila Klein's husband,
Andrew Loog Oldham (then manager of The Rolling Stones), to
see Hendrix perform; he was impassive, and later expressed his
concerns about relationship fallout. Then Keith approached the
producer Seymour Stein, who was also unmoved. She questioned
the indifference of music industry managers to Hendrix's talent,
which was so obvious to musicians.

Leaving Ondine's on 2 August, Keith met the bassist Chas
Chandler as he was arriving, and they chatted. Chandler was
touring the United States with The Animals, a British blues-rock
band from the mining town of Newcastle upon Tyne whose
quickly produced cover of 'House of the Rising Sun' (1964) had
sold millions. Chandler spoke of leaving the band to manage, with
a particular song in mind, 'Hey Joe', having heard a slow version
recently recorded by Tim Rose.

Keith suggested that she and Chandler go hear Hendrix
perform at Cafe Wha? Hendrix played a song he had just heard,
Tim Rose's slow 'Hey Joe'. The Animals' roadie James 'Tappy'
Wright noted: 'when he started playing with his teeth, and behind
his head, it was obvious that here was someone different.'[59]

The Animals were breaking up, but Chandler had found an act
to manage. He offered to return and launch Hendrix in London

after The Animals' tour ended. He arranged for a passport with some difficulty, because of Hendrix's early name change, but after arranging some dubious documentation the passport was issued. Chandler took care of the recording contracts that Hendrix remembered, but one he forgot was that with Ed Chalpin. Chandler and Hendrix with his carry-on bag flew together, first-class on Pan American, arriving in London on 24 September 1966; The Animals' roadie Terry McVay carried his guitar through customs at Heathrow.

Cafe Wha?, 115 Macdougal Street, Greenwich Village, New York.

Warhol's Pop activities were seeping through New York. Marshall McLuhan identified Andy Warhol's Factory scene on East 47th Street as a site of sensory overload and excess, in a media-saturated urban underground. In April 1966 Warhol's film *My Hustler* screened on West 41st Street at the Film-Makers' Cinematheque; and a show of inflatables as decor, the 'Silver Flotations' exhibition, with silver helium balloons and wallpaper patterned with cow heads, opened uptown at Leo Castelli Gallery on East 77th Street.[60]

In April 1966 Warhol staged the Exploding Plastic Inevitable with The Velvet Underground. Impressed by the reputation of The Beatles' manager Brian Epstein, Andy Warhol and Paul Morrissey played impresario, working with The Velvet Underground, a band they had first heard at Café Bizarre in December 1965. They had staged an early version of a happening called 'Uptight', at a New York Society for Clinical Psychiatry dinner at Delmonico's Hotel, Park Avenue and East 59th Street, in mid-January 1966; The Velvet Underground performed with Nico singing, and Gerard Malanga and Edie Sedgwick dancing. A show at the Film-Makers' Cinematheque, 'Andy Warhol, Up-Tight', had taken place in the second week of February, but after other gigs fell through, the Exploding Plastic Inevitable set up on the 'open stage' at the Dom club, run by Warhol and Morrissey at 19–25 St Marks Place, in April. In *Popism: The Warhol '60s*, Warhol and Pat Hackett write:

The Dom was perfect, just what we wanted – it had to be the biggest discotheque dance floor in Manhattan, and there was a balcony, too. We sublet it immediately . . . the very next day we were down there painting the place white so we could project movies and slides on the walls. We started dragging prop-type odds and ends over from the Factory – five movie projectors, five carousel-type projectors where the image changes every ten seconds . . . These coloured things would go on top of the five movies, and sometimes we'd let the sound tracks come through. We also brought down one of those big revolving speakeasy mirror-balls, etc. . . . we had no idea if people would come all the way down to St Mark's Place for night life. All the downtown action had always been in the West Village . . . by renting the Dom ourselves, we didn't have to worry about whether 'management' liked us or not, we could just do whatever we wanted to. And the Velvets were thrilled – in the Dom, the 'house band' finally had a house. They could even walk to work.[61]

The collective advertised in the *Village Voice* first as 'Come Blow your Mind, the Silver Dream Factory Presents the Erupting Plastic Inevitable with Andy Warhol, The Velvet Underground and Nico'. The dissonant montage of music, image, noise and sound was an improbable hit.[62] John Cale's viola drones imported avant-garde sonorities of La Monte Young and Marian Zazeela. The androgynous drummer, Maureen 'Moe' Tucker, turned out to be female. The Factory crowd obsessed over sex and drugs. Instinctively fusing glam and the abject, Lou Reed wrote songs about heroin and tied-off onstage using microphone wire. The dancers mimed shooting up and cracked whips. According to Paul Morrissey, 'We moved in on Friday afternoon at 3 o'clock and at 8 o'clock that night all these people showed up. It was packed. It was an enormous success from its very first night.'[63] Success was measured in cash: 'Warhol's EPI shows at the Dom turned out to be extremely popular – entry was $6 and they made $18,000 in the first week.'[64]

The Exploding Plastic Inevitable eventually toured. Marshall McLuhan used a photograph of one event to demonstrate echo-land, his term for contemporary auditory space, in his graphic paperback *The Medium is the Massage*, a widely distributed mass-

culture photo-book of 1967. The Warhol Factory collective refined
a camp parody of a media conglomerate. Artists in its orbit in
early 1966 may have been morally amorphous, superficial and
subversive, but the Factory was a disciplined machine when
it came to appraising, hustling and selling out. The Warhol
collective radar registered Hendrix as musical capital, at the
margins of their underground turf, when he occasionally touched
down with his own entourage, accompanied by Devon Wilson,
Jeannette Jacobs or Emmaretta Marks, in clubs such as Max's
Kansas City at 213 Park Avenue South.

# 4  LONDON: A PSYCHEDELIC SCENE

One thing I hate, man, when these cats say, 'Look at the
band, they're playing psychedelic music' and all they're
really doing is flashing lights on them and playing Johnny
B. Goode with the wrong chords. It's terrible.

Jimi Hendrix[1]

After a transatlantic flight and six hours in customs because
he had no work permit, Hendrix jammed on his first afternoon
in London, in September 1966, at the home of Zoot and Ronnie
Money, 53 Gunterston Road in Hammersmith, on the way from
the airport. That night he jammed at the Scotch of St James
club, and met an intern hairdresser and DJ, Kathy Etchingham.
They connected, and they remained sporadically together
until February 1969, when she announced plans to marry
Eric Clapton's driver, Ray Mayer. They lived until December
with Chas Chandler and his girlfriend Lotta Lexon at the
Hyde Park Towers Hotel, 41–51 Inverness Terrace, Bayswater.
Etchingham described the building as slowly disintegrating
from dry rot: a bed leg sank into the floorboards as she jumped
on to it.[2]

On 27 September Hendrix and Chandler returned to the
Scotch, a basement club in a small alley courtyard, 13 Masons
Yard, in central London. At the Scotch The Beatles had a table
with their name inscribed on a brass plate. In the same courtyard
was the Indica Gallery, opened by John Dunbar, Barry Miles and
Peter Asher in the summer of 1965. Initially the Indica bookshop
was in the basement below the gallery, and was where in October
1966 John 'Hoppy' Hopkins and Miles founded a counterculture
newspaper, the *International Times*.[3]

As a condition to his agreeing to leave New York, Hendrix had asked Chandler to introduce him to Jeff Beck and Eric Clapton. Clapton was in an exciting new power trio, Cream, with Jack Bruce and Ginger Baker, after leaving John Mayall's Bluesbreakers. Cream was a template for The Jimi Hendrix Experience.

Chandler soon brought Hendrix to sit in with Cream, on 1 October 1966, at a university gig on Little Titchfield Street. Leading London guitarist Eric Clapton described the impromptu event:

> Two months after our debut . . . we were booked to play at the Central London Polytechnic . . . I was hanging about backstage with Jack, when Chas. Chandler appeared . . . He informed us that Jimi was a brilliant guitarist, and he wanted to sit in with us on a couple of numbers.[4]

Clapton affirmed: 'It was just solid musicians, the whole club.'[5]

Onstage Hendrix played Howlin' Wolf's 'Killing Floor' (1964) with an accelerated tempo – blues churned to rock. Clapton's awe spread news of Hendrix's arrival as the virtuoso guitar performer in London:

> The stage was set for Jimi. It could have been anyone, but it had to be him. London was just coming into a kind of really heavy Soul thing. The Blues movement was dying, and really needed someone to bring it all back to life.[6]

Clapton also spoke of a lack in the London scene: 'That's what London wanted right then and he filled the gap perfectly.'[7]

London rock musicians were fascinated with American rhythm and blues. Aspiring musicians collected and listened to records, mimicking the Southern accents. The Yardbirds and The Rolling Stones covered blues tunes, lifting original guitar lines from recent rhythm and blues hits, and reusing them as if they were old folk songs, playing with the British contemporary rock sound. Led Zeppelin's transformative borrowing of blues and folk, injected into a new, heavy, psychedelic sound, eventually became so popular that the monetary rewards could no longer be ignored. The sources were tracked in detail, and since a sufficient number of words and riffs were from songs by American bluesmen Willie Dixon and Howlin' Wolf – no strangers to borrowed material themselves – Dixon and Wolf (Chester Burnett) successfully gained listed writers' credits. Dixon funded a blues foundation in Chicago with his proceeds.[8]

Brian Jones, Mick Jagger and Keith Richards were avid blues record collectors. Their first recordings copied, note for note, instrumentation, solo and arrangement. The Rolling Stones' version of 'Not Fade Away' recycled the Buddy Holly original. The singer Irma Thomas, billed as the Soul Queen of New Orleans, lost her taste for performing 'Time is on my Side' after The Rolling Stones' early cover of her arrangement sold millions. Her liner-note writer commented:

> That cover, which does not capture the mood of the original to any degree, annoyed Irma so much that she had an aversion to performing the song on stage except in response to persistent requests, but she has now mellowed her reaction and accords it a rightful place in her repertoire.[9]

The Rolling Stones' first hit was 'It's All Over Now', written by Bobby Womack and Shirley Womack in 1964. Womack had been reluctant to allow a Rolling Stones cover, but the royalties convinced him after its release in 1964:

> Their first number one single! I wasn't too crazy about the Stones covering that song, but [Sam] Cooke told me that it

would be one of the best moves I ever made. He was right, especially when the royalty checks started to roll in . . . but looking back, I probably got a small piece of what I was supposed to get, but it was big![10]

British guitarists were experimenting with distortion, fuzz and feedback as well. The Kinks guitarist Dave Davies wrote about exploring sound by reconnecting his amps in an elaborate sequence:

I discovered how to make my guitar scream . . . I managed to plug each amp into the other . . . and momentarily got the most crackling, distorted sound I had ever heard . . . that sound, which we used on 'You Really Got Me', that got the Kinks our first hit.[11]

Hendrix was a passionate blues listener and a record collector. He favoured Elmore James, a bluesman who worked as a radio technician and who developed a specific timbre using shop parts and pickup placement to get a screaming sound. Hendrix had first-hand experience with American blues musicianship, venues, audiences and psychedelic edge. His innovative, virtuoso new rock sound not only impressed London's music insiders, but compelled guitarists to update their sound. The social historian Matthew Frye Jacobson noted the incongruity in the English perception of Hendrix as an authentic rhythm and blues musician, while he was tagged as an alien in America.[12] This marginality could be seen as a variant on the chronotope idea, as his reception as musical anti-hero varied radically in differing places and contexts.

Hendrix explored London's second-hand shops and acquired ornate military jackets. From a shop called I Was Lord Kitchener's Valet (at 293 Portobello Road in Notting Hill), he bought a Royal Hussar jacket and a British Army Veterinarian Corps jacket.

Compared with the Cartesian numbered grids of American cities, London was a maze of sinuous streets in very different boroughs. Another labyrinthine novelty for an American was the prosody of accents – class-striated, local and regional – from Chandler's Geordie rumble, to Noel Redding's Kentish twang, to the Liverpudlian spoken by The Beatles entourage.

Hendrix met other musicians at clubs such as the Speakeasy, known as 'the Speak', at 48 Margaret Street near Oxford Circus. He wandered the city, visiting people, as Clapton remembered: 'At the beginning he used to come round to the flat and stay there.'[13] Clapton was living on the top floor of the Pheasantry, a Georgian building at 152–54 King's Road that had once been used to raise pheasants for the royal family. Clapton's flatmate was the Australian illustrator Martin Sharp; Germaine Greer lived at the same address, and George Harrison would also visit.[14]

On 29 September 1966 Hendrix played the upmarket Blaises Club in the basement of the Imperial Hotel (121 Queen's Gate, South Kensington), frequented by music-scene insiders.[15] Howard 'H' Parker, a roadie, listed early gigs and a flurry of word on the street:

> The first time I saw [Hendrix] was at a club called Blaises in South Kensington. His manager Chas Chandler had arranged the gig as a showcase for his new act. I'd seen Mitch [Mitchell, the drummer] in Denmark Street . . . He told me he was rehearsing with a guitar player and a bass player. Blaises, when we got down there, was packed full of the upper echelons of the rock and roll business . . . George Harrison was there, some of the Stones were there. He did a round of the London clubs, places like the Bag of Nails, the Speakeasy . . . a week in some place called the Seven and a Half, he did the Scotch of St James. I was with a band called the Pretty Things.[16]

The French rocker Johnny Hallyday heard Hendrix jamming in the Blaises Club with Brian Auger and the Trinity. Etchingham recalled a jam at the Cromwellian, at 3 Cromwell Road in South Kensington. The guitarist Vic Briggs remembered the venue as the Scotch, not with Hendrix sitting in, but rather in a pre-arranged jam, timed to take advantage of the presence of former Yardbirds manager Giorgio Gomelsky and Hallyday's manager Lee Hallyday (Lee Ketcham). As a result, Johnny Hallyday offered Hendrix a slot on his upcoming tour.[17]

Chandler speedily arranged auditions for a new band, to coincide with Eric Burdon's auditions for the New Animals. Noel Redding went to audition at a club called the Telephone Box for a position as guitarist for the New Animals. Eric Burdon had hired Vic Briggs already; Hendrix asked Redding to play bass and to jam. The next day, auditions were at a seedy basement club, Birdland, off Jermyn Street, near Piccadilly Circus. When Redding arrived the club was empty, so he walked to Michael Jeffery's ANIM office at 39 Gerrard Street, a few doors down from the Gunnell Brothers' management and booking agency at number 47. He learned that he had been hired. Hendrix had noticed that Redding picked up chord changes quickly, and thought his hair was cool: 'When I first picked them for the Experience, I picked Noel because he could play *anything* on that bass.'[18]

Chandler and Hendrix put together a power trio in the Cream mode: Noel Redding on bass and drummer John 'Mitch' Mitchell. Mitchell was casual about the process:

> I got a phone call from Chas Chandler, 'Hey, I got this guitar player coming over from America. Do you fancy having a play with him,' and he was the first person I knew, or ever heard, that knew who how to play that Curtis Mayfield style of guitar, and also, 'oh, you want Wes Montgomery – without being a flash git'.[19]

Hendrix envisaged a larger ensemble, possibly along the lines of
Little Richard's nine-piece band. This would have required more
resources, rehearsal and audition time. There was criticism of
the hasty auditions; Clapton later suggested that it would have
been worthwhile to scout for the most musically adept, and the
critic Will Straw mused whether it was a calculated exercise:
'The group's success suggested the commercial possibilities of
psychedelic pop. The trio was put together if not cynically then
at least with an eye to the market (it hardly sprang organically
from a musical scene or network); great care was taken with
the trio's image.'[20]

With the Hallyday tour on the horizon, rehearsals began
at The Animals' music publisher, Carlin, at Aberbach House,
17 Savile Row, a street known for bespoke tailors. At the offices
of Jeffery and Chandler, the musicians signed contracts with
Yameta, an offshore shell company that Jeffery had set up
while he was managing The Animals.[21] A working-class
Newcastle crowd enfolded Hendrix. The Animals suspected their
management company, ANIM, and Jeffery of embezzlement.
Briggs called Jeffery a crook, as did Eric Burdon; Andrew Loog
Oldham called him a scumbag. He had been to public school
and university, and ran a coffee bar, Marimba, and a jazz
club, the Downbeat, in Newcastle, which burned down
in a suspicious fire. Accounts of Jeffrey's Newcastle beginnings
usually mentioned the circumstances: 'After the Downbeat
Club was closed due to fire regulations, both establishments
burned down. Jeffery then opened the Club A'Gogo.'[22]
Chandler and Jeffery coordinated with the Gunnell Brothers,
who had owned the Flamingo jazz club on Wardour Street
(which closed in 1967). In January 1966 they opened the Ramjam
Club at 390 Brixton Road. Rik and John Gunnell promoted
the Woburn Festival in 1968 and the Isle of Wight Festival
in 1970.

At some point Decca Records executive Dick Rowe passed on signing Hendrix. Hendrix and Chandler returned to the Scotch of St James one evening and jammed with the VIPS (who later became Humble Pie), meeting Kit Lambert and Chris Stamp, managers of The Who. Lambert and Stamp, who were involved in intersecting film and rock worlds, were in the process of starting their own label, Track. They offered to be the new band's record label – and would have managed it as well. The Who were appearing regularly on the television music programme *Ready Steady Go!*, and Lambert and Stamp offered to arrange an appearance on the show for the Experience. Redding described how they were taken to the studio to meet The Who, and offered 'an irresistible deal'.[23]

As a management team, Lambert and Stamp circumvented the British hurdle of social class. Kit Lambert, Oxford-educated and gay, was the son of the composer Constant Lambert; Chris Stamp, born in Stepney, east London, was authentic London working class, the son of a Thames waterman and the brother of the actor Terence. The American record producer Joe Boyd summed up the team as 'cockney Chris Stamp and the Bohemian aristocrat Kit Lambert managing The Who'.[24] A mix of British hierarchies was in the spirit of pop London. In an interview the East End photographer David Bailey assailed the class snobbery that structured London media: 'Back then they didn't even use models who were working class. The number of times I heard: "Oh no, we can't shoot her, have you heard her speak?" It was class snobbery of the highest order.'[25]

The Who were among the top London bands. Pete Townshend had his own recording studio in a flat on the corner of Wardour and Brewer streets in Soho. Nurtured as a writer by Lambert, Townshend developed lyrical themes of class war, anti-consumerism and unruly proletarian youth, which drew on the working-class Mod social movement. Whether the members of The Who were real Mods remained open to debate. Townshend, having studied graphic design at Ealing Art College, affirmed the conceptual basis of the theatrical rebellion in the band's act, connecting to the Auto-destructive Art movement led by Gustav Metzger.[26]

Townshend followed closely Hendrix's early trajectory: 'The clubs . . . were all the same clubs where I had seen Blues musicians when I was sixteen – the Marquee Club, Blaises, Cromwellian, he played everywhere.'[27] Hendrix awoke mixed feelings in Townshend, of friendship and antipathy: 'I felt incredibly competitive with Jimi.'[28] He discussed the interplay of his stagecraft with Clapton and Hendrix:

[Hendrix] always felt that Eric, he and I had a sort of empathy . . . and complemented one another in a certain way . . . Where I fit in was . . . in the plastic bit . . . Eric was the very soulful bit, the musician bit . . . Mine was the blatant, the show biz.[29]

Townshend gauged the import of Hendrix in guitar sound and showmanship: 'What happened there was . . . important to me and fantastically important to The Who. It has just changed the sound of the electric guitar, completely turned the whole rock world upside down.'[30]

Hendrix and Mitch Mitchell set off for Marshall Amplification on 8 October 1966. Jim Marshall's first music shop, at 76 Uxbridge Road in Hanwell, west London, was a small, inventive manufacturer of guitar amplifiers. Mitchell had worked there as a 'Saturday boy', and had also taken drumming lessons from Marshall. Pete Townshend and Eric Clapton ordered customized amps there – Townshend 100-watt Marshall stacks, following John Entwistle. Townshend described an early amp:

My solos were often simply howling feedback, or stabbing noises, but never quite loud enough to suit me. One day in 1964 Jim Marshall delivered me an amplifier system I was reasonably happy with, a 45-watt amp that had a crisp American sound, but when you turned it up it screamed like a Spitfire.[31]

Both Townshend and Clapton came to depend on Marshall amps for their sound and act. Marshall promoted his role as an innovative supplier: 'I put it in a combo originally for Eric Clapton, who used to practise in my shop, and one day he asked if I could build him a combo version of the JTM 45 so it'd be easy for him to get into the boot of his car. So I did, and that's how the Bluesbreaker combo came about.'[32] The interviewer categorized its influence:

Its sound . . . would be heard on the landmark 1966 John Mayall album, Blues Breakers with Eric Clapton, as Clapton created the definitive electric blues guitar sound, mating a 1960 Les Paul with a Marshall model number 1962 combo amp.[33]

Townshend recommended the blast of Marshall stacks, as well as Hiwatt amps, when he first met Hendrix in October 1966, and so Mitchell accompanied Hendrix to the shop to acquire a similar set-up.[34] The former Animals and Experience roadie James 'Tappy' Wright mentioned that in the first year, touring smaller theatres, the Experience used the cheapest guitars – Höfners rather than Fender Stratocasters or Telecasters – but did not stint on amps.[35] Hendrix, who had limited hearing in one ear (as well as poor vision), became well known for destroying equipment by immediately turning it up to the loudest volume. He called the Marshall stacks 'the fridge': 'My old Marshall tube amps, nothing can beat them, they look like two refrigerators hooked together.'[36] At a gig Entwistle noticed Hendrix 'using a rack of equipment exactly the same as ours[,] and a wah-wah pedal'.[37]

The Experience joined Johnny Hallyday to play Evreux, France, on 13 October, the first gig on the tour, then Nancy on 14 October, with a 15-minute, four-song set. The Experience, at the bottom of the bill, opened for Hallyday on 18 October at the 2,777-seat Olympia (28 Boulevard des Capucines in Paris's ninth arrondissement), a distinguished 75-year-old venue known for its urbane interior with red curtain, carpet and seats.[38] Also on the bill were the Blackbirds, Brian Auger & the Trinity, and Long Chris. The Experience set list comprised 'Killing Floor', 'Hey Joe', 'Wild Thing' and the rhythm and blues hits 'In the Midnight Hour' and 'Land of a Thousand Dances'. The audience was warmly receptive, and French radio broadcast 'Hey Joe' and 'Killing Field' – a first for the Experience.[39]

On 23 October 1966 the Experience recorded 'Hey Joe' and Hendrix's first recorded composition, 'Stone Free', in the De Lane Lea basement studio at 129 Kingsway, wc2,[40] with background harmony vocals variously identified as the Breakaways – Margo Newman and Lissa Gray – and the Vernon Girls.[41] Hendrix commented: '"Hey Joe" is really a blues arrangement of a cowboy song . . . I'm surprised that it got so high in the hit parade.'[42]

The Experience made another appearance at the Scotch of St James on Tuesday 25 October 1966. The act, a few covers, was booked through the Harold Davidson Agency to play the Big Apple Club in Munich for four nights. Redding's acquaintance Gerry Stickells was hired as a roadie. Hendrix sent a postcard to his father to let him know that he had played Paris, and that he would have a record out in two months' time. At the Big Apple Club he performed a guitar smash, his first with the Experience, throwing the guitar onto the stage. According to Redding, 'it exploded into amazing sounds in response to the impact.'[43]

The Jimi Hendrix Experience was playing sporadic European jaunts and London after-hours clubs, the insider scene frequented by musicians. Redding said of the reaction:

> We started doing what we called the club scene in London, and suddenly we noticed we were filling the place, and then suddenly we'd see John Lennon in the corner, and McCartney, or Bill Wyman.[44]

A well-attended press performance at the newly opened Bag O'Nails, at 10–11 Kingly Street in Soho, on the afternoon of 25 November 1966 drew a London elite, including the Beatles John Lennon and Paul McCartney, the former Yardbirds guitarists Jeff Beck, Eric Clapton and Jimmy Page, Pete Townshend of The Who, Brian Jones and Mick Jagger of The Rolling Stones, and Donovan. The group's first television appearance, on *Ready Steady Go!*, aired on 16 December.

Television coverage helped to generate a crowd to fill a Chislehurst Caves gig on 16 December. Not a figurative cavern, like the famed Beatles base in Liverpool, Chislehurst Caves were literally under the ground, a network of tunnels in Old Hill near Bromley in Kent. Marc Spitz, a Bowie biographer familiar with the cave venue, wrote:

> Chislehurst caves were actual chalk caves, underground labyrinths of ancient chalk and flint mines dating back to 1250. The Chislehurst caves have a long and strange history. Man-made caverns of cretaceous chalk, according to legend they were built during the time of the Druids. The chalk had been mined since the 1600s. During World War I they'd been a place to store secret ammunition, and in World War II they were designated an air-raid shelter.[45]

On 6 December Hendrix, Etchingham, Chandler and Lexon moved into a flat that Chandler had sublet from Ringo Starr, in a Georgian terrace at 34 Montagu Square, Marylebone. Etchingham, whose social world included Brian Jones and Keith Moon, had learned of the empty flat, as Ringo Starr and his first wife, Maureen, had moved to the suburbs after their marriage, on the advice of The Beatles' financial counsel. Included with the tenancy was the use of a small, private park, exclusively for the residents of the street. According to Etchingham, their upstairs neighbour, an elderly lady, refused to lend them the key to the gated park. Hendrix had other problems:

> I moved into a flat with Chas Chandler. It used to belong to Ringo . . . In fact, they only took the drums away the other day. There's stereo all over the place – and a very kinky bathroom with lots of mirrors. Immediately complaints started to pour in. We used to get complaints about loud, late parties when we were out of town! We'd come back next morning and hear all the complaints.[46]

Chandler and Lexon took the main floor, and Hendrix and Etchingham the basement. The neighbours' complaints resulted in an eviction notice after a particularly loud party – possibly Chandler's birthday that December. By April they had moved, transporting their belongings on foot, to a flat on the fourth floor of a modern block at 43 Upper Berkeley Street.

In the short time he spent living in Montagu Square, Hendrix wrote 'The Wind Cries Mary', a lyric based on a quarrel. The cityscape became its setting. Etchingham recounted the story:

> I just picked up the plate and threw it on the floor. And a great row started from this. Jimi got the broom, sweeping it up before Chas came back . . . He's saying that he's sweeping up

the pieces of yesterday's life . . . then I ran out of the upper
stairs out of the apartment. And he followed me. And I was
standing underneath the traffic lights and I hailed a taxi.[47]

Hendrix explained a vaguely surreal, disjointed lyric:

And like the traffic lights turn blue tomorrow that means like,
tomorrow everything's gonna be you know, blue. Blue means
feelin' bad you know. In other words, like, first if you do your
everyday things like go across the street or something like that.
Instead of the traffic lights being red and green, you know, they'd
be blue, because in your mind. So it's a story about a break up.[48]

A few obscure phrases in 'The Wind Cries Mary' referred to television
visuals. Etchingham explained that the mention of jack-in-the-boxes
referred to the BBC broadcast sign-off: 'The BBC at the time used to
finish at 10:30 or 11 o'clock – when [it] signed off broadcasting in the
evening . . . the test card was a little girl putting a jack in a box.'[49]

The Experience continued recording at De Lane Lea on 2
November 1966, but Chandler sought a better quality of sound.
Kit Lambert suggested CBS Studios, in a former ballroom on
New Bond Street.[50] Although CBS offered the improvement in
sound, Chandler argued with one of its owners, Jake Levy, over
payment, with the result that the band returned to De Lane Lea
on 21 December. According to Chandler, most of the band's work
was refined at Olympic, London's leading independent studio,
where they worked from 3 February 1967. There they worked
with George Chkiantz, Andy Johns and Eddie Kramer. The South
African Kramer had worked at Pye Studios in 1964, recording such
artists as the Kinks. He was to work extensively with Hendrix
during the musician's brief career, learning his codes and cues –
green signalled reverb – and developing a rapport in the studio.
Kramer co-produced numerous posthumous Hendrix recordings.

In 1966 Olympic Studios, a four-track facility at 117 Church
Road in Barnes, southwest London, was newly opened. The
building had been constructed in 1906 as a theatre for the Barnes
Repertory Company, and had become the local cinema four
years later. In 1965 Olympic Sound Studios had purchased it and
converted it (under the direction of the architect Robertson
Grant) from a film studio into a recording venue. It was converted
back into an independent cinema in 2013.[51]

As the band was recording, Mitch Mitchell sensed rigour and
care in Hendrix's approach:

> He had very specific ideas about the sound he wanted to
> make. He was the first person ever that made me aware. He
> actually made me listen. It's very important to hear the lyrics
> before we actually did any tracks.[52]

'Hey Joe' entered the British chart in December 1966; it was
followed in spring 1967 by Hendrix's psychedelic anthem 'Purple
Haze', which he wrote in the dressing room of the Upper Cut
Club on Boxing Day 1966. (The Upper Cut was in east London,
beyond Stratford, so perhaps he had little to do but write while
waiting to go onstage.) 'Purple Haze' was inspired by a pulp
science-fiction novella by Philip José Farmer, Night of Light,
which Hendrix had read in a magazine. The story introduced
the atmospheric idea of a glowing night sky, purple and violet,
illuminating the nocturnal landscape, on a planet called Dante's
Joy. Fused with this imagery was a dreamscape that Hendrix
described as 'a dream that I had that I was walking under the
sea'.[53] Hendrix expressed frustration about the editing of the
lyrics, saying that he had written 'a thousand thousand words', so
that the lyrics no longer represented the original lengthy poem.[54]

'Purple Haze' was first performed live in January at the Mojo
Club in Sheffield, and was recorded at De Lane Lea Studios for

the album *Are You Experienced*, which was released in the UK in March 1967. Track Records' first release was not a Who song, but rather 'Purple Haze' backed with '51st Anniversary', released on 1 March 1967. The song uses a dominant seventh sharpened ninth, dissonant tones sometimes known as the Hendrix chord; as John Perry has written, 'Purple Haze is built round the 7#9 chord.'[55]

In January 1967 the electrical engineer Roger Mayer saw Hendrix at the Bag O'Nails, on an evening when the club was crawling with musicians, and offered him the use of his sound-altering devices. Mayer, who worked in vibration and acoustic research for the Royal Navy, had provided fuzz boxes for the guitarists Jimmy Page and Jeff Beck. The thudding opening of 'Purple Haze' used the Octavia, an effects pedal that reproduces the input signal one octave higher, mixed with fuzz to fatten the sound. Hendrix placed the Octavia after a fuzz and wah unit to react to the combined effects of both boxes in a 'feed forward' set-up. Mayer eventually toured with the Experience as a sonic consultant.

By 24 January 1966 an improbable estimate of 1,400 people were said to have squeezed into the Marquee Club on Wardour Street in Soho to see the Experience and hear their repertoire: 'Hey Joe', 'Stone Free', 'Like a Rolling Stone' and 'Wild Thing'. The queue reportedly extended from Wardour Street at Shaftesbury Avenue to Cambridge Circus. Chris Squire of Syn, the support band (and later of Yes), described watching Eric Clapton, George Harrison, Keith Richards, Pete Townshend and Steve Winwood arrive and take their front-row seats.[56]

Chandler arranged gigs, edited and selected riffs that had commercial potential as songs and sold his own bass guitars to finance the band. Hendrix kept lyric notebooks, matching them with session riffs, and read Chandler's pulp science-fiction paperbacks. Chandler and his co-manager, Michael Jeffery, arranged record contracts and booked tours, typically with two 45-minute shows per night. The band played central London clubs, music halls, multiple bills in supporting gigs in the London orbit, and toured British, French, Scandinavian and German venues.

Paul McCartney and Ringo Starr saw Hendrix play in Soho, at the Bag O'Nails gig on 11 January 1967 which Mayer had also attended. The newly opened venue, run by John and Rik Gunnell, was another club where McCartney had his own table. In *Melody Maker* of 25 February 1967, Paul McCartney reviewed 'Purple Haze' with gusto:

> Fingers Hendrix. An absolute ace on the guitar. This is yet another incredible record from the great Twinkle Teeth Hendrix! . . . It's breaking out all over the place . . . Hooray![57]

Andrew Loog Oldham commented: 'There was definitely a time period when what was London up to . . . what were they doing when they had time off – they were tracking Jim Hendrix.'[58] After the opening of the 7½ Club, a new venue at 5 Whitehorse Street in w1, the music journalist Chris Welch wrote:

> Everybody went again to see Jimi and the Experience, this time at the opening of a new club, the short-lived 7½ just off Piccadilly. The audience[,] sweltering but determined not to miss a note, included Mick Jagger, Marianne Faithfull, Pete Townshend, Eric Clapton, Anita Pallenberg . . . Once again Jimi's effect on audiences, consisting largely of musicians not exactly easy to impress, was staggering.[59]

Faithfull was part of the insider crowd following Hendrix, watching as he adjusted his act:

> I went out on my own at that time; every night I'd go to a club . . . On one of my sorties I saw Jimi Hendrix at a little club called the Seven and a Half. I'd gone because Mick [Jagger]

told me about him. He said he'd seen Hendrix in New York
and that it had taken his breath away . . . There were perhaps
a dozen people there, including a couple of roadies. I sat in this
tiny basement club for hours and watched him play. A Tantric
vision in crushed velvet pants and a ruffled shirt . . . He was
very awkward. He sang with his back to the stage [audience]
or into his guitar and mumbled so badly that you couldn't
understand one word. There were long unexplained gaps
while he discussed what he was going to play next with Mitch
Mitchell and Noel Redding or fiddled with his amps. He hadn't
got his persona together – he wasn't yet the voodoo chile – and
you could see he was *painfully* shy. But once he began playing,
he transformed. It became sexually charged and very direct.[60]

On 27 January 1967, a reported 2,000 people turned up to another
Chislehurst Caves concert. Mayer came to hear Hendrix again,
again offering him effect boxes.[61]

The Jimi Hendrix Experience played the Roundhouse on
Chalk Farm Road on 22 February 1967, supported by The Flies
and Sandy & Hilary. The Roundhouse was a cylindrical yellow
brick building, constructed in 1847 to house a railway turntable.
As a concert hall, it had a capacity of several thousand, and it
became a key venue for the London Underground movement.
On 15 October 1966 Soft Machine and Pink Floyd had headlined
its opening with an All Night Rave fundraiser that launched
the underground newspaper the *International Times*.[62] At the
Experience gig in 1967 Hendrix's black Fender Stratocaster was
stolen from the stage, and Chandler was forced to trade another
of his bass guitars to replace it.

Hendrix and Chandler were seen in March 1967 at the
Speakeasy in a German television documentary about Lambert
and Stamp, *Die Jungen Nachtwandler* (The Young Nightcrawler,
or Sleepwalker), a 54-minute film directed by Edmund Wolf

The Roundhouse, London, which reopened in 2006 after renovation by John McAslan & Partners.

for Rundfunk and broadcast on 3 July 1967. Segments included early footage of Pink Floyd playing excerpts from 'Interstellar Overdrive', live at the UFO Club in London on 24 February 1967. Clips of The Who showed Townshend playing, on acoustic guitar, a demo in his Wardour Street flat, and The Who, Lambert and Stamp interacting at a rehearsal in the Saville Theatre.[63]

At the Marquee Club on Wardour Street, on 2 March 1967, the Experience performed 'Hey Joe' and 'Purple Haze' for the German television show *Beat Club*, which was broadcast from Bremen on Saturday afternoons. The show consisted of segments with two other bands, including Geno Washington and the Ram Jam Band; it ended with The Who, which was introduced as England's most sensational group. The Who's finale featured a lengthy noise outro but no actual instrument breakage.[64]

## THE BBC SESSIONS

The BBC recording sessions in 1967 presented the band with a distinctly British opportunity to practise together and record as well as broadcast, in a series of sessions recorded in a few of the BBC's fourteen or so recording and rehearsal facilities in various locations. The Beatles, The Kinks and many London pop bands performed at such venerable BBC venues as the Aeolian Hall at 135–37 New Bond Street, or the Playhouse on Northumberland Avenue.[65] The largest of the facilities were the seven Maida Vale studios.

Regulations to protect live musicians essentially required live, in-studio performances, giving the Experience a kind of rehearsal. The band played the *Saturday Club* on 13 February 1967 at BBC Broadcasting House. The session was held in a tiny studio, referred to as S2, in the sub-basement, three floors below street level. The Experience caused the soundproof glass to vibrate, and was audible through the glass and the floors. Complaints issued from the concert hall two floors above, where a string quartet was being broadcast live on Radio Three.[66] The Experience played 'Love or Confusion', 'Foxy Lady', 'Hey Joe' and 'Stone Free'.

On 27 March 1967 the band recorded 'Purple Haze' at BBC Manchester, in the Dickinson Road Studios, and on 28 March 1967 they recorded 'Killing Floor', 'Fire' and 'Purple Haze'

Chas Chandler, Jimi Hendrix, Mitch Mitchell and Noel Redding during the taping of the German television broadcast *Beat Club*, at the Marquee Club, 90 Wardour Street, London, 2 March 1967.

at either the Playhouse Theatre or possibly BBC Broadcasting House. On 10 April 1967 they performed 'Purple Haze' and 'Foxy Lady' live at the Playhouse Theatre for a programme called *Monday, Monday Radio Show*, which was broadcast live in the early afternoon.[67]

There were a few more television appearances, including mimed songs for a Belgian show, *Tienerklanken*, on 7 March 1967, and a semi-live performance of 'Purple Haze' on *Top of the Pops*

The Jimi Hendrix Experience, Saturday Scene Concert, Chelmsford, Essex, 25 February 1967.

on 30 March 1967, with the vocal sung over a recorded track, at Lime Grove Studios in Shepherd's Bush, west London.

On 17 April 1967 the Experience played live on a BBC talk show, *Late Night Line-Up*, on the topic of psychedelic happenings, performing two songs, 'Purple Haze' and 'Manic Depression'. The show, of which only video documentation of 'Manic Depression' survived, was transmitted on 19 April.[68]

In May 1967 Track Records released the LP *Are You Experienced*. On the night of Friday 12 May, the Experience played the Manor House on Seven Sisters Road in north London; an audience member, Max Anthony, recalled Hendrix tossing a guitar out of a window:

> The final number ended in a crescendo of feedback, the band leaving the stage after turning the amps up full, Hendrix pausing briefly to lob his still plugged-in Strat out of one of the windows at the back of the stage. The band didn't return for an encore but I didn't really care. I was listening to the guitar banging against the outside wall in the wind.[69]

On 6 October 1967 the *Top Gear* session, hosted by blues veteran Alexis Korner, was broadcast on the BBC World Service and heard worldwide, including by American soldiers in Vietnam. In the studio corridors of the Playhouse Theatre during the *Top Gear* session, Hendrix encountered Stevie Wonder waiting to be interviewed, and they had a chance to jam briefly.[70]

## SUCCESS IN MOTION

'I am from Mars.'

Jimi Hendrix[71]

In March 1967 Chandler and Jeffery booked the Experience on a British package tour, which launched on 31 March. At the top of the bill were the Walker Brothers, who were breaking up; Engelbert Humperdinck and Cat Stevens were also on the bill, as were The Californians and The Quotations; the MC was Nick Jones. The package tour, a relic from the booking practices of music-hall vaudeville, kicked off at the ageing Finsbury Astoria. This vast

The Finsbury Astoria, Seven Sisters Road, London, 1936.

picture palace at 232–36 Seven Sisters Road, designed by Edward
Albert Stone and built in 1930, was one of a series of cinemas on
Seven Sisters Road, including the Electric Vaudeville (dating from
between 1909 and 1916) and the Finsbury Park Cinematograph.
The Astoria (which was renamed the Rainbow in 1971) was at the
junction of Seven Sisters and Isledon Road. Its octagonal entrance
lobby led to a large auditorium and balcony with some 3,000 seats.[72]

A 19.5-m-wide (64-ft) proscenium arch 10.7 m (35 ft) deep framed the stage, and there were twelve dressing rooms.

With so many acts cramming the bill, Chandler pondered how to upstage the other artists, steal the show and attract the attention of Fleet Street and the music press. Townshend was smashing his guitar at the end of The Who's set; The Move smashed television sets. (The Move were a Birmingham band influenced by The Who. They had a string of hit songs; in residence at the Marquee Club in 1966, their stage antics included taking an axe to a television set.)

At the Astoria Hendrix set his guitar on fire onstage, an act he had first tried in the USA in 1964, according to Bobby Womack.[73] Hendrix's flamboyant guitar performance, playing it with his teeth and rolling on the stage, culminated in the guitar burn, when he ignited if not the instrument, at least some lighter fluid, and whirled the flaming guitar around his head. Such destructive antics made news in the British press. Townshend destroyed his guitar in September 1964 at the Railway Hotel, after it accidentally broke when the neck hit the ceiling. He reacted by wrecking it. The Who kept it in the act with

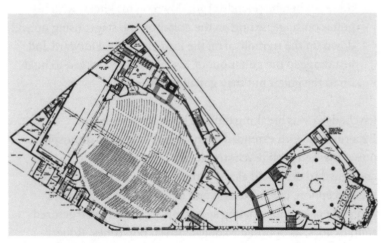

Finsbury Astoria ground plan.

their managers' approval. The film-maker Michelangelo Antonioni hired The Yardbirds to reproduce The Who's act, including smashing guitars onstage, in *Blow-Up* (1966), which was filmed in London and reimagined the daily observations of a character based on the photographer David Bailey. The Hendrix guitar burn caused a sensation, and proved pyrotechnics as a successful publicity stunt.

The 1967 tour landed on 9 April at the Empire in Lime Street, Liverpool. Some 46 years later the auction house Bonhams sold an Experience poster for that concert for £11,875.[74] The tour ended at the 3,000-seat Granada at 50 Mitcham Road in Tooting, south London, on 30 April.

Hendrix regularly upstaged the other acts, as the roadie Howard 'H' Parker recalled from a charged concert on 6 May in Lancashire:

> I did the last part of the Walker Brothers tour. We then went out and did one nighters around the country, getting really good reactions. I can remember playing the Imperial Ballroom, Nelson, a real cavern of a dance hall. The kids in the audience there – when he [Hendrix] got down on his knees, with his guitar on stage, sitting on the guitar on the stage, rising up and down on the tremolo arm, the kids just surged forward and just dragged the guitar out of his hand. He managed to hold on to the guitar but they got all the strings.[75]

Psychedelia was breaking out as a social phenomenon. Experiments with extended sounds, punctuated by atmospheric noise, meshed with psychotropic drug effects. Hendrix continued to drop acid along with his peers. Its use influenced the perception, consciousness and behaviour of performers and audience. Hallucinating spectators tolerated unstructured soundscapes, as opposed to quick, driven pop tunes. Robert Wyatt, drummer at the time for the Soft Machine, said: 'You could just play anything, for any length of time. And we did . . . There was a kindness in the audience.'[76]

The newness in contemporary pop and rock incorporated what R. Murray Schafer called a 'continuous flatline in sound'.[77] Thanks to a tour stopover in Mumbai where Ray Davies chanced to hear droning in local music, The Kinks' 'See my Friends' contained a drone a year before The Byrds' 'Eight Miles High' of 1966. The melange of sonic techniques in *Pet Sounds*, released that year by The Beach Boys, included the whirr and hum of a theremin. The Beatles' *Revolver* included an experimentally produced song, 'Tomorrow Never Knows', which used collectively handmade tape loops, mixes and drones. It was written and recorded in January 1966, and the album was released on 5 August.

Beatles John Lennon and George Harrison, along with Cynthia Lennon and Patti Boyd, dropped acid unwittingly in April 1965, when Harrison's 34-year-old cosmetic dentist added LSD to their after-dinner coffee in his flat at 12 Strathearn Place, w2. Harrison drove the couples, in Boyd's orange Mini, to the Pickwick Club at 15–18 Great Newport Street, wc2, then to the Ad Lib Club at 7 Leicester Place, near Leicester Square.[78] As they zoomed through the city, the delusional effects were intensified in a moving vehicle. Lennon and Harrison took a second LSD trip with Ringo Starr while the band was on a five-day break, at 2850 Benedict Canyon Boulevard in Los Angeles, at an afternoon party on 24 August 1965. Guests included the actors Eleanor Bron and Peter Fonda, The Byrds' David Crosby and Roger (Jim) McGuinn and the journalist Don Short. Lennon and probably Harrison plunged into frequent use. 'Within weeks of his first trip, John was taking LSD daily,' Cynthia affirmed.[79]

Drugs rendered Lennon radically unproductive, and so McCartney assumed prominence. He engaged with the London Underground scene as a bachelor living in the centre of the city. He set up a home studio in the attic at 57 Wimpole Street, the family home of his girlfriend, the former child star Jane Asher. Asher's mother, an oboist and professor of music with whom The Beatles producer George Martin had studied, taught McCartney music informally in her basement studio. Lennon and McCartney wrote early Beatles songs there. McCartney supported his friends Peter Asher (Jane's brother), Barry Miles and John Dunbar when they created the Indica Gallery and bookshop, and helped to finance the *International Times*. He left Wimpole Street in 1966, when he purchased property at 7 Cavendish Avenue, St John's Wood.

Lennon wrote 'Tomorrow Never Knows' in January 1966, having picked up a book at the Indica bookshop. The lyrics extol tuning out and drifting along, drawn from Timothy Leary and Richard Alpert's 1964 psychedelic rereading of the Tibetan *Book of the Dead*. Drones, backwards guitar sounds and found noise tapes synchronized the hallucinatory collage. *Revolver*, on which the song was released, was the album that brought 'avant-garde technique into the mainstream'.[80]

Lennon met Yoko Ono when she exhibited at the Indica Gallery in November 1966. She had arrived in London in September for Gustav Metzger's Destruction in Art conference. A Fluxus artist, Ono developed a conceptual approach to art, music and performance, addressing subjects of sexuality and collective city life. The appeal of her work straddled the intellectual world and the frothier pop sphere. Joe Massot, the director of the film *Wonderwall* (1968), a film made notable for its soundtrack by George Harrison, recalled an event at a gallery designed by the architect Cedric Price: 'I remembered her [Ono] from an opening at the [Robert] Fraser Art Gallery in Mayfair, where she had popped out of a brown paper bag naked, causing a bit of a sensation.'[81]

Pink Floyd, a band notorious for its hallucinogenic themes, played free-form jams at the UFO Club, 31 Tottenham Court Road, from December 1966. The American producer Joe Boyd and Cambridge graduate John 'Hoppy' Hopkins launched the club with original psychedelic light shows by the artists Mark Boyle and Joan Hills of Sensual Laboratory. Boyle described the mutating colour that illuminated the sound:

> Then I might be asked to make yellow projections while the current hit 'Mellow Yellow' [by Donovan] would be played and David Medalla and a group of dancers would fill an arena with more and more yellow objects, yellow cloth, yellow confetti, yellow paint etc.[82]

Pink Floyd was UFO's first house band. Boyd produced their single 'Arnold Layne', after which they signed with EMI. They wrote their experimental space rock soundscape 'Interstellar Overdrive' as Pete Jenner hummed to Syd Barrett the descending chords of Arthur Lee's 'Little Red Book'.[83] Except for Barrett, the members of Pink Floyd were studying architecture at the Regent Street Polytechnic, and would later commission spectacular inflateables for use onstage and floating over it.

Pete Townshend recalled watching Pink Floyd while on his third acid trip, on 6 January 1967:

> I went to see the Pink Floyd play for the first time at the UFO club. Syd Barrett was wonderful, and so were the rest of them. I fell in love with the band and the club itself, especially John Hopkins . . . who ran the club and worked the door. I went again the following night. This time I didn't use acid and took Eric Clapton to see Syd, who walked on stage (off *his* head on acid), played a single chord, and made it last about an hour using an electronic echo machine called a Binson.[84]

Hendrix dropped in to play central London clubs. As Pink Floyd grew successful and toured, The Move became the UFO house band. On 28 April 1967 Hendrix turned up at the UFO Club, jamming with Tomorrow, booked by Boyd at the last minute. He picked up a bass guitar that was feeding back while lying on the stage after John 'Junior' Wood put it down to 'loon around'.[85]

Tomorrow – Keith West on vocals, drummer John 'Twink' Alder and guitarist Steve Howe – was an early psychedelic group whose work, while not a commercial success, influenced an inner circle in its day. There is speculation that John Lennon wrote the 'Revolution' lyric, advocating not merely political but a personal revolution, in response to Tomorrow's single 'Revolution' and its lyric fomenting micro-scale individual and collective revolutions. Along with The Velvet Underground, Tomorrow was another band that Antonioni had originally intended to feature in *Blow-Up*. Mimes cavort in the film's enigmatic opening scenes, which are set on the plaza of Alison and Peter Smithson's Economist building. The film's final scenes on the green field recall Pink Floyd playing imaginary instruments and using instruments as games, miming along to 'See Emily Play'.[86]

In the ramp-up to the summer of love, large collective youth events and happenings included abstract displays of light and sound. Giant temporary events, sudden loud noise and large-scale, moveable sculptural installations, especially voluminous plastic inflatables, were quintessentially Underground and expressive of soft, mutable, whimsical, semi-translucent environments. Inflatable forms, usually made of plastic, presented a gelatinous sense of all the possibilities of instant fun, playful spatial enclosures. They also suggested phallic tumescence and detumescence in an age of sexual liberation.

A proto-rave, the Million Volt Light and Sound Rave on 28 January 1967, included experimental music composed by Paul McCartney. Working with the avant-garde composers' collective Unit Delta Plus, he completed a sound work called *The Carnival of Light* while The Beatles were recording 'Penny Lane' on 5 January

1967. The experimental sound collage, two overdubbed noise tapes, has remained unheard since. The rave took place at the Roundhouse and featured Soft Machine, Earl Fuggle & the Electric Poets, and a light show by Ray Anderson of San Francisco.[87]

The release of 'Strawberry Fields Forever' in February 1967 propelled psychedelia into mass media. The overall album framework of *Sgt. Pepper's Lonely Hearts Club Band*, released in June, was perceived as a conceptual revolution in the music of the vinyl record. Some critics found the album nostalgic, neo-Victorian and whimsical, and not psychedelic enough – too much Paul.

A police raid on the *International Times* was the catalyst for another enormous event, The 14 Hour Technicolor Dream on 29 April 1967, to raise funds to cover legal costs. It was held at Alexandra Palace ('The People's Palace'), a large nineteenth-century venue and north London landmark overlooking a park. Pink Floyd headlined, appearing at 5 o'clock in the morning. Some 10,000 people attended. Two bands set up at either end of the building, so that their sound collided in the middle; there was a centrally placed sound and light gantry and oversized inflatables. John Lennon made an appearance, arriving late with John Dunbar, and Hendrix may also have gone.[88]

Pink Floyd went on to headline the Games for May event at the Brutalist modern Queen Elizabeth Hall on the South Bank on 12 May 1967. The venue had opened two months previously. Posters advertised 'Space age relaxation for the climax of spring-electronic composition, colour and image projection, girls, and the Pink Floyd'. The seating for 900 spectators was damaged during the event, as 'bubbles produced from a machine while the show was in progress stained furniture in the hall [and] Pink Floyd were banned from ever playing there again.'[89] Performances ranged from wood chopping to proto-surround sound moved by an early joystick and early quadrophonic sound.

Meanwhile Hendrix was in and out of London while touring. From 17 to 19 March 1967 the Experience played three nights at the Star Club, a renowned dive at Grosse Freiheit 39 in the Reeperbahn, Hamburg's red-light district. The Beatles had made the club famous; they had played there for six weeks when it was newly open, in April 1962, and returned in November.[90]

By 4 April 1967 Hendrix, Etchingham, Chandler and Lexon were living on an upper floor at 43 Upper Berkeley Street, W1, near Marble Arch. Etchingham admitted to throwing parties there. It was agreed that Madeline Bell would join her at the flat when the band was away touring. Chris Welch interviewed Hendrix at the flat for an article in *Melody Maker*, published on 15 April 1967.[91]

After playing Copenhagen, and before Malmö and Stockholm, the Experience played Helsinki, on 22 May 1967, their only performance in Finland. They stayed at the Hotel Vaakuna. In the afternoon the band rehearsed and recorded at Ratakatu Television Studio, where they had to mime 'Hey Joe' for a show to be broadcast in September. There were three supporting acts. The Experience set list was 'Purple Haze', 'Hey Joe', 'The Wind Cries Mary' and 'Wild Thing'.[92] Biographers mentioned that 'the Experience and its road crew were harassed for their appearance.'[93] The venue was the 1,400-seat Kulttuuritalo, designed by the distinguished architect Alvar Aalto and opened in 1958. The German composer Karlheinz Stockhausen had played a concert there the night before. The critic Henrik Otto Donner, a musician and co-founder of Love Records, was in the audience for both performances and compared them, expressing his preference for the innovative sound of psychedelic rock:

Stockhausen and Hendrix work in many ways with the same material and same equipment. But Stockhausen has fallen into sterile observation of sound material whereas Jimi Hendrix creates vital music from that material . . . the way

Hendrix uses feedback, extended notes, humming of amps and echo effects and the way he mixes them with so vital [a] blues guitar . . . makes him an artist who in complexity can be compared to most of the serious composers.[94]

Stockhausen was an experimental electronic composer whose array of spatial propositions, from stereo panning to feedback, complemented the structure of his music. His work encompassed custom design of the venue, arranging the audience in circular mandala patterns (as in the 69-minute *Oktophonie* of 1991) or orchestrating the performance of a string quartet in four helicopters. His audacious formalism remains popular: *Oktophonie* was performed in nine sold-out shows at the Park Avenue Armory in New York in 2013.

The Experience returned to Stockholm to play the amusement park Gröna Lund on 24 May 1967. Their largest audience to date, with estimates ranging from 14,000 to 18,000, was then also the largest crowd to have filled that venue. There was a jam at the One More Club the next day, and a radio interview in Stockholm. With no hotel room booked, the band flew on to Copenhagen.

*Are You Experienced* was recorded during a five-month period between late October 1966 and early April 1967 and released in the UK on 12 May 1967. Its title song used overdubbed backwards tracks of guitar, bass and drum, and Hendrix played a percussive piano.[95] Photographs by Karl Ferris for the cover arranged the trinity of afro-coiffed young men in a cosmic pyramid. At the time of the album's release, Hendrix invited friends to his flat for an acetate listening party, including Brian Jones and Stanislas 'Stash' Klossowski de Rola, friends and fellow dandies in the Beau Brummell tradition. Stash, the son of the painter Balthus, was a hybrid, an avant-garde hippy aristocrat.[96]

The Jimi Hendrix Experience, *Are You Experienced*, 1967, cover.

The Jimi Hendrix Experience, *Are You Experienced*, 1967, back.

The Jimi Hendrix Experience continued a packed touring schedule at a variety of venues. The Australian feminist author Germaine Greer witnessed bedlam at a bank holiday gig, Barbecue 67 at the Tulip Bulb Auction Hall in the small town of Spalding, Lincolnshire, on 29 May 1967. The support bands were Cream, Pink Floyd, The Move and Zoot Money, and an improbable estimate of 4,000 people jammed the venue, which appeared to be a livestock auction shed. Greer was reporting for another, graphic-orientated underground tabloid, *Oz*:

> The first time I saw him . . . He was trapped by a huge dooby crowd on a high stage in a corner of a cattle shed in Spalding. The air was hot and rank because all the sliding cattle-doors were shut but one and there were no windows. As usual, an unlimited number of tickets had been sold and the promoters had split, leaving the kids to struggle in the heat and the dirt while police snooped around them with dogs trained to sniff out the drugs that none of them had the money to buy.
>
> We got in, in the chaos, for nothing, and there was Jimi caught like a bright bird underneath a corrugated-iron roof in the stink of cattle shit and sweating English youth. The crowd was so dense that those who fainted couldn't even fall down. Jimi was wrestling to get his guitar in tune and cursing the Orange gear that they had to use, as crappy then as now. The kids were festive and abusive. Jim began to play and the sound was terrible so he stopped. They jeered so he stepped downstage and yelled, 'Fuck you. I'm gonna get this guitar in tune if it takes me all night.'
>
> Then, as now, they didn't care whether 'Hey Joe' was in tune or not. They just wanted to hear noise and adulate.[97]

Hendrix attended a Pink Floyd concert at the UFO Club on 2 June 1967, and the Experience held a number of photo sessions, including one at the Upper Berkeley Street flat on 5 June.

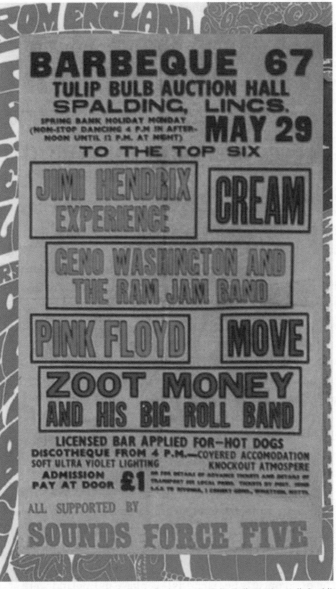

Poster for The Jimi Hendrix Experience, Barbeque 67, Tulip Bulb Auction Hall, Spalding, 29 May 1967.

In June the Experience rehearsed at the 1,426-seat Saville
Theatre, which was designed by T. Bennett & Sons and opened
in 1931 at 135–49 Shaftesbury Avenue. Tony Bramwell, part of
The Beatles' entourage, worked on preparing for the Saville stage
show while the Experience rehearsed for the June performance
at the Saville. He recounted:

> NEMS, which was owned by my boss Brian Epstein, was
> the booking agency for Hendrix. Through our connections,
> Hendrix often used the Saville for rehearsals. We liked to
> try and groom the acts a bit, suggest ways they could
> improve their performances. Hendrix was very open to
> ideas about stage presentation or lighting, so long as they
> didn't interfere with what he was doing musically. One thing
> we did was to make the legs on Mitch's drum riser weaker,
> by constructing them out of thinner wood, so that when
> Hendrix hit them with his guitar, they'd break more easily
> and send the whole thing crashing down. . . . Burning the
> guitar was becoming a standard part of the act, so Jimi
> warned us that he'd be doing that to climax his gig
> on the 4th [June]. All the theatres in the West End came
> under the control of the Lord Chamberlain's Office
> for safety regulations, so we had to arrange to have a
> fire blanket, a fire extinguisher, a fireman standing by
> in the wings, otherwise the show wouldn't be allowed
> to go on.[98]

The roadie Howard 'H' Parker identified the central role of the
Sunday evening rock concerts presented by Brian Epstein, and of
the Saville among London venues:

> The best concerts he [Hendrix] ever gave in England were at
> the Saville theatre concerts . . . It was more or less a hobby

for Epstein. It was the best presentation of rock and roll in London . . . he put on the bands that he liked.[99]

Parker also gave an account of the tumult:

Marshall had given us some new amplifiers to try out . . . none of it worked efficiently . . . We got a stroboscope on him . . . It came to 'Wild Thing'. I'd given instructions to the lighting engineer in the theatre to turn all the lights out. I put the Stroboscope onto its most hypnotic pattern . . . the only thing by which you could see anything was the stroboscope. When it came to 'Wild Thing' he just tore into those amplifiers, just knocked them, he took his guitar, swung it round his head, smashed them every which way. Mitch was on a double drum riser, which meant that he was sitting, like his feet would be four or five feet up in the air. Jimi was just smashing it, the drums were just starting to roll off the stage because he was knocking the legs of the drum riser. All this was going on, on just an every other frame level. It was like he was a demon running round. I think he was wearing a red velvet suit that night and he was running around the stage smashing everything just under the light of the stroboscope. And the audience rose up out of their seats like some tidal wave and just surged to the front. And he just threw the bits of the guitar out at them that night.[100]

Hendrix engaged in dialogue with the most influential music releases of the moment. At the Saville on 4 June 1967, the Experience performed The Beatles' psychedelic single 'Sgt. Pepper's Lonely Hearts Club Band', the title song and hit, released three days before, from the album that kept Hendrix's first album at number two. George Harrison and Paul McCartney watched from upper box seats; McCartney described it as the 'ultimate compliment'.[101]

Hendrix left London for New York on 13 June 1967, on the way to play Monterey, on the same flight as Chas Chandler, Mike Jeffery and the journalist Keith Altham. The night after they arrived in New York, Hendrix and Chandler attended a Doors concert at Steve Paul's The Scene at 301 West 46th Street. Noel Redding left London on 14 June, on the same flight as Brian Jones, who handed him a tab for his first LSD trip.

Jimi Hendrix on Stratocaster, performing on Dutch television show *Hoepla*, 11 June 1967.

## 5 THE NEW YORK–LONDON AXIS: A SERIES OF RETURNS

Jimi Hendrix said, 'I brought you something, acid, some acid.'

Lithofayne Pridgon[1]

Jimi Hendrix stopped in New York in June 1967 en route to and after Monterey, and again on leaving The Monkees package tour, which the Experience joined in midsummer. The Experience joined the tour in progress at the Coliseum in Jacksonville, Florida, on 8 July. The venue, seen in archival photographs, looks as though a stadium has landed like a cylindrical UFO in the middle of an enormous car park. For The Jimi Hendrix Experience, The Monkees tour was a gateway to a scale of concert where the sound quality was unlikely to be good, and where the audience's distance from the stage turned the musician into a miniscule puppet performing a sort of distant pageantry. An audience of 10,000 people attended. The Exprience played a 25-minute set. Then it was on to Miami.[2]

Hendrix summed up The Monkees as 'dishwater' in a 1967 *Melody Maker* interview; Chandler said he was appalled. The booking revealed Michael Jeffery's take on pop music: tools of management, The Monkees blended television and the record industry to optimize media coverage and profits. They were clean-cut versions of long-haired hippies, plucked from places like Laurel Canyon and packaged for television. A visually slick parody of a promotional movie, *Head*, written by Jack Nicholson, was released in 1968. On tour Redding noticed the session men: 'Not that they weren't good, but they had a "spare" group backing their set from behind the curtain.'[3] Some of the music was catchy, solid imitation Beatles. The problem for the bill was the 'death slot', as Hendrix called it. The shrieking power of teen girls whipped into a hysterical frenzy generated a shrill wall of noise that hit a climax just before the prefab four came on.

In Greensboro, North Carolina, Hendrix managed to get an earlier slot on the bill, and found an audience, as he explained in a telephone interview with the *New Musical Express*: 'Finally, they agreed to let us go on first and things were much better. We got screams and good reaction, and some kids even rushed the stage.'[4] The shift in order brought the audience under Hendrix's spell, according to Guion F. Stewart-Moore, who was at the concert in Greensboro with his anti-war activist brother:

Jacksonville Coliseum, Florida, capacity 12,000, demolished 2003.

My brother[,] who was 21 and very involved with the Vietnam
War moratorium, took myself, his girlfriend and her 12 years
old brother to see the Monkees. I was seated on the floor,
about 15 rows back on the right hand side of the stage. I can
remember vividly Jimi Hendrix playing but nothing about
the Monkees. We stood on our chairs the entire set of Jimi
Hendrix. It was my first concert and certainly the most
memorable concert I have ever been to. At 11 years old, I had
no idea who Jimi Hendrix was, but it was incredible. I can feel
the music and the crowd that night . . . I have no recollections
of anyone screaming for the Monkees to come on stage.
All I remember is everyone screaming, standing on chairs,
jumping up and down, waving their arms in the air, and being
entranced by Jimi Hendrix on that stage. The music was like
nothing I had ever heard and the crowd was in a fever when
he was on stage. The last thing I remember about the evening
was him setting his guitar on fire.[5]

Hendrix listed the problems with the tour to the *NME* interviewer:

We were not getting any billing – all the posters for the
show just screamed out – Monkees! Then some parents who
brought their young kids complained that our act was vulgar.
We decided it was just the wrong audience.[6]

Chandler was able to extricate The Jimi Hendrix Experience from
The Monkees tour after seven shows. The tour arrived back in
Manhattan on 16 July. The band stayed at the Warwick Hotel on 65
West 54th Street, playing three shows supporting the Monkees at
the Forest Hills Stadium in Queens. The Experience had played a few
dates in New York just before joining The Monkees' tour, staying
at Loew's Midtown Motor Inn, on Eighth Avenue between 48th
and 49th streets, where The Animals had lodged on their first tour.

Loews Midtown Motor Inn, New York, postcard *c.* 1960.

The band picked up gigs at small venues, including Midtown's hippest live music club, Steve Paul's The Scene, on 3 and 4 July 1967. The Scene was a grotty venue of about 465 sq. m (5,000 sq. ft) with absurdly low ceilings and very little headroom on its cramped stage, as photographs show. The manager had good control of the crowd, however, particularly who and how many were there. The Mothers of Invention were playing the Garrick Theater, above the basement Cafe au Go Go, for six months from March until September 1967. Hendrix heard Frank Zappa at the Garrick on 7 July; he spotted Zappa's new wah-wah pedal and bought one from Manny's Music.[7]

On Wednesday 5 July the Experience played a 40-minute show
at 10.30 pm at the Rheingold Festival, a concert series sponsored
by a beer manufacturer, held at the Wollman Rink in Central Park.
Nina Simone played the Monday evening, 3 July. Len Chandler and
The Jimi Hendrix Experience supported The Young Rascals, some

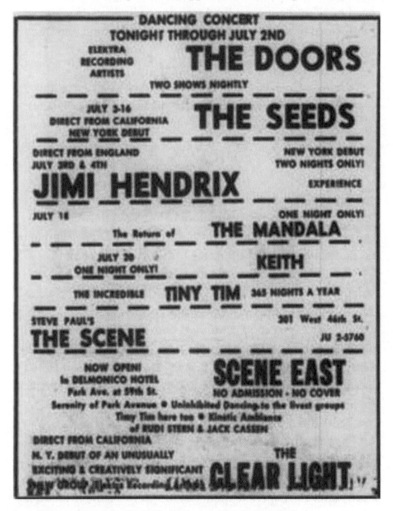

Poster for concerts at Steve Paul's The Scene, 3–4 July 1967, New York.

of whom were former Starliters. There was a significant audience of some 18,000 people. Linda Eastman (later Linda McCartney) photographed the performance, capturing a series of solo shots of Hendrix.

That day Hendrix, the Allen twins and Pridgon dropped acid together, with chaotic results. According to Pridgon, Hendrix was transformed by spending nine months in London and touring Britain and Europe:

> When he come back from London and he's playing all this music to me. It's really evident he made a hell of a change. There was even no hint of the old Jimi. You wouldn't know it was the same cat. I went to one gig at Hunter College after he was famous.[8]

One day that summer was devoted to recording at Mayfair Recording Studio, on an upper floor of 701 Seventh Avenue. On 6 July the Experience worked with the engineer Gary Kellgren in the studio recording 'The Burning of the Midnight Lamp'.[9]

Abandoning The Monkees' tour had its advantages, as Noel Redding joked: 'Getting thrown off the Monkees tour was as good as not being invited to the White House.'[10] Hendrix made it to a Frank Zappa and the Mothers photograph session on 18 July. He was included in the cover image of *We're Only in it for the Money*, Zappa's parody of The Beatles' *Sgt. Pepper's Lonely Hearts Club Band*, held at Mayfair Recording Studio, 701 Seventh Avenue.[11] Zappa was recording at the twelve-track Apostolic Studios at 53 East Tenth Street.

The band moved to the cheaper Hotel Gorham on 136 West 55th Street. Frank Zappa heard the Experience, with Hendrix playing his Flying V guitar, at the Cafe Au Go Go from 21 to 23 July, shortly after the Experience left The Monkees' tour. He found the volume unbearable:

I thought Hendrix was great. But the very first time I saw him perform, I had the incredible misfortune of sitting close to him at the Au Go Go in New York City and he had a whole stack of Marshalls. I was right in front of it. I was physically ill. I couldn't get out; it was so packed, I couldn't escape. And although it was great, I didn't see how anybody could inflict that kind of volume on himself, let alone other people. That particular show he ended by taking the guitar and impaling it in the low ceiling of the club. Just walked away and left it squealing.[12]

John Hammond Jr welcomed the guitar team of Hendrix and Eric Clapton on to the stage to join his band, the Screaming Nighthawks, at the Gaslight, a basement club on Macdougal Street in Greenwich Village. He described the circumstances:

Eric Clapton was in New York as well, and both of them jammed with us for two nights . . . It was amazing. What were the two of them playing? Blues, man, straight, heavy blues . . . I had put a little trio together . . . Charles Otis on drums and Lee Collins on bass, and I had met Eric Clapton in 1965 on tour in England when he was playing with John Mayall. Eric was in town with Cream and Jimi had just dropped out of this tour with The Monkees, so they came back to the Gaslight at the same time and they both came up on stage and played with me every night for a week . . . This was a tiny club that held maybe 60 people at one time.[13]

Eric Clapton said that he and Hendrix revelled in upstaging the bands they joined:

I used to go down to the Village with Jimi Hendrix, and we'd go from one club to another, just the two of us, and play with whoever was onstage that night. We'd get up and jam and just wipe everybody out.[14]

Paul Zullo, an audience member familiar with Hammond's album *Big City Blues* of 1964, described his astonishment and satisfaction when the two guitarists joined Hammond at the Gaslight:

Hammond did the vocals, played harp and steel, acoustic and electric guitars . . . backed by electric bass and drums . . . Their first set was a great collection of blues standards and the small weeknight crowd got their moneys [*sic*] worth (about $3) . . . The between set entertainment was provided by . . . Hugh Romney (aka Wavy Gravy) who tried to get us high with breathing patterns . . . After the bassist and drummer were back on stage Hammond made a little speech, 'please welcome, Mr Eric Clapton and Mr Jimi Hendrix.' . . . I had followed Clapton for a couple of years and wor-fm was playing 'The Wind Cries Mary' and the legend of Jimi's performance at Monterey was circulating.

A murmur went through the crowd (thirty to forty of us) and I looked to my right, two virtually twin shadows filled the whitewashed brick wall, massive afros, rail thin torsos and legs and guitars. They took the cramped stage, plugged into small amps and played the blues, Jimi on his Strat and Clapton on his sg (decorated by The Fool).

This was not a jam, with a tight rhythm section and a great blues singer, this was a show. They played Hooker, Dixon, Chuck Berry and Elmore James. jh & ec traded rhythm & leads, they did 'cut' each other in good fun, then they would play duel leads that were like nothing else I've heard since! This was a tight, clean, powerful performance . . . 'Spoonful' 'Smokestack' 'Brown Eyed Handsome Man' 'I'm in the Mood' . . . The small crowd just hung in the room when it ended, speechless.[15]

In August the Experience opened the Salvation Club, a small club with a circular dance floor and bar, at 1 Sheridan Square,

Greenwich Village. It had previously been Café Society, an innovative, historic and integrated club, where the jazz producer John Hammond Sr had first booked Billie Holiday, in 1938; it later reputedly became an organized crime den.[16] The Experience played a 35-minute gig nightly from 3 to 7 August 1967.

The Experience played for five days in the Adams Morgan section of Washington, DC, at the Ambassador Theater on 18th Street and East Columbia Road, beginning on 9 August 1967. The concert consisted of two shows of 40 minutes each, with support by Natty Bumpo. They stayed at the Shoreham Hotel and Motor Inn on Connecticut Avenue and Calvert Street, where Hendrix composed 'Bold as Love'. The first night of the run was a free community show for about 800 people; by the last night, the run-down former cinema, with its 1,300 seats, was filling up. Hendrix's biographer David Henderson recounted a running joke during 'Purple Haze':

> Jimi and Noel got into a joking thing . . . where they went up to each other and sang, ''Scuse me while I kiss this guy' as they puckered up and kissed at each other from a short distance.[17]

Electric Circus, a new nightclub, had opened a few weeks before in the same building as the Dom, the former East Village location of Warhol's Exploding Plastic Inevitable (19–25 or 19–23 St Mark's Place, between Second and Third avenues), premises that had in the interim been a hippy club, Balloon Farm. Electric Circus was hyped as 'the latest total environment, McLuhanist discotheque'.[18] The new club was opened by 28-year-old Jerry Brandt of Brandt Freeman International on 28 June 1967; it lasted until 1971. Brandt hired the graphic designer Ivan Chermayeff of Chermayeff & Geismar to create a series of psychedelic modern posters for the club.

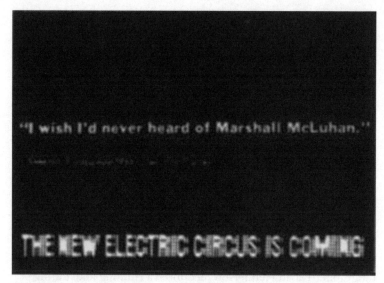

One of a series of posters, using blurred text, as if seen on a screen, to advertise Electric Circus by name-dropping McLuhan.

The interior of Electric Circus, the work of Charles Forberg & Associates, was a tent-like structure of white fabric, and there was a multimedia lighting installation by Tony Martin. The fabric, 'a giant Bedouin tent comprised of white stretch yarn', created a curved surface for projections 'of home movies, liquid lights and morphing glutinous blobs [which] glowed on the fabric. A gigantic sound system blasted rock.'[19] The electronic composer Morton Subotnick, whose work *Silver Apples of the Moon* (1967) used manipulated tape, contributed to the sound design of the club. He was invited by Jerry Brandt and Stanton J. Freeman, a manufacturer of high-fidelity equipment from Canada, who had bought the name 'Electric Circus'. Subotnick was working with new electronic instruments designed by Don Buchla, and appreciated the in-floor speakers that gave the Electric Circus the loudest sound in town:

I actually helped develop it. In the year before it opened, Stan Freeman and Jerry Brandt came to see me at my studio on Bleecker Street because I was doing all this multimedia stuff and they had bought the name 'Electric Circus'.

They had an idea about an electric circus, like a discotheque or a public space that was timely. They didn't know what it would look like . . . So I gave them a demonstration of what an electric circus would be in my studio that night. They started bringing people up to fund it and they were giving me $200 a day for doing it, which was a lot of money to me . . . they said, 'This is great. When we open, we'll give you $4,000 a year as long as the Electric Circus is open . . . you could become the artistic director.' . . . Don Buchla designed the whole sound system. The sub-woofers were huge, they were actually attached to the floor so you could feel the vibration of the sub-woofer. And of course people were moving, so once everybody moved together with that, it was pretty impressive.[20]

Andrew Loog Oldham described accompanying Brian Jones to the Electric Circus while they were in Manhattan. After a visit to the Upper East Side, to an infamous amphetamine 'doctor', 'Dr Feelgood' (possibly Max Jacobson), they went on to the club to meet Hendrix:

We limo'd down to the Village, to the Electric Circus on St Mark's [sic] Place. It was way past four, nearer to five, and the Circus was closed. Brian banged on the door and asked for the owner, Jerry Brandt, ex-William Morris agent, now trend-making host to Manhattan. Jerry came to the door, hugs passed all round and he welcomed us in.

Jerry left us alone. The 60s were nearly over as we made our way to the floor. There in the middle of this psychedelic arena, lying on his back on the floor, guitar in hand, plugged into the house sound system, oblivious to us, oblivious to all, lost in his sound coming back at him from a 360-degree soundaround blast, was the purple haze himself, Jimi Hendrix.

After fifteen minutes of this, my watch said five and I left Brian huddling with Jimi. I caught a cab outside and uptown to the hotel.[21]

Hendrix went on 17 July 1967 to see The Seeds; he said, 'We all went out to the Electric Circus which just completely blew my mind.'[22] Later, in Thomas Lopez's interview with Hendrix in his London flat, he discussed his interest in not just loud sound, but a three-dimensional, spatialized, lateralized sound, a proto-surround sound: 'I want stereo where it goes up, the sound goes up and behind and underneath. But all you can get now is just across and across.'[23]

## LONDON RETURNS: FADING PSYCHEDELIA, AUTUMN 1967

Hendrix returned to London in the autumn of 1967 with the electric Flying V and acoustic Epiphone guitars. The Experience played again on *Top of the Pops* on 24 August, performing 'The Burning of the Midnight Lamp'. Meanwhile, Kathy Etchingham described life in their flat-share as primarily musical: 'Jimi had music coming out of every pore. One minute he'd be eating his breakfast, the next he'd say "hey", pick up the guitar and play.'[24] He played 'continuously . . . he'd play the riffs in his head – only he could hear what he was hearing – and he would go through the words as well', and he practised in the bathroom: 'We shared the flat in Upper Berkeley Street with Chas and Lotte, but had our own bathroom. Ours was fully tiled and had no window but a beautiful echo, a good sound that Jimi liked so he would sit on the loo and play.'[25] The acoustic Epiphone served 'for almost everything he composed in this country, as he didn't use an amp until the move to Brook Street [in 1968], and in any case Chas would never have allowed it in case we disturbed the neighbours because we'd upset them in Montagu Square and Chas didn't want to be chucked out of a second flat. [Hendrix] would pick up and then play the acoustic, then pick up a Strat and play that unplugged, listening to it without an amp. He constantly played it to work out riffs and song arrangements including his own version of Dylan's "All Along the Watchtower".'[26]

Hendrix was one of a number of artists who received demo or unreleased tapes recorded at the Big Pink (eventually all released in 2014), or advance copies of Bob Dylan's album *John Wesley Harding* (1967). Tapes were passed to the Experience's publicist, Michael Goldstein, from Dylan's manager Albert Grossman. Dylan, who was writing profusely, made many songs available to select musicians to use for covers.

During the autumn Hendrix added 'All Along the Watchtower' to his repertoire, and on 21 January 1968 the Experience began recording it at Olympic Studios in London. The engineer Andy Johns recalled: 'Hendrix came in with these Dylan tapes and we all heard them for the first time in the studio.'[27] At one session a drug-intoxicated Brian Jones added a part that proved unusable. Hendrix went on re-recording and overdubbing guitar parts intermittently throughout June, July and August 1968, at the Record Plant in New York, sandwiched in between tour dates.

The song, released in September 1968, provoked a widespread reaction. Dylan continues to perform the version recorded by Hendrix. Hendrix's attitude to musical recording had evolved to emphasize drawn-out re-recording, the reworking of ideas. 'All Along the Watchtower' derived from the fatalist themes of Robert Johnson and Dylan, folded into biblical fantasy and a critique of the greed and corruption in the music industry. Hendrix identified once again with Dylan's lyrics of foreboding, as he grew to distrust and disdain his management. When asked for his reaction to Hendrix's version of 'All Along the Watchtower', Dylan said:

It overwhelmed me, really. He had such talent, he could find
things inside a song and vigorously develop them. He found
things that other people wouldn't think of finding in there.
He probably improved upon it by the spaces he was using.
I took license with the song from his version, actually, and
continue to do it to this day.[28]

The end of summer 1967 was marked by the passing of Brian
Epstein from a prescription drug overdose. The Jimi Hendrix
Experience (supported by The Crazy World of Arthur Brown,
and Tomorrow) played the Saville Theatre on Shaftesbury
Avenue in London on 27 August 1967. They played 'Summertime
Blues', 'Fire', 'The Wind Cries Mary', 'Foxy Lady', 'Catfish
Blues', 'I Don't Live Today', 'Red House', 'Hey Joe' and 'Purple
Haze'. The suicide of Brian Epstein that day caused the second
planned date to be cancelled. Arthur Brown considered it to be
the moment when a hippy audience rather than a teen audience
tuned in:

> All the underground people, from The UFO club and so on,
> came to see him [Hendrix]. He'd never actually played at The
> UFO, and they represented a different kind of audience from
> the pop fans who had been buying the singles.

When the Experience stretched and transgressed the pop formula,
Tony Bramwell heard the influence of acid:

> Performances were already starting to get a bit out of control
> by this time. He'd go off into long, jazzy improvisations
> that made the set difficult to follow. I also knew that part
> of the problem was that he was mixing a lot with the
> boys (John Lennon and Paul McCartney) and doing a lot
> of LSD.[29]

Jeffery was to become an acidhead, and Hendrix and Jeffery acid buddies. According to Chas Chandler, who remained oblivious to the drug excess,

> It was Tony Bramwell who told me – he was from Liverpool and was the youngest member of the Beatles' entourage, helping Brian Epstein to run the Saville. He was giving me hell in The Speakeasy for letting them do so much LSD . . . Jimi never seemed to be high or anything. I didn't find out until after we completed *Axis: Bold as Love* that he'd been taking acid. And this was a guy that was living in the same flat as me. You just couldn't tell with Jimi. He just seemed to cruise through anything that came along.[30]

Chris Stamp of Track Records maintained that softer drugs were prevalent: 'Everyone was sort of involved with pot . . . and LSD was very important at the time. Everyone was taking LSD, everyone was thinking about taking LSD . . . the actual hard drugs weren't important at all and they weren't around at all.'[31] Still, some members of the London insider scene known to be using heroin, which was available in pill form early on, included John Dunbar, the art dealer Robert Fraser, Ginger Baker and (later) Eric Clapton of Cream, Jimmy Page, John Lennon, Marianne Faithfull, Anita Pallenberg and Keith Richards. Epstein suffered from an addiction to prescription pills; Brian Jones reputedly took anything but heroin, chiefly Mandrax (methaqualone) and LSD.

Frank Zappa and the Mothers of Invention arrived in London to play the Royal Albert Hall on 23 September 1967. This elliptical red-brick building, which seats 5,000 and was completed in 1871, is topped by an immense dome of glass and wrought iron; its grand interior was renowned for its problematic acoustic doubling, since improved. It remains a prestigious music hall.[32] Graham Nash mentioned that he and Hendrix were both tripping on LSD at the

Mothers show. A spotlight followed them as they made their way to
Brian Jones's seat in order to get 'even higher with him'.[33]

On this occasion, the keyboardist Don Preston played the
Albert Hall organ, sounding the prodigious opening chords of
'Louie Louie'. Noise, rock and architecture reverberated and
synthesized within Queen Victoria's ornate memorial to her
consort. A concert-goer elaborated:

> The Royal Albert Hall has a stage in front of a tiered seating
> arrangement (for a choir) and in the centre of this is a large
> pipe organ. After Frank Zappa made the statement . . . Don
> Preston . . . opened a little gate, went rushing up the stairs to
> the organ and really let it rip.[34]

Frank Zappa, Pamela Zarubica (one of Zappa's several friends
who played the 'Suzy Creamcheese' character), Jimi Hendrix
and Jeff Beck visited the flat where Tomorrow lived. Zappa later
commented on the fact that Hendrix did not read or write musical
notation, suggesting that he hire a specialist to notate music for
him. However, Hendrix did have a precise method, a textual
narrative through which he noted musical ideas, and also used
portable tape recorders.[35]

The guitarist Mick Taylor was impressed with the switch-
handed playing technique Hendrix had developed:

> He came to this little club in London called the Speakeasy . . .
> it was that kind of club that musicians used to go to in the
> evening. He wanted to play, but there was no spare guitar . . .
> I'm right handed . . . and he's left-handed . . . and all he did
> was just turn it upside-down . . . It was amazing to hear
> someone play so well . . . and with the guitar backwards! Jimi
> Hendrix could play both ways . . . which is quite phenomenal.
> I've never met anyone else that could do that. It's like playing

the piano backwards . . . Because all the strings and notes are reversed . . . All the chords are reversed.[36]

During the recording of *Axis: Bold as Love* at Olympic Studios in October 1967, Hendrix did not just display his gift for playing the guitar upside-down, transposing the left and right hands. The notion of chirality, relating to a non-superposable mirror image form, lends insight into the specificity of Hendrix's virtuoso technique. Another unusual ability was his capacity to accompany and follow his backwards tracks. Mitch Mitchell wrote:

> It was about that time that I realized that Hendrix could play something forwards and know exactly how it would sound if it was played back in reverse. An amazing facility.[37]

Andy Johns confirmed this uncanny reverse sequential memory: 'He knew the stuff backwards . . . Somehow he knew where he was in a backwards track. Miles ahead of what was going on at the time, even the innovative stuff.'[38] Eddie Kramer was introducing spatial and psychedelic sounds in stereo. He explained the phasing in *Axis: Bold as Love* as 'where you get two sounds together [that] sound like water going down a funnel'.[39]

George Chkiantz of Olympic developed phasing, which can be heard on the Small Faces song 'Itchycoo Park', released in August 1967. It used flanging or phasing in mono. *Axis* was recorded in stereo, affording a more separated, spatial sound to the phasing.[40] Mitchell remarked on Hendrix's studio proficiency:

> Hendrix did have a natural capability of working in the studio. To him, that was like his palate of colours. There are some people who feel very comfortable behind the board and know how things work. He was just very natural with the technology that existed.[41]

Hendrix's spatial awareness allowed him to transform the reverberant volume of the studio into an extension of his sound, as Chris Stamp pointed out:

> He was the first musician to use the studio as another instrument, which Chas didn't get at all. Either Chas was going to go totally off the wall with Jimi or Jimi was going to have to do it on his own. That was inevitable; it could have been even better if Chas had somehow stayed in there.[42]

Rock and pop musicians were also using the studio and recording in innovative ways. In Los Angeles, Brian Wilson had by 1963 obtained complete freedom to experiment while recording for Capitol Records, as his biographer wrote: 'For the first time in the history of rock and roll the artist himself had absolute studio authority over his album-length output.'[43] The Toronto-based Canadian pianist Glenn Gould experimented with concepts of place and sound from his classically trained perspective. Gould came to consider live performance obsolete, and retired from concert performing in 1964 at the peak of his career; his interests shifted to recording and working in radio at the Canadian Broadcasting Corporation. He was iconoclastic in his radical adjustments of tempo, as well as in abandoning performance. Obsessed with the analogue recording technology of the era, he fantasized about splicing tape as single notes.[44]

The musician's artistic control did not extend to graphic depictions. The image on the cover of *Axis*, a graphic with the East Indian theme of rock star as Vishnu, left Hendrix cold. He commented dryly: 'I ain't that kind of Indian.'[45]

In late October 1967 The Jimi Hendrix Experience rehearsed in Studio B at the Denmark Street branch of the Regent Sounds Studio, garnering complaints about noise from the Labour Exchange next door.[46] In November Hendrix met Rahsaan Roland Kirk at Ronnie

The Jimi Hendrix Experience, *Axis: Bold as Love*, 1967, cover.

Scott's on Frith Street, and they played a number of jams together. Mitchell recalled Hendrix's enthusiasm for Kirk's playing:

> At the time, Jimi introduced me to Dylan and a few other people . . . like Roland Kirk. We'd all go off and play with other people and bring whatever you got from those people back into the band . . . it was only when Jimi began to go outside and play with other people like Roland Kirk that people became aware of really how good he was.[47]

Eric Burdon remembered Kirk performing at Birdland in New York, wired as a sonic tree: 'He was also covered in wires, pickups, and miniature tape machines, all plugged into amplifiers and echo units. He was, as he called himself, a sound tree.'[48]

In March 1969 Hendrix missed an opportunity to perform jazz and rock improvisation on film, in a studio recording called *Supershow*, which was filmed over two days in a former linoleum factory in Staines, just west of London. On 25 March performances included Led Zeppelin, Buddy Guy, Jack Bruce, Buddy Miles, Dick Heckstall-Smith and Chris Mercer; those performing the next day included Bruce, Clapton, Guy, Roland Kirk and his quartet, Miles, the Modern Jazz Quartet and Stephen Stills. Hendrix was scheduled to appear, but reportedly missed a flight from New York.[49]

The Jimi Hendrix Experience played a concert billed as the Alchemical Wedding at the Royal Albert Hall on 14 November. A spectator described the finale:

> He threw his guitar into the air above the stage. The Albert Hall is a huge space, and I can still see his white strat attached to a curly guitar lead almost levitating before crashing to the ground in a squeal of noise. He'd left the stage by then. What an exit![50]

The concert launched the band's largest UK tour, headlining and performing twice nightly on some fourteen dates with support by The Move, The Nice, Pink Floyd, Amen Corner, Outer Limits and Eire Apparent. The Blackpool concert of 25 November was filmed and recorded, and *Axis: Bold as Love* was rush-released in the UK on 1 December. Chas Chandler described a Newcastle concert as starting off with Hendrix throwing the Flying V guitar into an amp and impaling it there. The tour ended on 5 December at Green's Playhouse on Renfrew Street in Glasgow – the largest cinema in Europe at the time – a venue with some 4,000 seats, its upper floor a ballroom with a capacity of 1,500. The theatre was renamed the Apollo in 1973, and after fire damage was demolished in 1987, replaced by a multi-use commercial building with a pub and cineplex.[51]

Just before the tour began, on 12 November, the *New York Times* had reviewed *Are You Experienced*. The tone was positive despite some ambiguity and a negative title, 'A Genuine Nightmare'. The band members were called 'surrealistic hermaphrodites' and described as 'sneering through their bouffant hairdos'.[52]

Underground London converged at the end of 1967 for a three-day event, Christmas on Earth, Continued, at the Olympia Exhibition Hall of 1920, an immense venue on Hammersmith Road near Earls Court. The Experience headlined, supported by Traffic (instead of The Who, as advertised on the posters), Tomorrow, Soft Machine, Eric Burdon & The Animals, Graham Bond and The Move. It was Syd Barrett's final official gig at the head of Pink Floyd. He was visible onstage in front, with his guitar unplugged. The venue was set up with two stages, wall projections and the liquid light-show work of Mark Boyle and Joan Hills' Sensual Laboratory. When Soft Machine played, Robert Wyatt splashed in a basin of water. Hendrix played his Gibson Flying V, or 'Flying Arrow', as he called it. A clip of the Experience playing 'Sgt. Pepper's Lonely Hearts Club Band' shows him playing an engaging, energetic cover arrangement. According to a hippy who was in the audience, 'Flower Power was dying as a scene.'[53]

The Beatles' Apple boutique had opened at 94 Baker Street on 5 December 1967, with a colourful, psychedelic pop urban mural by The Fool. It presaged a future when merchandizing, known as merch, would overtake the profitability of music itself.[54]

The Jimi Hendrix Experience, filmed performing 'Sgt. Pepper's Lonely Hearts Club Band' on 22 December 1967 as part of the event 'Christmas on Earth Continued' at the Olympia, London.

The Experience finished the year with several television appearances, all lost. Television proved to be a disposable medium, since videotape was not archived systematically. On 8 December 1967 in Studio D at the Elstree Studios in Borehamwood, Hertfordshire, on *Good Evening*, Associated Television recorded Spanish Castle Magic', live to tape, for broadcast on 10 December. The Experience taped 'Purple Haze' on 16 December for a BBC survey of 1967, broadcast on *Top of the Pops* on Christmas Day.[55]

## 1968: 'THE END OF A BEGINNING'

> But what after all is one night? A short space, especially when the darkness dims so soon, and so soon a bird sings, a cock crows, or a faint green quickens, like a turning leaf, in the hollow of a wave. Night, however, succeeds to night. The winter holds a pack of them in store and deals them equally, evenly, with indefatigable fingers. They lengthen; they darken. Some of them hold aloft clear planets, plates of brightness.
>
> Virginia Woolf, *To the Lighthouse*

The year 1968 began with a Scandinavian tour in which the Experience played the dark winter nights in Gothenburg, Sweden. On their arrival, on 4 January 1968, after drinking at the Klubb Karl, Hendrix was arrested at 4 am by five police officers for damage to room 623 of the Hotel Opalen, at 73 Engelbrektsgatan (he had broken a plate-glass window with his right hand). He was charged for damage and taken to hospital for his hand injury. Photographs show him in a fluffy fur coat in the snow, surrounded by police, and also playing the Lorensbergs Cirkus venue with a bandaged hand. In uncertain English translation, Scandinavian reports detailed the ruckus: 'Jimi Hendrix . . . had to sleepover in detention'; the musician ran amuck in drunkenness in his room. Under a heavy drinking, where nobody was aware of anything, several glasses, bottles and furniture's got smashed. The tapestry was torn apart a couple of places. It all ended with Jimi Hendrix smashing a window with his right hand, so that blood dripped on the carpet.[56]

The police 'ordered him to report to the police station every day at 2 pm until his court appearance on January 16, 1968[,] when Hendrix received a fine of 3200 Swedish Crowns'.[57]

As the Experience toured, immense success was accompanied by exhaustion and burnout. Gimmicks and simple hit songs were tiresome performed night after night. American geography separated each stadium by vast distances, and the stadium booking lacked strategic logic. A concert almost every other night meant travel from hotels in New York or Los Angeles and flights to an anonymous city and stadium, with risks of equipment theft and crowd riots. Writing and recording were squeezed into downtime between tour dates. Hendrix considered *Axis: Bold as Love* hastily recorded. He intended to focus on recording. Chandler tired of the entourage surrounding Hendrix and was already losing interest while the band re-recorded *Electric Ladyland* and 'All Along the Watchtower'. Hendrix would remark, 'I hear it a bit differently' and rework another take.[58]

*Electric Ladyland*, the band's last album, was released without crediting Chandler as producer, despite his earlier involvement. Hendrix and Kramer indulged in flowing soundscapes, lengthier songs and psychedelic sonic interplay, and Hendrix's role as producer was innovative. As the guitarist John Perry pointed out, Hendrix, Sly Stone and Ray Davies were among the few self-producers in 1968.[59] Hendrix travelled America on tour, generally based in New York and returning sporadically to London; he also toured Europe. While in New York, Hendrix stayed with friends – such as Al Brown, at his apartment at 57th Street and Tenth

Lorensbergs Cirkus, Gothenburg, Sweden, erected in 1900 and demolished in 1969.

Avenue – or in luxury hotels, such as the Pierre at 2 East 61st Street or the Hotel Elysee at 60 East 54th Street, or in the apartment below Michael Jeffery's brownstone office at 27 East 37th Street. His management funnelled receipts through a holding company in the Bahamas. Ray Davies wrote 'The Moneygoround' (released on *Lola Versus Powerman and the Moneygoround, Part One* in 1970), a satirical lyric about The Kinks' money managers, in which he named his upper-class agents Grenville Collins and Larry Page.

The acerbic lines summed up the con of success: as the media consumed a performer utterly, the management could channel away the profits.

By February 1968 the Experience had started another American tour, travelling with the Mark Boyle light show. Soft Machine was the primary supporting act, playing some 60 dates, from Arizona on 5 February to the Hollywood Bowl on 14 September.[60] Noel Redding kept a detailed diary: 'We did 57 gigs in 55 days. We were playing bigger things. We were doing twenty to thirty thousand people.' The seating capacity of the venues ranged from 1,000 to 15,000. Transactions were in cash, and if there were any records, they were unrevealed, lost or destroyed.[61] Tickets sold out, even without television exposure, as a concert promoter explained:

> You could listen to him on the radio but you were not going to see him on TV. When he came to your town, you had to be at that concert. Because that was the only chance you would get to see him.[62]

Neville Chesters, having left the crew of The Who, joined the Experience's road crew with Gerry Stickells. In interviews Chesters described a nonsensical sequence of tour dates and locations:

> The 1968 tour was best described as complete madness. The gigs were far and wide. We would do Virginia Beach and then we would do Quebec and Cleveland and then we would be back in New York. We were all over the place . . . I recorded driving 19,000 miles in eight days. I didn't sleep at all; all I did was take Dexedrine or anything I could take.[63]

While in New York in March Hendrix stayed at the Warwick Hotel on West 54th Street. In April, ejected because of loud partying, he moved to the Drake Hotel on Park Avenue and 56th Street.

Hendrix recorded at Sound Center Studios, 247 West 42nd Street, on 13 and 14 March, with the harmonica player and guitarist Paul Caruso, Jimmy Maynes and Buddy Miles, Ken Pine of The Fugs and the guitarist Stephen Stills, indicating an ongoing interest in working with a variety of musicians. As his own producer, Hendrix developed his use of the recording studio as a spatial instrument. The engineer Tom Muccio observed his interest in futuristic detailing: 'Hendrix was infatuated by the recording console at Sound Center Studios, because it looked like the inside of a spaceship[,] particularly the sliding fader controls,' as opposed to Olympic's button controls. Muccio added: 'When Hendrix came by . . . there were only 3 or 4 people with him. It would just be Hendrix, Noel Redding, and Mitch Mitchell usually. Noel always had a girlfriend with him.'[64]

Hendrix continued to record jams and amass tapes for his personal files. He made a reel-to-reel home recording known as the Dirty Tape in his room in the Drake Hotel, some time in March 1968.[65] It featured Mr Wiggles teasing Paul Caruso. (A friend of Hendrix, Mr Wiggles, real name Alexander Randolph and also known as Dickie Diamond and August Moon, was a DJ, songwriter, producer and owner of labels, including Sound of Soul.) The record producer Alan Douglas explained the importance of the tape recorder for Hendrix, who had never learned musical notation, as a way to keep track of new writing: 'Every time Jimi had an idea for a song he had to sit down, play it, and make a tape if he wanted to keep it . . . he also had to write out in longhand what he heard, which was very time-consuming.'[66] The art historian Pepe Karmel later remarked on the detailed musical precision of Hendrix's notes:

> The paper bore a simple lyric and elementary chord patterns (E, B, F-sharp, and D, A, E) and the words 'Repeat twice – then break with guitar and Bells – Guitar first string E String ring open as B and G strings playing slight oriental pattern together. B string notes start on 7th fret with G string on 6th . . . Repeat

with low click of bass and slide guitar coming from down notes to up – Then vocal, and at the same time guitar hitting G chord and bass string and bass guitar hitting A . . . then syncopate chords of B min, C# min, D, up to G . . . then to B.' . . . He knew in advance exactly what he wanted to do in each solo, and could articulate it quite precisely. All the fog and fuzz of slides and wails and feedback were precisely calibrated in advance, and articulated to the band. That's fundamental . . . when he wanted to transcribe his musical ideas he had to do it in this way – as a narrative, a little memo to himself.[67]

On 19 March 1968, near the beginning of the tour, the Experience, supported by Soft Machine and the liquid light-show projections of Mark Boyle, played the Capitol Theatre at 230 Bank Street in Ottawa.[68] The Capitol was one of the larger venues in town, with 2,580 seats. Joni Mitchell was performing that same night at a modest folk club called L'Hibou ('the owl') on Sussex Drive. As it happened, they were all staying in an elegant hotel, the nineteenth-century Chateau Laurier – a monumental 430-room Canadian Pacific railway hotel – at 1 Rideau Street, near the Canadian Parliament. Joni Mitchell described their meeting:

> After his set, [Hendrix] came down and he brought a big reel-to-reel tape recorder. He introduced himself very shyly and said, 'Would you mind if I tape your show?' I said, 'Not at all.' And later that evening we went back, we were staying at the same hotel. He and his drummer, Mitch, the three of us were talking. It was so innocent. But [the hotel] management, all they saw was three hippies. We were outcasts anyway. A black hippie! Two men and a woman in the same room. So they kept telling us to play lower. It was a very creative, special night. We were playing like children.[69]

Hendrix's diary entry for 19–20 March noted:

> Arrived in Ottawa – beautiful hotel . . . strange people . . .
> beautiful dinner. Talked with Joni Mitchell on the phone.
> I think I'll record her tonight with my excellent tape recorder
> (knock on wood). Went down to the club to see Joni, fantastic
> girl with heaven words. We all got to party. Ok, millions of
> girls . . . We left Ottawa city today. I kissed Joni goodbye.[70]

Mitch Mitchell described all three musicians listening to the tapes
together after midnight, being chased from room to room:

> Hendrix and I both had these portable Sony tape recorders,
> huge things, that we dragged around the world. So we went
> to this little folk club, after our gig[,] with Hendrix's tape
> machine. We were amazed, she was wonderful. So we taped
> the show and went back to the hotel.
>
> Turns out, not only is she staying in the same hotel, but
> she's on the same floor. So we went to his room, just the three
> of us, played the tape back, compared notes, that kind of
> thing. It's two in the morning, but we're keeping things low
> and we'd been there about an hour and the manager comes
> up. He went berserk . . . so we moved everything into my
> room. We got chased out of there and went to Joni's. This
> went on all night. Unfortunately the tape recorder and the
> tape were stolen the next day.[71]

Joni Mitchell lived at 41 West Sixteenth Street, New York.
Leonard Cohen recalled encountering Hendrix with her:

> I was walking up Twenty-third Street, which is the street the
> Chelsea Hotel was on, and I was with Joni Mitchell, a very
> beautiful woman, and a big limousine pulled up and Jimi

Hendrix was in the backseat and he was chatting up Joni from the back of the limo.[72]

The Jimi Hendrix Experience block-booked the Record Plant, a new twelve-track recording studio at 132 West 44th Street, from April until July 1968. The studio had been built by Gary Kellgren, Chris Stone and the producer Tom Wilson. They hired Eddie Kramer, who joined them on 18 April 1968. Hendrix was working with Al Kooper playing the piano on demo tracks for 'Long Hot Summer Night', and gave Kooper a Stratocaster. Traffic was also recording at the studio, leading to intermingled contributions from various musicians. Chris Wood, for example, played the flute on '1983 (A Merman I Should Turn to Be)' on *Electric Ladyland*.[73]

In May, at The Scene, the crowd – including Hendrix, Mitch Mitchell, Kramer, Steve Winwood, the bassist Jack Casady and Larry Coryell – went to the Record Plant to record 'Voodoo Chile'. Kramer observed this composing through jamming, and recognized its planned spontaneity:

> The classic example of this was 'Voodoo Chile' . . . after Chas left, Jimi had wonderful aid and assistance from a quite unlikely source: The Scene club . . . around the corner from the Record Plant. Having booked the session for seven o'clock, we'd be sitting there . . . wondering when he was going to show up . . . He'd be over at The Scene at ten and show up at the studio at twelve or one, dragging behind him an entourage that included musicians whom he had sussed out as being the key players to try out that evening . . . There was a certain sound he was looking for, and he'd eyeball the musicians very carefully to make sure that they were going to be compatible with what he wanted to do . . . there were some phenomenal musicians around, and 'Voodoo Chile' was a classic example of Jimi figuring 'OK, I'm gonna get these guys in to play this particular song'. He'd bring

them in at midnight or whenever, and everything would be ready: the amps, the mics, the headphones – I'd tested everything. Then he'd show them the song, and there'd be one run-through and one take, maybe two. Bam! It was done. So, to the outside observer there were the hangers-on and the whole rigmarole with onlookers, and sometimes that made it a bit challenging to work, but it never detracted from Jimi's goal. Chas may have commented 'Oh, he's playing to the gallery,' but it didn't seem to bother Jimi . . . maybe that was the vibe he was looking for.

Chas was absolutely essential to Jimi's development as a writer and as a performer, as well as in terms of putting the band together, producing the records and giving Jimi the necessary discipline to come up with the goods. But with the *Electric Ladyland* album his role diminished as soon as the sessions moved to the States. You could tell there was a sea change in Jimi's behaviour, in his attitude.[74]

In an interview, Casady described the sleek transition from club to recording studio:

We were playing the Fillmore Auditorium a lot and since it was our hometown we got to meet a lot of the acts that came through. I met Jimi there. Sometime later we were in New York taping The Dick Cavett Show. That night we went to a local club to check out Stevie Winwood and Traffic and Jimi happened to be there too. In those days we carried our guitars around with us everywhere we went because there was always a chance to play. We went over to the studio . . . and hung out all night. At about 7:30 in the morning Jimi asked me if I wanted to play a blues he was recording and I said sure. We ran over it one time and he broke a string. Ran over it again and then I think part of a third time and that was it. I was as surprised as anybody that it ended up on the record.[75]

Mitch Mitchell enthused over improvised, ad hoc jams at the Scene in 1968:

> We had the Scene Club, just around the corner, two blocks away (from Record Plant) where some of the best jam sessions ever took place. You'd find people like [Rahsaan] Roland Kirk, Gébor Szabó, playing with Albert King, who was out in the road – with a 400 foot lead playing outside in the street. It was a tiny basement.[76]

The quasi-documentary *Groupies*, a film that made the hangers-on appear highly unappetizing, used The Scene as a location not long before the club closed in 1970.

On 3 May 1968 Jimi Hendrix and Mitch Mitchell jammed with Joe Tex and his seventeen-piece band for a Black Power Benefit at the Town Hall, 123 West 43rd Street between Sixth and Broadway, a distinguished 1,500-seat venue founded by Suffragists in 1921 and which had played host to performers and composers from Billie Holiday to Igor Stravinsky. Mitchell recalled that they appeared unrehearsed, long after midnight:

> I ended up playing one thing in New York with Joe Tex and his big band – and this ain't Count Basie! Jimi woke me up in the hotel in New York and it was about 2 o'clock in the morning, 'Mitch, come on. You've got to come.' [And we played] in some ballroom.[77]

On 8 March 1968 the impresario Bill Graham opened the Fillmore East, at 105 Second Avenue at Sixth Street. The 2,700-seat auditorium in a converted vaudeville theatre of 1925–6 was recognized for its acoustics and became the venue for many live recordings, including Miles Davis's so-called lost quintet.

A bootleg circulated of Davis's electric quintet performing on 7 March 1970 on a bill supporting Neil Young and Crazy Horse. The venue closed in June 1971.[78]

The Experience played a double bill with Sly & the Family Stone there on 10 May 1968, and at the end of the year Hendrix headlined the Fillmore East with Billy Cox and Buddy Miles. The trio also recorded the album *Band of Gypsys* with four landmark performances as a high-profile black rock power trio, live on New Year's Eve 1969 and New Year's Day 1970.

In 1967 Colette Mimram and Stella Douglas, the Benabou sisters, had opened a boutique with no name at 321 East Ninth Street, not far from the Fillmore East. At that time Douglas was married to the producer Alan Douglas. With the shop as a hang-out, a private social circle developed. It included Betty Mabry Davis, Miles Davis, Devon Wilson and the sisters Colette and Stella, who created stage costumes for Hendrix, notably a white jacket, blue-beaded and fringed, which he wore at Woodstock. Carlos Santana referred to this female pack as 'the monitors'; he also mentioned 'lady swapping' and referred to a group of about ten, known as the 'Cosmic Family', that orbited Hendrix and Miles Davis: 'like moons they would just gravitate.'[79] Douglas described meeting Hendrix and Davis through the social scene of the boutique. Other accounts told of Hendrix meeting Miles Davis through their hairdresser, Finley.

Hendrix continued to jam at Midtown clubs, particularly the Scene, throughout April 1968. Another favourite basement club was the Generation at 52 West Eighth Street in the Village, where he jammed with B.B. King and Buddy Guy some time between 7 and 15 April 1968, after the assassination of Martin Luther King Jr. Janis Ian mentioned meeting Hendrix there around that time.[80]

The Experience played the Civic Dome in Virginia Beach on 3 April and 21 August 1968. A spectator with a keen interest in the sound of Soft Machine described the concert, stressing that the geodesic dome, 'a horrible venue', did nothing for the acoustic experience. He described Soft Machine's set, beginning with the line-up:

> The band was three musicians: Robert Wyatt, Kevin Ayers, & Michael Ratledge. As for the set: an extremely intense and loud set ensued featuring music from the first and second Soft Machine records. At the end of the set, Ratledge pushed his organ off the stage causing . . . severe feedback . . . Hendrix performed and did various acrobatic stunts . . . he left his guitar intact by the end of the first show, [at the end of the] second set, Hendrix burned his guitar. Hendrix became the first of two hard rock bands in the 60s to be banned forever from the state of Virginia.

The spectator continued with a fragmented summary of the guitar smash and lob:

> Jimi smashing the guitar . . . a Sunburst Strat . . . Jimi is on his knees operating the wah pedal with his hand, guitar between his legs . . . he smashes the guitar . . . against the amps, then you see three quarters of the guitar's body sailing over the cop[']s hands and into the crowd.[81]

There is some debate about the dates of a celebrated jam at 52 West Eighth Street on or after the night of 4 April 1968. It may in fact have taken place on Sunday 7 April, the opening night of the Generation Club, or in the days that followed. The scheduled programme started with a performance by Big Brother & the Holding Company, followed by B.B. King. After an intermission musicians gathered onstage for a tribute jam to King. D. A. Pennebaker filmed the jam, which has become known as 'Wake at Generation'.[82]

Civic Dome, Virginia Beach, demolished 1994.

The Experience performed in Virginia Beach the night of the assassination, and played Newark the next night at the request of the local police force. Mark Boyle reacted to an extraordinary improvisation Hendrix played on the occasion:

> A vast crowd gathered at the auditorium – if he didn't show up they'd burn the city down . . . Soft Machine did a great set then Hendrix came out to enormous applause and then he said, this number is for a friend of mine. He abandoned completely his normal set and the band played an absolutely hauntingly beautiful . . . lament for Martin Luther King. Within minutes the whole audience was weeping. The music had a kind of appalling beauty, a harrowing beauty.[83]

The assassination of Dr King provoked a radicalization of the militant movements of the time. The writer Michael Herr emphasized its repercussions on Americans in Vietnam: 'The death of Martin Luther King intruded on the war in a way that no other outside event had ever done.'[84]

On Saturday 18 May the Experience headlined the two-day
Miami Pop Festival, attracting an audience of 25,000 to Gulfstream
Racetrack in Florida. Supporting bands included Chuck Berry,
the Mothers of Invention, John Lee Hooker, Mississippi Fred
McDowell, Blue Cheer, Steppenwolf and The Crazy World of
Arthur Brown. The Experience made a spectacular entrance by
helicopter and performed on a flatbed truck, one of three arrayed
on the racetrack by the promoters Marshall Brevitz and Michael
Lang. A Warner Brothers Records executive summed up the swift
ascent of the band:

> In less than a year from the time Jimi Hendrix came over to do
> Monterey Pop to the time he headlined Miami Pop, he became
> the biggest concert attraction in the country. That's fast.[85]

An epic jam took place at the Wreck Bar in the Castaways Hotel,
Miami, with John Lee Hooker, Noel Redding, Frank Zappa,
Arthur Brown and Jimmy Carl Black. Rain washed out the second
concert, and in a limousine en route Hendrix wrote 'Rainy Day
Dream Away'.

The Experience was back at Fillmore East on 8 June 1968,
to sit in with Electric Flag, and on 10 June, at the Record Plant,
Hendrix continued to harvest musicians from nearby clubs or
adjacent recording studios. For 'Rainy Day' he recruited the
drummer Larry Faucette, the saxophonist Freddie Smith and the
keyboard player Mike Finnigan. Finnigan explained:

> Tom Wilson had discovered and produced my little r and b
> band. He introduced us to Hendrix and Jimi asked me, Larry
> Faucette, and Freddie Smith to jam on this tune he had in
> mind. He said, 'We're going to do a slow shuffle in D. You be
> Jimmy Smith and I'll be Kenny Burrell' . . . He used a small
> thirty-watt Fender Showman amplifier.[86]

# 6 HEAVY TOURING

The road of excess leads to the palace of wisdom.

William Blake, 'Proverbs of Hell', in *The Marriage of Heaven and Hell* (1790)


[Michael Jeffery] and Jimi figured out, to tour a band round [the] United States using air transport was really not that much different from London using road transport. So we zig-zagged to and fro, up and down, north, south, east, west, across America. You'd be swimming in Arizona in the morning. The afternoon you'd get out in a blizzard in Canada.

Mark Boyle


The Jimi Hendrix Experience continued its extended recording session at the Record Plant until 29 July 1968. With reports of crowds in the studio, Noel Redding had faded into the background: 'On a lot of the albums it was done with just two people with Jimi playing bass and playing guitar. It was faster working that way.'[1]

The band returned to the tour grind, kicking off in Baton Rouge on 30 July. Early in the tour, at Moody Coliseum in Dallas on 3 August, Hendrix covered Traffic's 'Dear Mr Fantasy' as an instrumental, a telling choice. After a Record Plant recording session on 7 August, the Experience gathered in Central Park to pose with the statue of Alice in Wonderland, atop a giant bronze mushroom, surrounded by a group of racially diverse children, for photographs by Linda Eastman and David Sygall.

Another packed slate of tour gigs winged through Connecticut, Massachusetts, Salt Lake City, Colorado and Dallas in late August and early September. On Saturday 17 August 1968, at the Atlanta Municipal Auditorium, the Experience's supporting bands included Eire Apparent (from the Chandler and Jeffery stable), the Amboy Dukes and, supporting the second show, Vanilla Fudge. The Fudge, an intimidating band with a manager connected to the Lucchese crime family, joined the supporting acts regularly until the end of the tour.

As the Experience's renown expanded, supporting acts seemed weaker, more conventional choices. Many of the later acts, managed by Jeffery, were rock epigones, mediocre rather than innovative or experimental music-makers. In November Cat Mother & the All Night Newsboys joined the support line-up. Hendrix, who was involved with producing their album, gently mocked the band's long, clunky name, calling them some variant of Madam Flipflop and her All Night Social Workers.[2] The band shortened its name to Cat Mother, and eventually fled to the West Coast to escape Jeffery.

In the autumn of 1968 the Experience performed in prestigious venues on the East Coast. On 2 November they played the early twentieth-century Woolsey Hall, the main auditorium at Yale University in New Haven, Connecticut. Woolsey Hall, on the Hewitt Quadrangle, was a 2,691-seat hall whose architects, Carrière and Hastings, also designed the New York Public Library. An audience member expressed his discomfort with the loudness of the band:

> Whenever Hendrix hit his wah-wah foot pedal, not necessarily to use it as a wah-wah but to increase his high end by leaving it in the treble position, he was absolutely ear-shattering and difficult to listen to. It was unbelievably piercing and I definitely had to cover my ears a few times during the show.[3]

On 28 November there was a concert billed as an Electronic Thanksgiving in the 2,738-seat Lincoln Center Philharmonic Hall, designed by Max Abramowitz of Harrison & Abramowitz, the first building, opened in 1962, of the Lincoln Center campus. It was renamed Avery Fisher Hall, then renamed again for David Geffen after his $100 million gift in 2015. Steve Paul, owner of the New York club The Scene, was impresario for a double bill by promoter Ron Delsener: Jimi Hendrix and the harpsichordist Fernando Valenti. An audience member rhapsodized over the sound quality:

> The sounds that came out of that guitar . . . it was as if it was swirling around and around over your head – especially when he did Voodoo Chile. The guitar riffs were out of this world . . . I sat just a little to the left of the middle of the stage and Hendrix was in front of me and all I could do was watch how he played that guitar – which mesmerized me. I can still remember the music just flowing around and around the tops of our heads – best stereo surround sound ever heard (of course it was 1968).[4]

Carnegie Hall in New York, however, refused to book The Jimi Hendrix Experience. An undated newspaper cutting, 'Carnegie Won't Experience', revealed that the hall's managers were averse to the risk posed by a Hendrix audience, even with a surety bond posted. The booking manager said:

> We have information that in his [Hendrix's] other appearances in other places the audience got very much out of hand. They destroyed furniture and draperies. We cannot afford to take that chance.[5]

Back in London, Hendrix seized the opportunity to subvert live television and salute the break-up of Cream on 4 January 1969, during a live televised performance of 'A Happening for Lulu'. The Experience began playing the hit 'Hey Joe', then, at a signal from Hendrix – 'We're going to stop playing this rubbish' –

the sound morphed into 'Sunshine of your Love', causing the broadcast to run over its time slot. Hendrix later commented:

> I dream about having our own show where we would have all contemporary artists as guest stars. Everybody seems to be busy showing what polished performers they are and that means nothing these days – it's how you feel about what you are doing that matters.[6]

Two sold-out concerts at the Royal Albert Hall, on 18 and 24 February 1969, marked the group's success in Britain and, at the second show, one of the final Sunburst Strat guitar smashes.[7] Noel Redding fell off the stage during the debut of his new band, Fat Mattress, at the second concert. The Experience's appeal had arrived at the lucrative scale of the stadium. The sold-out Royal Albert Hall performances were documented, with scenes from the musicians' daily life, in 106 minutes of film, the release of which was held up for decades in legal disputes.

## A LONDON FLAT

Chas Chandler left the Record Plant and his role as Hendrix's producer in May 1968. In interviews he gave his reasons, admitting finally that he no longer contributed and did not see the point of more than forty takes of 'Gypsy Eyes'. Chandler said, 'We'd be going over a number again and again and I would say over the talkback, "That was it, we got it." He would say, "No, no, no," and would record another and another and another. Finally, I just threw my hands up and left.'[8] He maintained his role as Jeffery's partner for a while and attended the Experience's tour concerts on the West Coast. There he and Lotta Lexon met the journalist Sharon Lawrence. Chandler left New York on 8 May, returning to the Upper Berkeley Street flat with Lexon, who was pregnant.

He asked Kathy Etchingham to find a new place for herself
and Hendrix, renting a bedsit in Earls Court to make sure she
complied, but she rented a central London flat for Hendrix and
herself, at double the Earls Court price.

Etchingham found the flat at 23 Brook Street, a modish
Mayfair address, in a classified ad in the *Evening Standard*.
She wrote: 'We knew we wanted Mayfair so we could walk to
gigs, but the prices were high, even though it was a little seedy
– £30 a week.' The management firm paid, as when she booked
recording sessions: 'I used to ring them up to book time. Thirty
quid an hour and they'd want the cheque there and then.'[9]
Etchingham suspected embezzlement when the rent was paid
in cash:

> Mike [Jeffery] was siphoning off the money and depositing
> it somewhere abroad because when I complained to his
> assistant, Trixie Sullivan, that the rent hadn't been paid she
> turned up at the flat with a briefcase stuffed with American
> dollars. She peeled a few off and gave them to me before
> snapping the case shut and disappearing again.[10]

The flat was on the top two floors of a terraced house identified
by its blue plaque as the former residence of the German-born
Baroque composer George Frideric Handel. He had bought the
building new in 1723, lived there until 1759 and composed *Messiah*
there. In fact, Handel had lived next door, at number 25; the
plaque had been placed between addresses. Still, Hendrix and
Etchingham thought of their flat as Handel's house and bought
a recording of *Messiah*.

The narrow building has a modest plan, with typical front and
back rooms and staircase. On the ground floor was a shop called
Mr Love, which sold snacks and cigarettes, and a photographer,
Carl Niekirk, rented the middle storey. The top flat, on the top

The house at 23 Brook Street, London. Hendrix occupied the top two floors.

two floors, had a small garret room with a spare bed in which such friends as George Harrison and Billy Preston stayed. A practice room held a drum kit, and Hendrix played through an amplifier without complaints from neighbours. There was a kitchen, although typically the couple ate at the Bag O'Nails. Hendrix experts have counted the days the musician could have spent at the flat and have arrived at fewer than 60. Still, a large public assembles to visit the modest rooms. Jane de Mendelssohn conducted an intense two-day interview for the *International Times* at the flat between 27 February and 12 March 1969.[11] A televised interview, with Hendrix speaking to Hugh Curry while lounging on his bed in the flat, survives. It was filmed on 7 January 1969 for the Canadian television series *Through the Eyes of Tomorrow*, and broadcast by the Canadian Broadcasting Corporation.[12] In the 1990s Etchingham organized a campaign to have a blue plaque affixed to the building, and the plaque was unveiled at a ceremony in 1997. In 2015 the Handel House Museum commissioned an architect to renovate and extend the building in order to open the flat to public view.

During the time Etchingham and Hendrix occupied the flat, in 1968, the Experience had one gig in England, on 6 July at the Woburn Festival, held on the Duke of Bedford's estate, where Humphry Repton had proposed naturalistic landscape gardening in 1805. A young fan called Hendrix's set 'exquisite', then spent a cold night walking to the nearest village. Others stayed on the estate and built fires, causing £20,000 worth of damage.[13]

On 1 September, in America once more, the Experience played the 9,450-seat natural amphitheatre of Red Rocks outside Denver, Colorado. The surreal landscape of red sandstone monoliths and the panoramic view of Denver may have ensured a positive vibe.[14] In Denver the band stayed at the Cosmopolitan Hotel on Broadway and 18th Avenue; the hotel was demolished

The rear of 23 Brook Street.

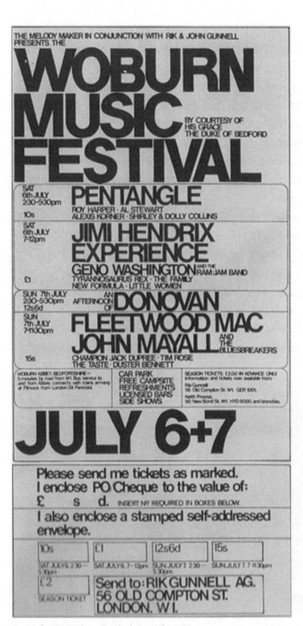

Poster for the Woburn Festival, 6–7 July 1968.

by implosion in 1984. Hendrix's response to the area was upbeat: 'I had a lot of fun at the Denver, Colorado place. We played there at Red Rocks, that was groovy, that was nice 'cause people are on top of you there, or at least they can hear something. That's where it should be, natural theatre-type thing.' While there, Hendrix was finishing off the specifications and liner notes for the band's new album, *Electric Ladyland*. He sketched out a layout for the cover on Cosmopolitan Hotel stationery, and instructed the record company to use Eastman's and Sygall's photography for the cover image.[15]

*Electric Ladyland* was released on 16 October 1968 in the United States and 25 October in the United Kingdom. The cover of the album as released in the UK featured a staged studio photograph of a group of reclining female nudes as hapless groupies, an image Hendrix disavowed. He said, 'I didn't have nothing to do with that stupid LP cover they released.'[16] Stamp and Lambert had paid scant attention to his sketch of the Experience perched with children on the mushroom in Central

Postcard showing the Red Rocks Amphitheatre near Denver.

Denver Cosmopolitan Hotel, 18th Street between Broadway and Lincoln, built 1926, demolished 1984.

Park, instead hiring a photographer to make a cover that would generate publicity. The women were paid a few pounds extra to doff their underwear, repeating dreary pop attitudes that undermined young women as consumers of pop music. For sport, pop media ridiculed women, especially those who acted on their creative ambitions, as Yoko Ono and Linda Eastman (McCartney) learned.

## MCLUHANIST TOTAL ENVIRONMENTS OF LIGHT AND SOUND

By 1968, when on tour, Hendrix usually performed without a light show, as the sound engineer Abe Jacob confirmed: 'There were no lights, there [were] three follow spots and the three spots stayed on the three band members.'[17] Hendrix appreciated light shows and immersive total listening environments if not for his own concerts. He developed a rapport with the collective artists Mark Boyle and Joan Hills (later known as the Boyle Family), whose pulsating colours were featured at UFO in London. In the autumn of 1967 Hendrix jammed with Soft Machine at UFO and became familiar with their imagery. Hills indulged Hendrix's passion for control panels when she let him observe her work the controls at the Speakeasy light shows. Boyle wrote: 'When we played the Speakeasy on Margaret Street, Jimi Hendrix would come in and watch, sitting beside Joan in the light box, gazing intently at the screen. A very sweet and gentle man.'[18] When Boyle accompanied Soft Machine on tour, Hendrix supported their reluctance to discuss their technique. Boyle recounted a discussion in a bar where Hendrix argued for secrecy and said: 'In the early days of jazz in New Orleans, Louis Armstrong used to play with a cloth over his hands so that the other trumpeters couldn't see what he was doing!'[19]

In New York in the last months of 1968 an experimental performance club, Cerebrum, opened at 429 Broome Street, Soho, near the corner of Crosby Street. Hendrix noted the address on his handwritten script for a film called *Moon Dust*.[20] The architect of the club was John Storyk, a Princeton graduate who had found the job in a classified ad in a newspaper. Cerebrum issued from a collaborative group that was eventually connected with Charles Ludlam's Ridiculous Theatrical Company.[21] The club hosted participatory theatre, with an aesthetic of ether. A hybrid of discotheque, live venue and ad hoc performance space, it hosted a nightly Soho party, a happening on demand. The underground theatre held two three-hour sessions per night, for which booking was required. Patrons entered a door at pavement level, paid, undressed, put on translucent robes and descended. They described a pale, dim space:

> A white room, trippy projections on the wall, distortions of a wide variety of music buzz around you, a thin, scented fog sitting in the air. There's no liquor, only water and marshmallows, served by the so-called 'Cerebrum guides',

who led visitors through this strange psychedelic spa, elevated platforms which you could visit to experience the unique stimulants taking place there – headphones with groovy music, musical instruments, balloons, kaleidoscopes, children's toys – reclining on white pillows on lush white carpeting . . . 'guides' came along and smeared menthol on your lips or tingly lotions upon your skin.[22]

During its nine months of operation, Cerebrum, which had 'no dance floor, no band, no alcohol', prompted reviews and comments from monthly magazines *Life* and *New York*, the weekly *Time* magazine and the daily *New York Times*, and from Alvin Toffler, the author of *Future Shock* (1970). *New York* magazine called it 'voyeuristic' in March 1969, and on 13 December 1968 the article 'A Mattress for the Mind' in *Time* called Cerebrum a 'McLuhan Geisha House'.[23] Club patrons, wearing headphones and white gowns, gesturing in fog with translucent balloons and parachutes, appear both obsolete and futuristic in videos of the period. Storyk thought the lack of a bar in Cerebrum confounded organized crime for a while. He recalled that the club was broken into and trashed. The club folded abruptly in June 1969, apparently (according to a member of the collective) because there was no money for air conditioning.

## BEYOND MAY 1968

Hendrix was becoming a symbol of nonchalant rebellion, with an amorphous impact on a sociopolitical revolutionary moment. The events of May 1968 in Paris sparked insurrections in other European urban centres, and remained pivotal throughout the late 1960s. Unrest emanated from a social crisis in student residences in Nanterre, in the western suburbs of Paris, where

male and female students were segregated at night, and spread
to become a wider social critique of sex roles, consumerism,
daily life, the unresponsive government, militarism and
capitalism.

Students occupied iconic, centrally located public places
such as the Théâtre de l'Odéon, scene of marathon collective
discussions. They also occupied the universities, in particular
the Sorbonne, and the École des Beaux-Arts became a militant
poster-printing studio. A general strike paralysed France as
workers aligned with students to explore hedonism and contest
government by the elite, in a movement that paralleled those
opposed to the Vietnam War in the United States. Students of
architecture and urbanism created defiant posters and proposed
temporary inflatable structures as new kinds of environment for
change. Militants in Berkeley, California, protested in concert with
the French proto-revolution. Its impact on continental intellectual
life was far-reaching, and Hendrix figured symbolically in a
loosening of rigid social conventions.

On 23 May 1968 the Experience embarked on a mini-tour in
Europe, possibly making the trip just for a few well-paid dates.
They played first in small, exclusive clubs in Milan and Rome,
and the Bologna Palasport, then went on to play a large arena in
Zurich. The Zurich Beat Monster Concerts of 30–31 May took
place in an ice rink with a capacity of 13,000. The Experience
had top billing, with support by Eric Burden & The Animals,
The Koobas, The Move and Traffic providing opportunities
for jamming. The arena was in the northeast of the city, at
Wallisellenstrasse 45, and had been designed by Bruno Giacometti,
brother of the Swiss sculptor Alberto Giacometti. This was one
of the first Swiss pop concerts with a large audience, estimated at
10,000 people. Given the wider social unrest in Europe at the time,
the police transformed the stage into an 'impregnable fortress',
meeting the audience with a line of police dogs. Rioting during

Monsterkonzert, Zurich, 1968.

the show was controlled, but it spilled out into the streets in the darkness after the concert.[24]

Hendrix returned to London in June. The Experience rehearsed on 4 June; the following day (at Studio D in Elstree Studios) they recorded a performance for the ITV television series *This Must Be Dusty!*, for broadcast on 12 June. The band played 'Stone Free', dedicated to Brian Jones, who had been arrested for possessing cannabis. Although Hendrix was sometimes uncomfortable as a vocalist, he played the guitar and sang with the respected singer Dusty Springfield, who was no stranger to schmaltzy material. Their duet was a soul tune popular in 1963, 'Mockingbird', once an Inez & Charlie Foxx hit. The Experience also performed 'Voodoo Chile (Slight Return)'. All that has survived is a ghostly image, filmed from the television screen, of a rare showbiz-style duet, as well as a high-quality soundboard recording.[25]

On 28 June Hendrix demonstrated his commitment to social justice by attending a benefit for the Martin Luther King Memorial Fund at Madison Square Garden in New York, which drew a crowd of 14,000. The performers included Joe Tex and King Curtis & the Kingpins; the concert was headlined by Aretha Franklin and by Sam & Dave, accompanied by a thirteen-piece band. Hendrix was invited on to the stage and applauded for his donation of $5,000.

The Experience went on to play Tampa twice, with a sold-out show on 18 August and one that was almost sold out on 23 November. The venue was the modern Curtis Hixon Hall (opened 1965; demolished 1993), which was styled to resemble a playfully futurist space station. Interviewed at the time of the first show, Hendrix said: 'I've had almost no private life at all in the two years we've been on tour . . . We haven't had a practice session in almost four months.'[26] At the November show Hendrix gave the audience the finger after too many flashbulbs popped, saying: 'It's too bad you spent all that money for one picture. I thought you came for sound.'[27]

In September 1968, in an interview with Terry David Mulligan in Vancouver, Hendrix politely explained how mind-numbingly dull it can be to repeat the same repertoire:

We've been playing 'Purple Haze', 'The Wind Cries Mary', 'Hey Joe', 'Foxy Lady', we've been playing all these songs, which I really think are groovy songs, for two years, so quite

Jimi Hendrix and Mitch Mitchell during an interview in Vancouver, September 1968.

naturally we start improvising here and there, and there's other things we want to turn on to people.[28]

In 1969 the Experience began a final tour with the original power trio line-up, opening in North Carolina on 17 April. Noel Redding's band Fat Mattress (which Hendrix jokingly called 'Thin

Pillow') joined the supporting bill for fifteen dates. Hendrix, who was actively seeking a bass player, got back in touch with Billy Cox in Nashville, as Cox explained: 'The only telephone number Jimi had for me was for Mr Wright's television repair shop, because neither of us had a phone in the old days and we could get messages there.'[29] They arranged to meet in Memphis after the concert on 18 April:

> He wanted me to be his bass player. I went back to Nashville, closed my music publishing company, and dropped everything else and left for New York . . . He didn't have an apartment in New York and was staying in a hotel. He had a little amp there and we would work day in, day out, with little patterns, trying to put together some good music.[30]

Mitch Mitchell summed up the musical problems with Redding and his diverging musical interests:

> The only music Noel listened to was two albums by the Small Faces. The Small Faces were great, but that's not where our heads were at. Noel had no knowledge of [the legendary soul bassist] James Jamerson or the guys that played with James Brown. The bigger problem was that he had no interest, either. Billy, on the other hand, was a bassist; he had put the work in on the instrument. Noel, God rest his soul, had no interest in the bass as an instrument.[31]

Hendrix arrived in Toronto on 3 May, crossing the border after playing the Cobo Arena in Detroit. He was arrested for narcotics possession, held and interrogated for hours at Toronto Pearson Airport, a space-age glass-walled cylinder equipped with constant piped-in muzak.[32] Publicists for the Experience suppressed news of the arrest, but word reached Lawrence through her entertainment reporter network. She contacted Hendrix's lawyer Henry Steingarten, relaying her crucial notes taken during a United Press International interview and providing a credible eyewitness account of a scene in a hotel room when a hippy girl tossed Hendrix a pill container, which ended up in his open carry-on bag.[33]

Hendrix was released on $10,000 bail and performed at Maple Leaf Gardens that night. He was required to return to Toronto on 5 May on an arraignment. Hendrix appeared impassive about his arrest. Bored with rock concert bookings, he looked forward to collaborating with other musicians, saying, 'I plan to use different people at my sessions from now on . . . It really bugs me that there are so many people starving, musicians who are twice as good as the big names.' On 9 May 1969, in an interview about a concert at the Charlotte Coliseum, in Charlotte, North Carolina, Mitch Mitchell spoke of his plans for jazz performance to Ray Brack of the *Charleston Gazette*: 'I want to do a concert at Carnegie Hall with

James Marshall Hendrix, Toronto Police mugshot, taken the day of his arrest at Toronto airport on a charge of possessing narcotics, 3 May 1969.

Miles Davis and Roland Kirk. We're trying to get that together right now. We just can't go on playing concerts like this.'[34] Hendrix spoke of a getaway: 'After this tour is over and our album is ready, I'm going to take a long vacation – maybe in Morocco or Sweden or way in the South California hills.'[35]

After playing fourteen concerts in a month, culminating in the Indianapolis Fairgrounds Coliseum on 11 May, the Experience had four days off. Hendrix recorded with Stephen Stills and guitarist Johnny Winter, releasing a jam with Winter, a version of Guitar Slim's 'The Things that I Used to Do'.[36]

In June an eleventh-floor apartment at 59 West 12th Street, New York, was rented for Hendrix. He stayed there intermittently, storing his equipment there, sometimes sharing with Devon Wilson. Mitch Mitchell mentioned staying there as a guest. The architect of the building, which dated from 1929, was Emery Roth & Sons, prolific designer of the Manhattan skyline.[37] He returned to Los Angeles on 7 June to work with Billy Cox on new material using a method of establishing patterns, and moved into a penthouse suite in a small hotel in Beverly Hills, the Beverly Rodeo Hyatt on North Rodeo Drive.[38]

On about 17 June Hendrix met the independent film producer Chuck Wein, former habitué of Warhol's Factory and credited as dialogue writer for Warhol's film *My Hustler* of 1965 (a dubious credential, considering Warhol's work was often ad-libbed). After a tarot card reading, Hendrix talked with Wein, discussing an idea Hendrix had, to stack up a huge number of amps and play the Grand Canyon. Hendrix also met the artist Emilie Touraine at Help, an all-night restaurant. According to *Rainbow Bridge* actor and art director Melinda Merryweather, Hendrix, Touraine and Wein dropped acid together. Merryweather called Emilie 'Terrain':

Terrain was living on Orion Street in the valley. She, Chuck and Jimi all took acid together in that house . . . Jimi had told Terrain that he was from another planet located near an asteroid belt off Mars.[39]

The Experience's final gigs on tour were at the Newport Pop Festival at Devonshire Downs on 20 June and the Denver Pop Festival on 29 June. At Devonshire Downs they played a

The building at 59 West 12th Street, where Hendrix lived in an 11th-floor apartment.

substandard 30-minute show in front of a crowd estimated at
100,000; the band headlined the 20–22 June festival in Northridge,
California. An outstanding selection of 32 acts booked for the
festival included (on 21 June) guest star Albert King, Ike & Tina
Turner, Taj Mahal, Albert Collins, Buffy Sainte-Marie and Love,
and (on 22 June) Booker T. & the MG's, Marvin Gaye and The
Byrds. The promoter recalled paying the Experience $100,000 for
the show, while the other bands played for between $2,000 and
$25,000. To make amends, Hendrix returned at the promoter's
request to jam for two hours on the last afternoon with Buddy
Miles, Eric Burdon, Mother Earth and a full stage of musicians
with what appear from videos of the event to be spontaneous
dancers.[40]

For the Denver Pop Festival, at the Mile High Stadium, the
Experience was supported by Aum, Zephyr, Three Dog Night
and Joe Cocker. Hendrix played a somewhat subdued version of
'The Star-Spangled Banner' as he announced that each performer
would go in different directions.[41] The stadium had been enlarged
in 1968 to hold 50,000 spectators, and the massive capacity may
have led to a lack of crowd control.[42] The weather was hot – over
33°C (92°F) – and the Denver audience was rowdy. The event ended
in chaos, and the local police resorted to tear gas to subdue the
crowd. Gusts of wind blew the gas towards the stage, and Gerry
Stickells recalled scooping the band into a van in a toxic haze:

In Denver once we nearly got killed . . . It was the last gig
the original Experience played . . . The air was so thick with
tear gas . . . you had a job to see. Everybody was reeling. Just
in the last number the crowd broke through the stage with
no security . . . in the middle of a football field, suddenly like
thirty thousand kids come rushing around . . . They could get
all the way round the stage. I managed to get them [the band]
in the back of the equipment truck and padlock them in, in

complete darkness in the back of the equipment truck and we
had to try to get out with these kids. They squashed [the] big
truck . . . including the roof of the cab – we couldn't get the
back doors open when we got back to the hotel. They'd been
all over it and squashed it.[43]

In the summer Hendrix broke into mainstream American televised
mass media as a guest on two major talk shows, *The Tonight Show
starring Johnny Carson* and *The Dick Cavett Show*. Flip Wilson guest-
hosted Hendrix on *The Tonight Show* on 11 July, among guests
including Joe Tex and Wilson Pickett, who were appearing in
concert at Madison Square Garden. On that show Billy Cox made
his first public appearance as a bassist with Hendrix, playing 'Lover
Man' with the drummer Ed Shaughnessy (of the *Tonight Show*
band). During the performance, which Hendrix dedicated to the
late Brian Jones, an amplifier blew and had to be replaced.[44]

Hendrix appeared twice on *The Dick Cavett Show* on ABC-TV.
On 7 July he performed 'Hear my Train a Comin'' with the house
band, and discussed his Electric Church ideas. On 9 September he
made a second appearance, in which, along with an interview, he
played 'Izabella' and 'Machine Gun' with Billy Cox, Mitch Mitchell
and the percussionist Juma Sultan.[45]

After spending the last days of summer in Woodstock at a
rented house known as Shokan, Hendrix moved into the Hotel
Navarro, at 110 Central Park South, close to the Record Plant.[46]
This 260-room hotel, a favourite haunt of Keith Moon, was built
in 1928; it subsequently became the Ritz-Carlton.

Hendrix's interest in stadium concerts and mass public
appearances had diminished, although he remained enthusiastic
about events that drew an African American audience. On
5 September the large collaborative band that Hendrix had
assembled to play the Woodstock festival, called Gypsy Sun
and Rainbows, played a street festival benefit at 139th Street and

Lenox Avenue for Harlem's United Block Association, arranged through his long-time friends the Allen twins. Hendrix spoke publicly about making tickets available to those on lower incomes and to children. In a press conference at Frank's, a restaurant on 125th Street, he said: 'A lot of kids from the ghetto, or whatever you want to call it, don't have enough money to travel across the country to see these different festivals, what they call festivals. I mean, seven dollars is a lot of money.'[47] Hendrix took to the stage after a local favourite, Big Maybelle, and backed by members of Sam & Dave's band. Gypsy Sun and Rainbows – Hendrix, Cox, Larry Lee, Mitchell, Sultan and Gerardo 'Jerry' Velez – won over and engaged the crowd.

After playing the small Salvation Club, at One Sheridan Square, on 10 September 1969, the new band's last performance, Hendrix left with the owner of the club, cocaine dealer Bobby Woods. That night Hendrix was abducted in a baffling kidnapping that lasted about 48 hours. After being held for a night at what was described as an apartment in Little Italy, then at a Brooklyn warehouse, Hendrix turned up at the Shokan house. There was no credible explanation for the incident, which has been the focus of much speculation. Hendrix, seemingly unshaken, jammed on bass with Mountain at Ungano's, at 210 West 17th Street in New York City, some time between 9 and 12 September 1969.[48] Suspects for the kidnapping ranged from manager Jeffery, who had insisted Hendrix play the Salvation, to inexperienced mobsters. In February 1970 Woods was found murdered with five bullets in the head, in what appeared to be a gangland execution.

Mitch Mitchell returned to London in mid-September. Hendrix asked Billy Cox and Buddy Miles to perform with him as Band of Gypsys. The band was formed in order to perform live and to produce an album in fulfilment of a contractual arrangement with Capitol Records, required to release U.S. royalties suspended by American courts as a result of the legal manoeuvring by Ed

Chalpin. During this period of transition Hendrix and Jeffery
reportedly communicated only through a secretary, Kathy Ebert.
Aspects of Hendrix's creative and personal life remained unstable,
as he struggled with management and lawyers.

While avoiding his manager, Hendrix began to work with
Alan Douglas, a jazz and spoken-word producer who had a
reputation for associating with gifted artists – he had recorded
John Coltrane, Billie Holiday, Lenny Bruce and Allen Ginsberg.
Hendrix asked Douglas to produce a series of Record Plant
sessions, including impromptu sessions with Stephen Stills and
with the Last Poets. The Last Poets produced an innovative
spoken-word piece, *Doriella du Fontaine*, with Lightnin' Rod
(a stage name, along with Alafia Pudim, of Jalaluddin Mansur
Nuriddin), Hendrix and Buddy Miles, recorded in November 1969.
It remains linked to the development of rap. It was a fortuitous
moment that Douglas described as utterly spontaneous:

> When Jalal goes into it Buddy starts up with a beat. Then Jimi
> walks in, he hears it and says, 'Hey stop let me play!' We put
> Jalal in a booth with a window. Jimi gets out his guitar, sits
> down in front of the booth and cues Jalal all the way through
> it. One take, non-stop, not a flaw.[49]

Betty Mabry Davis held a dinner party for Hendrix at Miles
Davis's brownstone, 312 West 77th Street, later in 1969, before
her divorce from Davis in December. Miles Davis did not attend,
but he left a sheet of music out and telephoned Hendrix from
his recording studio to discuss it. Hendrix was unable to read
music, but a conversation about music took place regardless.[50]
In their approach to place, improvisation and sound the two
men appeared to be on the same wavelength. Davis wrote in his
autobiography:

What we did on *Bitches Brew* you couldn't ever write down
for an orchestra to play. That's why I didn't write it all out,
not because I didn't know what I wanted; I knew that what
I wanted would come out of a process and not some pre-
arranged shit. This session was about improvisation . . .
Any time the weather changes it's going to change your
whole attitude about something, and so a musician will
play differently, especially if everything is not put in front
of him. A musician's attitude is the music he plays. Like in
California, out by the beach, you have silence and the sound
of waves crashing against the shore. In New York you're
dealing with the sounds of cars honking their horns and
people on the streets running their mouths . . . Hardly
ever in California do you hear people talking on the streets.
California is mellow, it's about sunshine and exercise and
beautiful women on the beaches . . . People there have color
in their skin because they go out in the sun all the time. People
in New York go out but it's a different thing, it's an inside
thing. California is an outside thing and the music that comes
out of there reflects that open space and freeways, shit you
don't hear in music that comes out of New York, which is
usually intense and energetic.[51]

A promising but unfulfilled initiative was a proposed
recording session with Hendrix, Davis and the drummer Tony
Williams, scheduled, then cancelled at the last minute over
financial demands by Davis and Williams. Davis and Hendrix
were reportedly jamming together informally at Davis's
brownstone and at Hendrix's Twelfth Street apartment. At
the time, both Davis and his collaborator and arranger, the
jazz musician Gil Evans, shared a fascination with the Hendrix
sound, eventually resulting in the album *The Gil Evans Orchestra
Plays the Music of Jimi Hendrix*, released in 1974.[52]

At the end of 1969 a pivotal event in Hendrix's career, the trial in Toronto, took an innocuous turn. Hendrix flew to Toronto accompanied by his friend Jeannette Jacobs, of the a capella band Cake, and appeared in court there on 8 and 9 December. Chas Chandler and Sharon Lawrence testified on his behalf. On the witness stand Hendrix replied to a request to define the concert tour pattern, saying: 'You play different one-night stands in different cities every night. Say about four or five cities, then you rest two or three days and I guess we do about thirty cities a tour.'[53] Hendrix revealed his existential condition of rootless-ness with sly humour, in response to a question about drug fumes and an incense tile. When asked whether he used incense to mask kitchen or any other odours, he replied: 'No. I don't have a kitchen.'[54] Unlike The Rolling Stones' London drug busts of 1967 at Redlands in West Wittering, West Sussex, or the arrests of Brian Jones and Stash Klossowski de Rola at Jones's Courtfield Road flat in Kensington, Hendrix was acquitted, and he returned to New York to prepare for the Fillmore East Band of Gypsys concert.

In this era of an emerging Black Power movement, Hendrix's friend Al Brown stressed that it was 'important to gain acceptance of a Black audience'.[55] Buddy Miles also emphasized the significance of an African American band: 'The Band of Gypsys was a strong statement from three brothers.'[56] Band of Gypsys rehearsed at Baggy's Studio, a space with no control room, at 71 Grand Street in New York, on 18 and 19 December. Buddy Miles recounted Hendrix's eagerness to rehearse.[57] Mitch Mitchell, a slight man and a manic drummer, admired the strength in Miles's power 'fatback' drumming, calling him a 'cement mixer'.[58]

Band of Gypsys performed the required original material, and the live album they owed, recorded by Wally Heider at the Fillmore East, was delivered to Capitol Records. In these four sold-out concerts over two evenings – 31 December 1969 and a

New Year's show on 1 January 1970 – the band moved away from psychedelia towards an earthy funk sound. Billy Cox mentioned Hendrix's use of pedals during the concerts:

> In previous gigs with the Experience he used a Fuzz Face and a wah-wah pedal, then at Woodstock he used a Fuzz Face, wah-wah pedal, and a Uni-vibe, but at the Fillmore East he used a Fuzz Face, wah-wah pedal, Uni-vibe, and Octavia and it was incredible. In fact you could hear all of it kicking in on 'Machine Gun'.[59]

The future of the band now appeared uncertain, as handlers and management were at odds with the new direction.

Hendrix agreed to play a Winter Festival for Peace on 28 January 1970 at Madison Square Garden, a venue whose sound he had criticized. Acts including Harry Belafonte and the cast of *Hair* donated their time to raise funds for the Anti-Vietnam War movement, in a concert organized by the folk singer Peter Yarrow and put together in under a week. Hendrix began performing at about 3 am and played only two songs, 'Earth Blues' and 'Who Knows', before becoming visibly ill and leaving the stage. Afterwards, Michael Jeffery fired Buddy Miles, ostensibly as part of a management plan to re-form the Experience with the old line-up.

Hendrix worked at Juggy Sound, New York, in January 1970, and during February at Sterling Sound, as well as extensively at Olmstead Recording Studios, a white penthouse on 54th Street, selecting songs from the second show of 1 January for the Band of Gypsys album. He alternated with Record Plant sessions, where in a jam on 23 January he conjured thunder and lightning sounds from his guitar.[60] In February he jammed with Johnny Winter, Stephen Stills, Eric Burdon, Buddy Miles and Jack Casady, the Jefferson Airplane bassist.

It seemed that additional touring was necessary to continue to pay for the construction of the Electric Lady Studio. 'He got a big advance from Warner Brothers, his American label, to finance the building of Electric Lady Studios, and of course they wanted some return for their investment,' said an industry man.[61] Cox and Hendrix continued their creative jag. As Cox explained, 'When we were out on the road, we were on the road. When we were back at home or in town, we spent all our time in the studio.'[62]

*Rolling Stone* journalist John Burks met the Experience for an interview on 4 February, at the management office on East 37th Street, and was told that Noel Redding would resume as bassist. Instead Hendrix chose Cox for the band's next tour, Cry of Love, in spring 1970. This time the tour was organized more rationally, on a fly-out basis, so that the band was primarily playing concerts at weekends, leaving time for recording.

Hendrix hired Ballin' Jack, a Seattle band formed in 1969 by two of his childhood friends (who had played in the Velvetones), Luther Rabb on bass and vocals and Ronnie Hammon on drums, to join part of the tour. The band, with a horn section – saxophonists Jim Coile and Billy McPherson, trombonist Tim McFarland and trumpeter Jim Walters – opened for eight Experience concerts, in Dallas, Houston, Tulsa, Memphis, Baltimore, Ventura and Denver, and at the Forum in Los Angeles in April, considered to be a highlight of the tour.[63]

When Rabb was vocal about Hendrix's drug use, Hendrix said he would stop using, but it was apparently just to keep him quiet. Ballin' Jack found themselves staying in a different hotel on the next leg of the tour.[64] The film *Woodstock* was released in May 1970, during the tour, ensuring the band's media profile.

The last date of the tour was 1 August, in Honolulu. While in Hawaii, Hendrix and the Experience were drawn into the morass

of *Rainbow Bridge*, the only film directed by Chuck Wein, whose
previous film experience had been at Andy Warhol's Factory.
Warhol's films were collectively made, avant-garde, real-time
cinematic transcriptions, often of mundane pseudo-activities in
the studio – the polar opposite of what was traditionally required
of a film director. A typical Warhol art film involved setting up
the 16 mm Bolex camera for a static shot that lasted until the film
cartridge ran out; Lou Reed recalled a three-minute screen test
when Warhol turned the camera on and walked out of the room.
For compound scenes, sequences were structured using formal,
situational or deadpan humour, such as the five-hour take of the
film *Sleep* (1964). *Rainbow Bridge*, an unsuccessful hybrid, merged
the deadpan approach of the Factory with the complex logistics
of a large-budget film, shot on location. Wein's approach to the
script seemed Warhol-based, allowing non-actors to improvise
in front of the camera.[65] Melinda Merryweather described her
own on-camera role, saying, 'I am just myself.'[66] Warhol used the
16 mm film format, the film technology of the day, to impose a
system of production on his filmed oeuvre, sometimes slowing
the film speed for projection. Media theorist Friedrich Kittler,
who interpreted the music and lyrics by Hendrix as Dionysian,
has contended that contemporary media technology dictates its
own logic – we are subject to our gadgets, goes the catchphrase.[67]
Kittler's critique of Marshall McLuhan recognized technology
not as extending or amplifying the human body, but rather as
determining situations and circumstances. In Kittler's terms,
the body, 'wetware', a sack of bodily fluids, networked with the
analogue camera and the limits and possibilities of 16 mm film.

The scenes of the live Experience concert are the most
interesting of *Rainbow Bridge,* a film otherwise unwatchable and
a tedious psychedelic experiment. As a media failure, it prompts
speculation about the mix of contemporary art, music and film.
Jeffery financed a disorganized, profligate film with Warner, while

obliging Hendrix to tour when he wanted time to develop and record new material. Merryweather described pitching the film with Wein:

> It was an opportunity . . . the people at Warner's said – 'Go ahead, do what you want to do.' I'll never forget when Chuck first threw the concept at them . . . one guy turned to the other and said, 'I don't know what the hell he's talking about, but give him the money.'[68]

The expanding Los Angeles film industry attracted music-industry executives who were eager to connect mass-media film and music profits. Hendrix also made amateur films, in Kodak's Super 8 film format. Some of them he called Goodbye films, sequences of short takes showing departing lovers. They are unavailable, possibly lost, prompting speculation about their artistic value, measured against the era's experimental moving image work, using Super 8 film. They might be interesting compared with the early sculptural, performance-based body prints of the artist David Hammons, made in Los Angeles in 1968, and the work of contemporary, then-emerging African American and underground filmmakers, from Charles Burnett to Shirley Clarke.

The spectacle of the Los Angeles film industry drew both Stax and Motown record companies. *Wattstax* (1973; reissued in 2004), the uplifting film commemorating the Watts Uprising of 1965 in Los Angeles, contrasted strikingly with the Motown biopic *Lady Sings the Blues* (1972), a commercial dramatization of the life of Billie Holiday, which strayed comically from her autobiography. Film critics suspected Berry Gordy, Motown's founder, had not read the book, and waif-like Diana Ross, although her 'round sound' was admired by Miles Davis, was miscast as the womanly, streetwise Holiday. The Motown attitude to music carried over

Roger Mayer, Mitch Mitchell, Jimi Hendrix and Noel Redding with film cameras in Arizona, February 1968.

to cinema, and took to extremes the formula of the underrated backing musicians and the over-valued soloist.[69]

On 30 July 1970 the Experience performed in front of several hundred local hippies in a magnificent location with views of the Pacific Ocean, on a pasture on the slopes of Haleakala crater, a dormant volcano on the island of Maui, Hawaii. The concert location, to be filmed for *Rainbow Bridge*, was set in a visually stunning landscape. Acoustically, however, the gales made recording impossible. The strong winds combined with problems with the generator to interfere with the recording. At the end of the film shoot, Hendrix spent more than a week with Merryweather, and wrote a song for her, 'Scorpio Woman', giving her the tape when he left Maui on 13 August.[70] Merryweather sold the tape twenty-eight years later to Experience Hendrix, the Seattle-based company that controls Hendrix's estate.

In an interview Abe Jacob discussed the simple approach to concert sound and the small amount of gear that was needed to create a sound that set off an avalanche of bootlegs:

In those days the touring acts left it up to the local promoter to provide the sound equipment, provide lights, and anything of that sort. So they really only just carried themselves and maybe their musical instruments . . . Our touring experience was very limited compared to what we saw just even ten years after Jimi's death. All of the musical equipment, all the PA equipment, the band gear, a little bit of wardrobe and a few lights, all fit in one 19-foot U-Haul truck . . . The idea still worked because it was the quality of the show. [Hendrix's] musical ability just outshone any of the other physical limitations that we might have had as far as putting on the show. Jimi's live performance desires and wishes basically was that he could be playing for all these people in his living room. That was what he intended to make this concert feel like. For almost the entire time that we did his sound there was only eight microphones used: a vocal mic for him, a vocal mike for Noel, four mics on the drums, and a mic at the mixing desk where I could introduce him. That was the entire setup for the Experience . . . The rest of it was all between the three great musicians . . . Even with the lack of equipment . . . they were still able to perform because . . . he was a master of dynamic. When he wanted to have that vocal of his come across, everything came down automatically in level, so that one microphone was able to carry . . . Towards the end of the Experience's run, Hendrix became huge . . . The difference was basically the size of the audience and the size of the room. The stuff onstage was basically the same.[71]

The Experience played the New York Pop Festival Friday on 17 July 1970, at Downing Stadium on Randall's Island. Supporting bands included Grand Funk, Jethro Tull, Steppenwolf and John Sebastian. Hendrix brought an entourage, his friends Devon Wilson, Betty Mabry Davis, Deering Howe, Colette Mimram and Alan and Stella Douglas. He went onstage at 5 am and endured radio frequency interference, with police reports broadcasting through the amplifiers, and a rowdy crowd who drowned out his dedication of a song to his friends. The band performed the songs 'Stone Free', 'Fire', 'Message to Love', 'Lover Man', 'All Along the Watchtower', 'Foxy Lady', 'Ezy Rider', 'The Star-Spangled Banner', 'Purple Haze' and 'Voodoo Chile'. The concert had been the object of protest and picketing by a collection of 21 militant groups, including the Puerto Rican equivalent of the Black Panthers, the Young Lords Party. A pseudo-documentary entitled *The Day the Music Died* was created to dramatize these conflicts, mixing genuine footage with

post-produced fictional re-enactment. The film included two
performances by Hendrix, of 'Foxy Lady' and 'The Star-Spangled
Banner'.[72]

## TOURING AFTERMATH

*Ceci tuera cela* ('this will kill that'), wrote Victor Hugo in *Notre-Dame
de Paris* (1831), predicting that the book would prevail over
architecture in the nineteenth century. In the digital era, music
outlasts both books and architecture. Posterity depends on
electricity. The pop music industry itself has mutated through
decades of such trends as raves, techno and EDM, and the historic
status of rock.

Many venues where Hendrix played have fallen to urban
renewal, have been reckoned obsolescent and replaced. The
Spanish Castle, halfway between Tacoma and Seattle on the
Pacific Highway, immortalized by Hendrix in 'Spanish Castle
Magic' as a destination arrived at by dragonfly, was closed in
1968 after a road accident involving several fatalities. Humble
venues from the Experience's tour of 1968 have been erased
or transformed. The Paul Sauvé Arena in the working-class
Rosemont district of Montreal, an ice rink that held 4,000,
was demolished in 1996. The Capitol Theatre at Queen and
Bank streets, Ottawa, a 2,580-seat picture palace built in 1920,
was demolished in 1970 (but not before George Harrison had
travelled there incognito in 1969 to see a performance by
Eric Andersen, whom he was considering for inclusion in the
Apple stable).

London's club scene remains in constant flux. The
architecture that has disappeared includes the Imperial Hotel in
Knightsbridge, with Blaises Club in its basement, demolished in
1992. The Marquee on Wardour Street was also demolished and
has been replaced by a restaurant. In London the uses of buildings

change along with the character of each district. Soho, still trendy but no longer as seedy, has lost much of its reputation as a site for emerging music and turned largely upmarket, along with much of gentrified London.

Manhattan venues were also fated to change. The Harlem club Smalls Paradise has become a branch of the pancake restaurant IHOP. In Greenwich Village, the Cafe au Go Go is now a condo, the Electric Circus is a Chipotle restaurant and the Fillmore East is a bank. The building that housed Steve Paul's The Scene was demolished in about 2014 to make way for a new condo tower and Sound Center had met a similar fate a few years before. On Music Row in Nashville, condos are planned to replace the RCA Victor Nashville Sound Studios.

At Brown University in Providence, Rhode Island, the Marvel Gymnasium on Elmgrove Avenue, a neo-Georgian building dating from 1927, was demolished in 2002. The Jimi Hendrix Experience played there on 8 March 1968, supported by Soft Machine, with the Mark Boyle and Joan Hills Sense Laboratory appearing on the poster. The 3,000-seat art deco Sam Houston Music Hall, at 801 Bagby Street in Houston, was demolished in 1998. A fan said of the venue: 'The acoustics were wonderful and there was not a bad seat in the house. It was my favorite place to see a concert.'[73] The Experience played there on 4 June 1968, supported by Soft Machine, the Moving Sidewalks, Neal Ford and the Fanatics.

The Experience played the 7,000-seat Curtis Hixon Hall in Tampa twice in 1968, on 18 August and 23 November, selling out the first date and almost selling out the second. The building, an example of Southern futuristic modernism, opened in 1965 and was torn down in 1993.

The modern, glass-walled, cylindrical airport with 24-hour muzak in Toronto, where Hendrix was held and searched in 1969, was demolished in 2004. While on trial in the city in December 1969, Hendrix stayed at the flagship Four Seasons Motor Inn at 415

Jarvis Street. It was designed by the architect Peter Dickinson in 1961 to launch the Four Seasons brand, and was demolished in the mid-1980s. Maple Leaf Gardens, an ice rink convertible for concert use (an acoustically infernal custom), where the Experience played after Hendrix posted bail, is no longer used for concerts.

Press releases described the garish metal panels that clad the Seattle Experience Music Project, designed by the Los Angeles-based architect Frank Gehry in 1999, as inspired by a smashed guitar. Instead the building resembles a bagpipe intersecting a jellyfish, along the lines of a surrealist ironing board and sewing machine. An electric guitar, whether a high-end Fender Stratocaster or a bottom-of-the-line Danelectro model, holds utilitarian value, as do the ordinary houses and streets of inner-city Seattle. Some of Hendrix's many addresses linger on the map. Saving an entire wood-frame house or two would be worth more than slicing it into souvenirs, as one developer proposed. Baudelaire wrote of the changing face of the city, and its destiny of change; the urban theorist Françoise Choay argued that buildings should be torn down according to whether they are good or bad architecture, not whether they are new or old.[74] What gets press for architecture is rarely architectural quality. While it may seem counter-intuitive, Choay advocated evaluating and eliminating based on quality, not newness, and conserving and repurposing parts of the city that endure in value. On that basis, a few of the remaining former Hendrix homes would serve as more informative memorials to his humble origins than the right-handed statue and uncommunicative architecture in Seattle. Perhaps the Gehry building will be updated by architects engaged with Hendrix's substantial legacy, to provide opportunities for popular electric music in an inner-city environment and reinforce a landscape responsive to urban sound.

## WOODSTOCK AND ENSUING FESTIVALS

Hendrix tried to use Woodstock, and headlining a major three-day event, to launch a large, collaborative band with complex percussion. Instead his Woodstock solo was to become one of his best-known improvisations. The sheer size of the Woodstock, Isle of Wight and Fehmarn festivals introduced logistical problems that would remain unsolved as long as the aim was to attract the largest possible audience. The prospect of attracting a massive audience still appeals to some festival promoters, some now settle for smaller events with audiences of a thousand or so, such as Basilica SoundScape in New York State, founded in 2012.

In July 1969, in order to rehearse for the Woodstock Festival, Hendrix occupied a rented eight-bedroom house, Ashokan (complete with stables and two horses), at 77–79 Traver Hollow Road, near Shokan, nearly 20 km (12 miles) from Bethel and about 160 km (100 miles) north of New York City. It was near Jeffery, and not far from West Saugerties, where Bob Dylan's manager, Albert Grossman, lived. Dylan had been living on Camelot Road, near the Big Pink, the rural house at 2188 Stoll Road, where Dylan and the Band recorded the Basement Tapes, from May to November 1967. Johnny Winters was living near the nearby settlement of Rhinebeck. Woodstock was associated with pastoral bohemianism, summer holidaying and a rural cross-disciplinary aesthetic avant-garde aesthetic. David Tudor premiered the John Cage composition 4′33″ at a hall called the Maverick, near Woodstock, in the late summer of 1952.[75] In summer 1969, when Woodstock Festival was held, the town buzzed with musicians.

Hendrix recruited musicians to rehearse with him, inviting Billy Cox and the rhythm guitarist Larry Lee, both based in Nashville, where Cox tracked down Lee – who had recently returned from Vietnam. Larry Lee explained in an interview: 'I think I had been home about maybe two weeks. I had just come

from the unemployment office when the phone rang and it was
Billy.'[76] At Shokan they rehearsed and there was time to discuss
the Vietnam War and the anti-war movement.

Cox, his wife, Brenda, and Lee moved into the hilltop
house, joining the percussionist Jerry Velez. Velez knew the
area because his sister Martha, a singer, lived in Woodstock with
the trumpeter Keith Johnson, a member of the Paul Butterfield
Blues Band. Another percussionist, Juma Sultan, was connected
with a local avant-garde artist colony, Group 212, and played
with the Aboriginal Music Society. Sultan had been jamming
with Hendrix at a studio above the garage at Jeffery's home
in Lower Byrdcliffe.[77] Hendrix left on impulse for a vacation,
flying to Morocco via Paris, visiting Marrakesh and Casablanca
with Deering Howe, Colette Mimram and Stella Douglas.
He returned on 7 August to woodshed with the new group
of musicians.

On 10 August 1969 a small converted church in the town
of Woodstock, where Sultan played with the Aboriginal Music
Society on Sunday evenings, was the location for the Tinker
Cinema jam. The musicians included Sultan, Velez, the trumpeter
Earl Cross, the drummer Ali Kaboi, Michael Carabello on congas
and the percussionist José 'Chepito' Areas. Velez mentioned
Hendrix's interest in a larger ensemble playing African and
Afro-Cuban music, and Sultan spoke about ideals of a collective
experience in 'a cooperative group'.[78]

Hendrix and the housekeeper and cook at Shokan, Claire
Moreice, visited Jeffery at home, 1 Wiley Lane, Woodstock, to
discuss business. While they waited they looked through his
record collection and realized there was nothing but commercial
pop product, as Moreice remembered:

> Jimi went to play some music and Michael had a record
> collection like from one end of the wall to the other and Jimi

couldn't find anything to play, it was all kiddy pop and bad rock 'n' roll, you know, no real music. There was something that disgusted Jimi about that.[79]

Mitch Mitchell arrived at Shokan to rehearse with the group. Perhaps surprised at the emphasis on percussion, he observed that the group did not gel despite the rehearsals. Mitchell recalled: 'We rehearsed up at the house which wasn't in Woodstock by the way, it was about 12 miles from any kind of civilization, for about a week or ten days. It was probably the only band I've ever been involved with that simply did not improve over that length of time.' He added, 'I have a realistic view of this period and, for me, my memories of the Woodstock situation are that it was not brilliant, musically. It was fortunate that Billy and I had played together a little bit beforehand.'[80]

Woodstock was a music festival, spectacle and instant city with an ephemeral population of 400,000, complete with monumental traffic jam. Over the weekend of 15–18 August 1969, crowds accumulated, then dispersed. After permission for the first site was refused, a large, very tall stage was rapidly built on an extensive dairy farm in Bethel, nearly 100 km (60 miles) southwest of Woodstock, at the base of a sloping field, making use of a natural amphitheatre that fell away to a pond.

The acts included Richie Havens, Country Joe McDonald, Santana, Canned Heat, Janis Joplin, Sly & the Family Stone, The Who, Jefferson Airplane and The Band. Crosby, Stills, Nash & Young played at 3 am on the Sunday, and the Paul Butterfield Blues Band played at 6 am. Delayed by rain, Hendrix made the stage about 9 am on Monday; he was the last act to perform and closed the festival. He introduced his group as Gypsy Sun and Rainbows, and they performed a two-hour set while the remains of the Woodstock audience, about 30,000 people of an estimated 400,000, straggled off.

Late in the set – which included loose jamming and an original number, 'Mastermind' by Larry Lee – Hendrix unleashed an improvisatory guitar solo based on 'The Star-Spangled Banner'. His rendition showered cascades of sound like missiles, and crystallized a sociopolitical cultural event. The West Coast writer Sherman Alexie's short story 'Because my Father Always Said he was the Only Indian who Saw Jimi Hendrix Play "The Star-Spangled Banner" at Woodstock' (1993) testifies to the popular influence of this musical event. Alexie wrote: 'Twenty years later, my father played his Jimi Hendrix tape until it wore down.'[81] At a press conference in Harlem a month later, on 5 September, when asked by an interviewer about his rendition of 'The Star-Spangled Banner' at Woodstock, Hendrix said: 'We play it the way the air is in America today. The air is slightly static.'[82]

Hendrix with Gypsy Sun and Rainbows, onstage at Woodstock, 18 August 1969.

Hendrix wrote a poem commemorating Woodstock, entitled '500,000 Halos', a gesture to the peaceful solidarity of the throng. He appreciated the performances by Stone and Havens. Many musicians found Woodstock disorganized. Because of the rain, Robbie Robertson found it 'swampy'. Mitch Mitchell was unimpressed by what he saw as a commercial event. Unconvinced by the quality of the Crosby, Stills, Nash & Young performance, Neil Young refused to allow his image to appear in the film. Grace Slick of Jefferson Airplane was flippant:

> Woodstock everybody remembers with a little more fondness than I do . . . It was not that well organized. But it was unique in that there were a half-million people not stabbing each other to death. And it was a statement of, look at us, we're 25 and we're all together and things ought to change.[83]

Joni Mitchell wrote a song about Woodstock after she tuned into television footage of the festival. Her agent had convinced her to stay away from the traffic. Her lyric and music expressed a poetic generational identity that saw itself as golden stardust. Stephen Stills boldly asked her for the song, which became a hit for Crosby, Stills, Nash & Young.[84] The documentary film that came out in 1970, directed by Michael Wadleigh and with camera work and editing by Martin Scorsese, diffused the festival to a mass public audience. Havens's solo performances and Hendrix's 'Star-Spangled Banner' stood out, bookending the film. Despite its shortcomings, the Woodstock Festival became a powerful social ideal, representing a curious youth cult of social harmony in a temporary outdoor soundscape, resulting from an intersecting quality of music and an overwhelming, disorganized, undressed mass of young people. For some, the event defined a new communal youth era.

The 'refugee camp conditions' at Woodstock inspired a
chain reaction of ambitious young promoters who improvised
festivals.[85] The Isle of Wight invited Hendrix for its third year in
1970, having scored Bob Dylan in 1969. Organizers expected an
audience of 125,000 to the event, which was held on East Afton
Farm near Freshwater, but 600,000 turned up, including petulant
militant anarchists from France. It was the Experience's largest
audience – and probably was for Miles Davis, too, who at the time
was seeking a wider public.

Artists included Joan Baez, Leonard Cohen, Miles Davis,
Donovan, Emerson, Lake & Palmer (making their debut), Kris
Kristofferson, Jethro Tull and The Who. A makeshift crowd-
control system consisting of a corrugated-metal fence crossed
the meadow and obstructed the hillsides. The surplus audience
camped rough on what came to be called Devastation Hill. The
sheer numbers overwhelmed the patrolling guards, who were
accompanied by German shepherds. Interviewers captured an
American spectator, dubbed Yogi Joe, describing the relationship
between performers and audience as between 'the pop kings
in power and serfs'. Yogi Joe also claimed to have attended
Woodstock, which he 'dug very much', as well as ten other
festivals, and declared that the festival business was becoming a
'psychedelic concentration camp'. Joni Mitchell sang her festival
anthem 'Woodstock' to the audience, looking momentarily
fearful and then recovering as a demented Yogi Joe rushed the
stage, grabbed the microphone, was dragged off and recited her
Woodstock lyrics to security guards on camera.[86]

Hendrix probably missed the joyous set played by the
Brazilians Gilberto Gil and Caetano Veloso on the second day
of the festival. They appeared on stage with a tribe dressed in a
bright red collective stage costume, designed by artist Nicola L.
to be worn by eleven people and resembling a nest or umbrella.
The two musicians, both exiled from Brazil, were living in a

commune at 16 Redesdale Street in Chelsea, and were befriended
by the band Hawkwind. Veloso later said he learned in London
that 'great rock was not about volume and wildness, but about
precision and spareness.'[87] The Experience's performance was
glum in comparison. Hendrix said later that it was dark; all
he could see were hillside bonfires and he preferred to see the
audience. He said, 'it was dark . . . we was playin' at nighttime.
I couldn't see [laughs] . . . everybody. You know if I could see the
people instead of just lines of bonfires up there.'[88]

Hendrix headlined the last festival he played, held on
Fehmarn Island in the Baltic Sea, off Germany. The Fehmarn
Open Air Love and Peace Festival was inspired by the island
location of the Isle of Wight – but the weather, the location and
the organization were all worse. The festival ran from Friday
evening to Sunday, 4–6 September 1970. The line-up included
the British progressive rock band Aardvark, Ginger Baker's Air
Force Mark One, Mungo Jerry, Sly & the Family Stone, as well as
the German bands Cluster, Embryo, Frumpy and Inga Rumpf,
and Limbus 4. Bad weather caused a few cancellations.[89] An
audience member named Gunni described the weather as
defining the event:

> It rained for almost the entire festival. Three days in the
> mud . . . we had come mainly to see Jimi Hendrix. We waited
> three days for Hendrix. When Jimi came out on stage, the
> sun suddenly came out, the concert was unbelievable.[90]

A roadie and assistant stage manager, Ford Crull, criticized the
proximity of the stage to the ocean in the rain and wind. He
pointed out a basic danger – that the wet stage could electrocute
the performers: 'If you think the Isle of Wight was a mess, you
should have been to Fehmarn . . . Whoever built the stage was
an idiot. There were gales, so the sea just kept blowing on stage.

The Jimi Hendrix Experience, Isle of Wight Festival, 31 August 1970.

The whole place was wet and so she [Sandy Denny] kept getting shocks.'[91] The funk rock of Sly & the Family Stone revived the freezing audience, after which the German electronic group Cluster played through the night. The crowd dismantled parts of the wooden stage and lavatory facilities to make campfires.[92]

As Gunni remembered, sunshine appeared when Hendrix, Cox and Mitchell took to the stage early on the Sunday afternoon to play to an estimated crowd of 15,000. The Experience played for 90 minutes and left the island as soon as the show ended. The festival did not turn a profit, and the island's officials subsequently banned open-air music festivals until 1995.[93]

After Hendrix played his version of 'The Star-Spangled Banner' at Woodstock, his sound and his iconic image became prominent as a symbol of youth resistance to the Vietnam War, even though his political stance was pragmatic, vague and

elliptical. Hendrix rather engaged with and expressed his thoughts
on urban, environmental and spiritual issues. In *Dispatches*,
Michael Herr described the amulets and icons worn by soldiers,
positioning Hendrix in a pantheon of Vietnam anti-heroes:

> They carried around five-pound Bibles from home, crosses,
> St Christophers, mezuzahs, locks of hair, . . . snaps of their
> families, their wives . . . pictures of John Kennedy, Lyndon
> Johnson, Martin Luther King, Huey Newton, the Pope, Che
> Guevara, the Beatles, Jimi Hendrix.[94]

Ordinary Americans were aghast at media images of their
nation's role in the war in Vietnam, televised in the nightly news.
Herr wrote off the official discourse on the war as 'psychotic
vaudeville'. As crazy became normal, Hendrix's soft, articulate,
African American working-class diction was a voice of normality,
his speech rhythms saturated with meaning for blue-collar
American soldiers in battle. Herr reported:

> One day I went out with the ARVN on an operation in the rice
> paddies . . . There was no way of stopping their [the enemy's]
> fire, no room to send in a flanking party, so gunships
> were called and we crouched behind the wall and waited.
> There was a lot of fire coming from the trees, but we were
> all right as long as we kept down . . . I suddenly heard an
> electric guitar shooting right up in my ear and a mean,
> rapturous black voice singing, coaxing, 'Now c'mon baby,
> stop actin' so crazy', and when I got it all together I turned
> to see a grinning black corporal hunched over a cassette
> recorder. 'Might's well,' he said. 'We ain't goin' nowhere till
> them gunships come.' . . . That's the story of the first time
> I ever heard Jimi Hendrix, but in a war where a lot of people
> talked about Aretha's 'Satisfaction' the way other people

speak of Brahms' Fourth, it was way more than a story; it was Credentials.[95]

Herr mentioned the underground diffusion of the music by cassette tape: 'We packed grass and tape: Have You Seen Your Mother Baby, Standing in the Shadows, Best of The Animals, Strange Days, Purple Haze.' He stressed the unofficial, grass-roots rock soundtrack to the war, and a sense of falling out of phase: 'Whenever one us came back from an R&R we'd bring records, sounds were as precious as water: Hendrix, the Airplane, Frank Zappa and the Mothers, all the things that hadn't even started when we'd left the States.'[96]

## ELECTRIC LADY STUDIOS, NEW YORK, FEBRUARY 1969 TO AUGUST 1970

That's what being a musician's about. Playing anywhere. That's why we can play Madison Square Garden and come down and play at the Experience, then go back over and play the Whisky, and then play the Hollywood Bowl. See, once they get all those ideas about what building is which, they're saying 'Oh, they'll play down there, it might not be very good because they're not known to play there!' That's silly. It's fun anyway to me. It's groovy that we get paid . . . regardless of where you're going, just check it out. You've gone there to hear the music. It's terrible to have to rely on the Madison Square Garden all the time, 'cos those places are not for real good rock music. Then you have to go to the small clubs and get your ears blasted away. I think that they should make special buildings, like they make special buildings for restaurants and hotels. They should make special buildings for loud, or whatever you want to call it, electronic rock music.

Jimi Hendrix, December 1969[97]

The publicist Michael Goldstein owned the Generation at 52 West Eighth Street, where Hendrix jammed. When the club closed after six months in around September 1968, Hendrix and Jeffery co-purchased it for $50,000. The first plan proposed a club to be called Jimi's Place. Another name Hendrix mentioned to a journalist was Godiva's studio and club.[98]

The prospect of opening a bar raised concerns about protection money, since New York nightclubs had to contend with the mob. Jim Marron, the manager hired from Steve Paul's The Scene, observed that 'Eighth Street was Mafia-run, and four nightspots there were already under their control.'[99] Hendrix commissioned John Storyk, whose playful, immersive work he had seen at the Cerebrum Club, to design the new venue. Storyk prepared plans for a meeting held on 23 February 1969, without Hendrix, who was in London. Storyk learned that a project for a recording studio had replaced the plan for a club. Marron, who had been hired to run a new club, convinced Hendrix and Jeffery that a studio was fiscally sound. Hendrix used the Record Plant, an expensive recording facility, as a practice space; an audit revealed that the block booking cost $300,000.[100]

Hendrix, whom Storyk described as distant, requested 'soft, curvaceous' space and 'no right angles', also using the term 'womb-like'. In an interview Storyk said Hendrix 'had very specific ideas about what it would look like and feel like . . . Construction started and stopped a few times, usually having to do with money . . . a case full of money would appear and a month later we'd start again.'[101] Storyk worked with Bob Hansen, an industrial acoustician who was hired to develop the details of acoustic isolation. Eddie Kramer – who in 1968 had moved to New York to the Record Plant and would go on to engineer Hendrix's entire production, including *Electric Ladyland* – was hired to oversee the design; he became director of engineering at Electric Lady Studios from 1970 to 1974. Kramer called for extra ceiling height and a drum room. The recording artist's control of sound recording in the studio was not unheard of. Ray Charles built his own RPM studio in 1964; Brian Wilson worked in a home recording studio from 1967 to '72. Still, in the music business it was something of a novelty – an indulgence or oddity – since studios owned and operated by record labels were the norm. The Electric Lady Studios were contemporary with The Beatles' fashionable, ineptly artist-run production facility, Apple Studios in London; Hendrix, along with The Beatles, led a trend towards artist-run recording.

Apple Corps, first proposed by Brian Epstein in April 1967, was an ambitious, multi-pronged venture. By January 1968 it comprised Apple Records, Apple Electronics, Apple Films, Apple Publishing, Apple Retail, an Apple Boutique on the corner of Baker and Paddington streets and a new headquarters in a Georgian terraced house at 3 Savile Row, with offices for each Beatle. A recording studio was to be created in the basement, and there were rumours of a 72-track recording studio, electric paint, a flying saucer, a sonic force field and various other trippy devices. The inventor, a friend of Brian Jones, shared a flat in Bentinck Street with John Dunbar. The film director Joe Massot recalled Lennon discussing wallpaper speakers. The recording studio was left unfinished, having already veered off course, when The Beatles broke up, and the project ended when manager Allen Klein closed down Apple in 1969.[102]

The Kinks opened the recording venue Konk Studios in Crouch End, north London, in 1971. Of the creative environment of the time, Ray Davies said: 'The idea of the 1960s, the way it happened, was a cumulative thing. It wasn't about just the Beatles or the Kinks, it was about lots of people doing things differently.'[103]

## ELECTRIC LADY STUDIOS: A CONTINUING CONSTRUCTION STORY

While applying for the building permit for Electric Lady Studios, John Storyk learned about its media history. The Viennese architect Frederick Kiesler, who had moved to New York in 1926, designed the Film Guild Cinema on the upper floor of a new three-storey building by the architect Eugene De Rosa for the client, Film Guild Cinema founder Symon Gould. The 490-seat cinema, which opened in 1929, had a screening room that eliminated the theatre-derived proscenium, and an eye-shaped projection screen; an innovative proposal for a 'projectoscope' with simultaneous projections on multiple surfaces was not built. The cinema became a notable avant-garde film house in New York.[104]

From 1938 to 1958, the Abstract Expressionist painter Hans Hoffmann had his studio in the building. In the basement a polka club, the Village Barn, lasted for more than 30 years (1930–67); it was replaced by the Generation Club, then by Electric Lady Studios. In the 1970s the Eighth Street Playhouse, dedicated to independent film, took over the cinema. According to Storyk, the Playhouse retained some elements of the original Kiesler interior, including the cove lighting.

The studio was identifiable for two decades by its curved brick exterior wall, in the shape of a guitar body. This was excised in the 1990s. Since then the various layers of cultural use have turned an ordinary-looking building into a cultural hub, amplifying the metropolitan intensity of artistic life. Artists frequenting the studio have ranged from Aretha Franklin to Frank Zappa, from Erykah Badu to Stevie Wonder, from David Bowie to Jay Z.

Electric Lady Studios became a legendary psychedelic lair with its own mystique. It is not clear why the long, thin slot of space turned out to be so successful. Storyk's projects are

Electric Lady Studios, 52 West Eighth Street, New York.

typically square in proportion. The construction lasted twice as long as the original estimate and cost double. A year-long delay resulted, not just because of financing trouble; water infiltrated from heavy rains during the excavation undertaken to provide extra ceiling height, as well as to stabilize the base below the drum kit. While digging down, construction crews discovered the Minetta Brook below, requiring a sump pump and acoustic isolation. There is speculation that the flow of water directly below may affect the acoustics of the recording studio, perhaps influenced by the travel time of sound through water, which is about four or five times the speed through air. Storyk, now a partner at Walters Storyk Design Group, went on to develop over 2,500 studios, radio stations, clubs and theatres.

As construction on the Electric Lady Studios neared completion in the spring of 1970, Hendrix was eager to use the

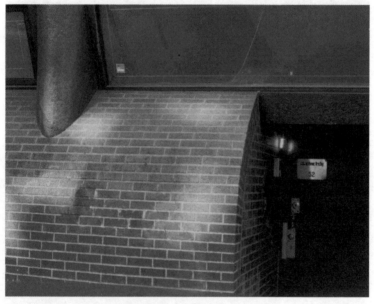

Electric Lady Studios, 52 West Eighth Street, original curved brick entrance, removed c. 1995.

space. He had recorded 30 songs there by June 1970, most of
the album *First Rays of the New Rising Sun* and jams with Steve
Winwood and Chris Wood of Traffic. The studio officially opened
on 26 August 1970 with a party organized by the 'Limbo King'
Mike Quashie. Hendrix spent much of the time in the second-
floor offices. A then-unknown Patti Smith recalled sitting on the
stairs speaking to him. Hendrix flew back to London on an Air
India flight that night with his road manager Eric Barrett. Three
weeks later, he was dead.

# CONCLUSION

I play amplifier.

Jimi Hendrix, overheard by Richie Havens[1]

This era of music sparked off by the Beatles has come to an end. Something new has to come.

Jimi Hendrix[2]

The economist Jacques Attali wrote, in the context of a political economy of music, of 'sound as a way of perceiving the world'.[3] The composer R. Murray Schafer's World Soundscape Project extended and developed that perception. The term 'soundscape' has entered common parlance, being widely used in contemporary music, along with the sense that a concert plays, always already, in any natural environment. It reframes the ideas of sonorous chance in John Cage's silent avant-garde piece, 4′33″. Performance by Schafer has come to be linked to contemporary symphonic music staged in a natural environment – such as trombones in canoes – on lakes or in forests or meadows. An early Schafer composition was influenced by the work of Marshall McLuhan and the modular dreamscapes of the psychedelic era. Schafer created the soundtrack to Kaleidoscope, a psychedelic exhibition pavilion conceived and constructed for Expo 67 in Montreal and dismantled soon afterwards. The architect of the pavilion was Irving Grossman, and the Toronto-based film-maker Morley Markson designed the pavilion interior as an immersive sound and image environment, a raised cylinder containing three theatres. A grid of mirrors clad the interior floor, ceiling and walls, and on to it kaleidoscopic patterns were seamlessly projected, accompanied by Shafer's soundtrack.

In the tradition of Bach's 'Well-tempered Clavier', Hendrix tuned his instrument, the electric guitar and amplifier, and his recording studio to arrange and render musical the atmosphere of the natural environment, as well as the atonal sonority of the motorized world. The background noises of cities and suburbs, of rumbles, squeals and grinding, the whirring sounds of acceleration and deceleration and the Doppler effect of drones in motion, the sensation of moving fast through the streets inside a metal vehicle, its interior coated with sound-absorbing textile, the babble of crowded inner-city pavements, and all kinds of reverberation, bounce, sustain and echo, were integrated in the formula of popular song. Tonalities of motion used honed improvisation and repetition within the architectural environment to transform noise in the mixing chamber of the analogue recording studio.

Lyrics of purposeful movement, as in 'Crosstown Traffic', coexisted with the contemplative motion and layers of feedback of the posthumously released 'Drifting'. As for the reception of sound, Hendrix was also interested in varying his rapport with the audience. He liked to see the audience moving and roving. He mused about multimedia cacophony and simultaneous events. He imagined reciprocity in performance, in the oscillating attention and inattention of an audience and their movement with respect to that of the performers. In a late interview, he said:

There's no reason why these huge crowds should not be entertained by side attractions as well. They should make them like three-ring circuses, booths, movies – even some knights jostling.

The interviewer asked, 'You mean jousting?' Hendrix replied, 'Right – and freak shows!'[4]

Hendrix has had a lasting impact on popular and guitar music, and on sound performance in general. The barriers separating genres have dissolved, rock music has fractured and the concept of an album, detached from the vinyl record, seems obsolete. Hendrix released four albums of original material during his four-year recording career. Now there are over 500 releases and countless Internet posts. The Hendrix sound was new. Master tapes stored in cans had to be labelled 'The sound distortion is intentional'. Electronic dissonance in popular music, the snap, crackle and tape hiss, was considered noise that recording technicians would eliminate. Hendrix spoke of a continuous 'stream of consciousness' of music, as opposed to the sudden illumination of an idea out of nowhere. His visual sense influenced musicians, artists and design architects, who tend to adopt not corporate suits but, rather, more idiosyncratic attire, such as colourful, vintage or repurposed garments, following Hendrix's dishevelled, feminine style in ornate military or floral jackets, just as Hendrix adapted Little Richard's costumes.

Hendrix commissioned an urban recording studio, the layout and controls of which were accessible to and designed for the artist's collaboration with the sound engineer. It paralleled the synthesis of songwriter and performer. Mitch Mitchell commented: 'The studio was where Jimi lived; in truth, if he could have lived in the studio 24 hours a day, he would have. The studio was a natural instrument for Jimi, one with which he possessed an uncanny ability to express himself.'[5] Creation of experimental studio space was ahead of the official, intellectual research: in Paris in 1970 the architect Renzo Piano was commissioned by the French government to design an underground recording studio as part of IRCAM, an institute for sound and music research.

The artist's private recording studio influenced contemporary pop, perhaps most directly Prince's Paisley Park studio complex, built in 1988 in Minneapolis, Minnesota. While Electric Lady remains and enjoys renewed success, other legendary recording

Jimi Hendrix photographed by Baron Wolman in New York City, February 1970.

studios – such as Goldstar in Los Angeles – closed as the music industry restructured radically. Digital recording may be highly portable, but sound will still be located in a particular place and time, however temporarily. Music outlasts the ordinary backdrop buildings used for recording studios and live recording in clubs. In the mid-1960s musicians wandered the city streets to find districts and clubs frequented by other musicians. Recording artists sold out to pseudo-businessmen, shills, lawyers and accountants in a record industry that was often connected to organized crime. Today the dissemination of music is immaterial and decentralized, carried out via social networks.

Hendrix the city-dweller, wanderer, loner, nighthawk and 'indoorsman' favoured modest surroundings, ordinary buildings and public places, seeming indifferent to ostentatious signature architecture. He wandered urban neighbourhoods in search of clubs to visit as a performer and listener. His rock-star friends purchased aristocratic palaces as homes and recording studios,

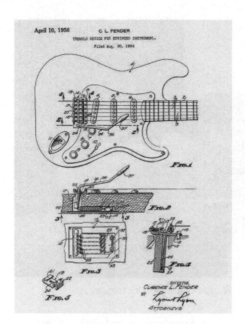

Fender Tremolo backplate, patent diagram.

such as George Harrison's Friar Park estate in Oxfordshire or The Rolling Stones' rented Villa Nellcôte in the south of France, temporarily used as a recording studio. By contrast, the traditional city and its urban places fed Hendrix's creativity: the semi-public urban space, the tropes of the seedy basement club and the artist's garret – separated by the Atlantic.

In what might be interpreted as a critique of the virtuoso, Hendrix was comfortable innovating with simple tools to make sound, using a comb for a kazoo on 'Crosstown Traffic', for example. He created an eerie wind noise, making sounds by tapping on the back of his guitar. Hendrix explained his technique:

> I just turn the amp up very loud and it's mostly feedback and the way you control the knobs. And the back, see, I play a Fender Stratocaster guitar, and you can take the back off. A little small plate and you can tap the springs. There's little

springs back there. And it makes these weird little sounds sometimes.[6]

Mike Bloomfield mentioned his astonishment as Hendrix tapped the back springs while they were jamming backstage:

> Once we played a gig at The Shrine in Los Angeles, and we were backstage fooling around with our guitars. Hendrix was playing with his toggle switch. He was taking the toggle switch of the guitar, tapping the back of the neck and using vibrato, and it came out sounding like a sirocco, a wind coming up from the desert. I have never heard a sound on a Hendrix record that I have not seen him create in front of my eyes.[7]

The media, especially digital media, may not extend human reach in the manner that McLuhan predicted. Still, an aphorism associated with McLuhan – 'hearing is believing' – works for Hendrix.[8] Hendrix told a journalist in Chicago:

> Two shows a night are tough . . . we usually start jamming on stage . . . Right now when it comes to actual playing, I like to do really funky clubs. Nice, sweaty, smokey, funky, dirty, gritty clubs, 'cause you can really get to people then. All this stuff where you stand 2,000 miles away from the people and all that – I just don't get any feeling at all.[9]

# CHRONOLOGY

**27 November 1942**
Jimi Hendrix is born in Seattle; at birth he is named Johnny Allen, and later renamed James Marshall.

**February 1958**
Hendrix's mother Lucille Jeter dies; Jimmy repeats ninth grade.

**1958–60**
Hendrix plays in The Velvetones, Rocking Kings, Thomas & the Tomcats.

**31 October 1960**
Hendrix drops out of Garfield High School.

**May 1961**
Hendrix is caught joyriding, and on 31 May enlists in the United States Army and is posted to Fort Ord, Monterey, for basic training.

**November 1961**
Hendrix's basic army training ends and on 8 November he joins the 101st Airborne (headquartered at Fort Campbell, Kentucky), starting parachute training (making 25 jumps). He meets bassist Billy Cox, and together they play the Pink Poodle Club in Clarksville, Tennessee, that month.

**July 1962**
Hendrix, discharged from Fort Campbell, moves to Clarksville and forms the King Kasuals with Billy Cox, playing the Pink Poodle, Elks Lodge and the Disabled Veterans Hall, and follows weekly gigs by guitarist Johnny Jones, who played with Junior Walker and Freddy King, listening for Jones's Delta sound.

## December 1962–February 1963
Hendrix visits family in Vancouver.

## 1963
Hendrix travels on rhythm and blues package tours with musicians including
Solomon Burke, Otis Redding and Joe Tex.

## March 1963
Hendrix meets MC Theophilus Odell 'Gorgeous George' in Atlanta, and backs
him touring with Hank Ballard & the Midnighters and Aretha Franklin.

## May 1963
Hendrix and Cox reform the Kasuals and play local Nashville clubs the
Del Morocco, the Sandpiper, the Black Poodle and the Jolly Roger.

## Autumn 1963
Hendrix tours the Chitlin' Circuit with Bob Fisher & the Bonnevilles, The
Marvelettes, Curtis Mayfield & the Impressions, Bobby Womack and Sam Cooke.

## December 1963–January 1964
Hendrix stays at the Hotel Theresa in Harlem, New York City, and wins the $25
First Prize at the Apollo Theater Wednesday Amateur Night contest.

## March–April 1964
Hendrix joins The Isley Brothers, and tours with them in Canada, Bermuda and
the USA, including Seattle.

## May 1964
Hendrix records 'Mercy, Mercy' at A-1 Sound on 56th Street, New York, with
Don Covay & the Goodtimers. He records 'Testify' (Parts 1 and 2) with
The Isley Brothers on their T-Neck label and continues touring with them.

## Late summer–Autumn 1964
Hendrix leaves The Isley Brothers in Nashville and joins Gorgeous George on
tour. He sends a postcard to his father with an Atlanta address.

## c. 1965
Hendrix, on a package tour in Memphis, meets Steve Cropper and trades
guitar riffs.

### December 1964–January 1965
In Atlanta Hendrix (as Maurice James) auditions successfully for Little Richard's backing band, and tours with him.

### January 1965
In Alabama Hendrix plays on the same package tour as B.B. King and jams with Albert Collins on tour in Houston.

### February–March 1965
Hendrix records 'My Diary' and 'Utee' at Revis Studio, Los Angeles, with Rosa Lee Brooks, Arthur Lee and a drummer and bassist.

### April 1965
On 16–17 April Hendrix performs at the Paramount Theatre in New York with Little Richard's backing band, billed as The Royal Company, on a bill with a dozen acts.

### July 1965
Hendrix appears on the *Night Train* television broadcast, in Little Richard's backing band, The Royal Company, behind Buddy & Stacy. In New York Hendrix records at A-1 Sound with Alexander 'Mr Wiggles' Randolph.

### Summer 1965
Hendrix tours again with The Isley Brothers and records 'Move Over and Let Me Dance' backed with 'Have You Ever Been Disappointed' with them.

### October 1965
Hendrix meets Curtis Knight at the Hotel America in New York, and joins Curtis Knight & the Squires. On 15 October Hendrix signs a recording contract with Ed Chalpin's PPX Enterprises; Hendrix gives his address as Hotel America, 145 West 47th Street. In New Jersey Hendrix auditions for Joey Dee & the Starliters, and tours with them during November and December, including in New York state, Connecticut, New Jersey and Massachusetts.

### 1965
Hendrix gets his first credit as composer, with Curtis Knight for the single 'Hornet's Nest' (the B-side is 'Knock Yourself Out'). He records with Ray Sharpe and the King Curtis Orchestra on 'Help Me (Get the Feeling)' Parts 1 and 2, and records with Jimmy Norman on 'You're Only Hurting Yourself' (B-side 'That Little Old Groovemaker').

## February 1966

Hendrix tours with King Curtis & the Kingpins.

## May 1966

Hendrix performs at an Atlantic Records launch at the Prelude Club, New York, in the backing band King Curtis & the All Stars, with Cornell Dupree behind Wilson Pickett and Percy Sledge. He also plays at Cheetah with Curtis Knight & the Squires and Carl Holmes & the Commanders. He meets Linda Keith that month.

## July 1966

Hendrix forms Jimmy James & the Blue Flame at Cafe Wha? in New York, with Randy 'California' Wolf, Randy 'Texas' Palmer and the drummer Danny Casey.

## August 1966

Hendrix meets Chas Chandler at Cafe Wha? on 4 August, and plays with John Hammond Jr at Cafe au Go Go on the 27th.

## September 1966

Hendrix arrives at Heathrow Airport, London, on 24 September, stays at the Hyde Park Towers Hotel, 41–49 Inverness Terrace, meets Kathy Etchingham and jams at the club Scotch of St James. On 29 September Noel Redding auditions at the Telephone Box and goes to Birdland the next day, then the ANIM office.

## October 1966

On 1 October Hendrix sits in with Cream at the Central London Polytechnic; on the 5th he rehearses with Redding and Mitch Mitchell auditions at Birdland. The Jimi Hendrix Experience is formed. The first performance of The Jimi Hendrix Experience (JHE) takes place on 13 October at Cinéma Novelty in Evreux, France, supporting Johnny Hallyday; on 17–18 October in Paris, the JHE rehearse and perform at Olympia, supporting Johnny Hallyday.

## November 1966

On 8–11 November the JHE play the Big Apple Club in Munich; Hendrix throws his guitar – a first guitar toss with the band.

## December 1966

In London Hendrix moves into 34 Montagu Square with Chas Chandler, Lotte Lexon and Kathy Etchingham. On 16 December 'Hey Joe' (B-side 'Stone Free') is released on Polydor. On the 26th Hendrix writes 'Purple Haze' in the Upper Cut dressing room.

## January 1967

The JHE play the 7½ Club in London's Mayfair on 12–18 January; the Speakeasy Club on the 19th; Chislehurst Caves in Kent on the 27th; and the Saville Theatre on the 29th, with The Who at the top of the bill, and The Koobas and The Thoughts.

## March 1967

On 2 March the JHE record 'Hey Joe' and 'Purple Haze' at the Marquee Club in London for the German television show *Beat Club*, for broadcast on 11 March and 22 May. On 17 March the 'Purple Haze, 51st Anniversary' (second single in the UK) is released on the Track Records label. On the 22nd Hendrix moves to 43 Upper Berkeley Street in London, with Kathy Etchingham, Chas Chandler and Lotta Lexon. That month the JHE tour Belgium, France and the Netherlands. On the 28th in London BBC Radio hold the Saturday Club recording, which is broadcast on 1 April. On 31 March the JHE play the Finsbury Astoria in London. This month sees the beginning of The Walker Brothers' package tour, and the first guitar burn by Hendrix in the UK. The tour continues with over twenty dates, two shows nightly, across the UK in April, ending on 30 April at the Granada in London.

## May 1967

*Are You Experienced* is released in the UK on 12 May on the Track Records label. The JHE perform in the UK and continental and northern Europe, including Helsinki on the 22nd, where they play the 1,400-seat Kulttuuritalo, designed by Alvar Aalto; on the 29th they top the bill at Barbecue 67 in Spalding, Lincolnshire.

## June 1967

On 4 June the JHE top the bill at the Saville Theatre, London. On 13 June Chandler, Hendrix, Altham and others arrive in New York. Hendrix hears Richie Havens at Cafe au Go Go. On 18 June the JHE play the Monterey Pop Festival, California, and on 20–24th the Fillmore Auditorium in San Francisco, supported by Gábor Szabó; Jefferson Airplane is top of the bill on the first night.

## July 1967

On 1 July in Santa Barbara the JHE headline at Earl Warren Showgrounds, supported by Moby Grape and Tim Buckley; from 3–4 July they play on a bill with Tiny Tim and The Seeds at Steve Paul's The Scene in New York. On 8 July they join The Monkees' tour partway through, providing support at seven concerts in Florida, North Carolina and New York. They exit the tour on 16 July. On 17 July in New York Hendrix hears The Seeds at the Electric Circus. Hendrix meets up with Frank Zappa at the Tin Angel, next to The Bitter End on Bleecker Street in Greenwich Village, and on the 18th he participates in the album cover photo shoot for Frank Zappa and Mothers of Invention's *We're Only in it for the Money*, at Mayfair Recording Studio. The JHE play Cafe au Go Go on the 21st; on 28 July Hendrix and Eric Clapton jam at the Gaslight Cafe with John Hammond Jr and his band The Screaming Nighthawks.

## August–November 1967

The JHE perform in the UK, Germany, Sweden and the Netherlands. On 3–7 August the JHE play the opening of the small Salvation Club in Greenwich Village; from 9–13 August they top the bill at the Ambassador Theater in Washington, DC, supported by Natty Bumpo; in Los Angeles they support The Mamas & the Papas at the Hollywood Bowl. Hendrix possibly meets Jeanette Jacobs of Cake and Devon Wilson during a JHE film shoot in Los Angeles. On the 27th the JHE top the bill at the Saville Theatre, London, supported by The Crazy World of Arthur Brown and Tomorrow.

On 14 November they headline the Alchemical Wedding, at the Royal Albert Hall in London, supported by Pink Floyd, The Move, Amen Corner, The Nice and Eire Apparent; it is the beginning of the band's second UK tour.

## December 1967

*Axis: Bold as Love* is released in the UK on 1 December. On the 5th the JHE play the 4,000-seat Green's Playhouse in Glasgow, the last date in the tour. On 22 December they top the bill at Christmas on Earth at London's Olympia; support includes Pink Floyd, Soft Machine, Traffic, Eric Burdon & The Animals, The Move, Graham Bond and Tomorrow.

## January 1968

On 4 January the JHE play Lorensbergs Cirkus in Gothenburg. Hendrix injures his hand, and is arrested for wrecking his room in the Hotel Opalen, detained and fined. The band tours Sweden, Denmark, the UK and France.

## February–March 1968

On 2–4 February the JHE top the bill at the Fillmore Auditorium, San Francisco, where support acts include Albert King, John Mayall's Bluesbreakers and Soft Machine; on 4 February Hendrix films Janis Joplin backstage. They tour the west and southwestern U.S., and then several north-central and northeastern states, including Philadelphia, Michigan and Massachusetts, supported by Soft Machine.

In March Hendrix jams at Steve Paul's The Scene in New York, and records on a portable tape recorder; the music later is released, with tracks variously titled 'Woke up this Morning and Found Myself Dead' and 'High, Live and Dirty', and featuring 'Bleeding Heart', The Beatles' 'Tomorrow Never Knows', Cream's 'Outside Woman Blues' and 'Sunshine of your Love', and Jim Morrison's drunken rant 'Morrison's Lament'. On 19 March in Ottawa the JHE play the Capitol Theatre, supported by Soft Machine. Hendrix records Joni Mitchell at the folk club L'Hibou.

## April 1968

On 3 April in Virginia Beach the JHE play the Civic Dome, supported by Soft Machine. On 4 April Martin Luther King Jr is assassinated in Memphis.

## May 1968

On 8 May Chandler leaves New York and his role as producer of the JHE. Hendrix assumes the role of producer on the album *Electric Ladyland*. In London Kathy Etchingham locates a flat at 23 Brook Street to be leased as Hendrix's residence. On the 10th the JHE play a double bill with Sly & the Family Stone at the Fillmore East in New York, filmed by ABC (film lost). On the 18th in Hallandale, the JHE headline the Miami Pop Festival at the Gulfstream Racetrack; rain cancels the second day. From 24–26th they play concerts in Milan, Rome and Bologna, and on 30th–31st in Zurich top the bill at the Hallenstadium Monster Konzert; support includes The Move, Traffic, Small Faces, John Mayall's Bluesbreakers, Eric Burdon & The Animals, The Koobas & Eire Apparent.

## July 1968

On 6 July the JHE headline the Woburn Music Festival at Woburn Abbey, Bedfordshire. On the 30th they top the bill at the Lakeshore Auditorium, Louisiana Independence Hall, supported by Soft Machine; the tour continues to cities including New Orleans, Dallas and Houston.

## August 1968

On 17 August the JHE headline the Municipal Auditorium, Atlanta, supported by Soft Machine, Eire Apparent and (for the first time) Vanilla Fudge; the tour continues, to cities including Florida, New York and Utah.

## September–October 1968

The tour continues to Arizona, California, Vancouver, Washington, Oregon and Hawaii; on 1 September the JHE tops the bill at Red Rocks, Denver. In October the band records at TTG Studios in Hollywood; on the 16th *Electric Ladyland* is released in the U.S. (UK release 24 October).

## Autumn 1968

Hendrix acquires a 50 per cent interest in the former Generation Club on West Eighth Street, New York, the eventual address of Electric Lady Studios.

## October–December 1968

The JHE tour continues, playing cities including Kansas City, St Louis, Boston, Miami, Providence and Chicago.

## January–February 1969

The JHE tour Sweden, Denmark, Germany, France and Austria. On the 4th the band salutes Cream on live television (BBC, in London), during 'A Happening for Lulu'. In February Hendrix commissions John Storyk to design the Electric Lady recording studios. On 18 and 24 February the JHE top the bill in a filmed concert at the Royal Albert Hall, London, supported by Soft Machine, Mason, Capaldi, Wood and Frog. Van der Graaf Generator and Fat Mattress debut at the second concert.

## April 1969

Jimi does an interview for *Life* magazine in New York (published as 'An Infinity of Jimis' on 3 October); on 11 April in Raleigh, North Carolina, the JHE headline the Dorton Arena, supported by Fat Mattress; the tour continues to Philadelphia, Memphis and includes dates in Texas and California.

## May–June 1969

On 2 May the JHE top the bill at the Cobo Arena, Detroit. On the 3rd Hendrix is arrested at the airport in Toronto for possession of narcotics before being released on $10,000 bail. The band's tour continues to cities in New York, Alabama, North Carolina, Virginia, Indiana, Maryland, Rhode Island, Washington and California. On 30 May–1 June they headline the Waikiki Shell in Oahu, supported by Fat Mattress.

In June an eleventh-floor apartment at 59 West 12th Street, New York, is rented for Hendrix, while in Beverly Hills, Los Angeles, Hendrix works on new material at the Beverly Rodeo Hyatt House Hotel, with Billy Cox. On 20–22 June the JHE headline the Newport Pop Festival in San Fernando Valley, California; 29 June sees the last concert by the original JHE line-up at the Denver Pop Festival, Mile High Stadium.

### July–August 1969

Hendrix holidays in Marrakesh, Essaouira and Casablanca with Colette Mimram, Stella Douglas, Luna Douglas, Deering Howe and Michael Jason. On 10 August Hendrix jams at the Tinker Cinema in Woodstock with percussionists Juma Sultan and Jerry Velez, Earl Cross on trumpet, Ali Kaboi on drums, Michael Carabello on congas and José Chepito Areas on percussion. Gypsy Sun and Rainbows (with Billy Cox, Larry Lee, Mitch Mitchell, Juma Sultan and Jerry Velez) headline and close the Woodstock Festival, which is attended by an audience of 300,000 that dwindles to an estimated 30,000 by the final morning. On 22 August in Harlem, New York, Hendrix speaks at the press conference for the United Block Association at Frank's Restaurant on 125th Street; on the 26th he records at the Hit Factory.

### September 1969

In Harlem, New York, Gypsy Sun and Rainbows play the United Block Association Concert at 139th Street and Lenox Avenue. Their last performance takes place on 10 September at the Salvation Club. That month Hendrix is interviewed for *Rolling Stone* by Sheila Weller (published 15 November).

### 31 December 1969–1 January 1970

Band of Gypsys (Hendrix, Billy Cox and Buddy Miles) headline the Fillmore East, New York, supported by Voices of East Harlem.

### March 1970

On 17 March Hendrix records at Olympic Studios in London with Arthur Lee on 'The Everlasting Love' for the album *False Start*.

### April 1970

The JHE, composed of Jimi Hendrix, Billy Cox and Mitch Mitchell, begin the Cry of Love tour at the Forum in Los Angeles on the 25th, continuing to cities in California, Wisconsin, Minnesota, Oklahoma, Texas and Pennsylvania.

## May 1970
The JHE play the Berkeley Community Theatre on 30 May.

## June 1970
The Cry of Love tour continues to cities including Dallas, Tulsa, Memphis, Albuquerque, Denver and Boston.

## June 1970
Touring on weekends, during the week Hendrix records at the Electric Lady Studios in New York as the facility nears completion; on 12 June *Band of Gypsys* is released in the u.s., released in the uk three months later due to legal wrangling.

## July 1970
On 4 July the JHE headline the Second Atlanta International Pop Festival in Byron, Georgia, with an audience estimated at 200,000, and then play Miami, Florida, on 5 July. On the 17th they headline the New York Pop Festival at Downing Stadium, and a film (released in 1977 as *The Day the Music Died*) documents the event. The band plays San Diego on 25 July and Seattle the next night; on the 30th they perform the *Rainbow Bridge* concert in the Haleakala crater, Maui, billed as Vibratory Colours – Sound Experience, for an audience of 200–300 people.

## August 1970
The Cry of Love tour ends on 1 August, at the Honolulu International Center, Oahu, Hawaii. On the 26th Hendrix attends the Electric Lady Studios opening party in New York before flying to London. On 30 August at Afton Down, near Freshwater, Isle of Wight, the JHE headline the Isle of Wight Festival, with an audience estimated at 600,000.

## August–September 1970
The JHE tour Sweden, Denmark and Berlin. The band headlines the Open Air Love and Peace festival on 6 September in Fehmarn Island, Germany. On 16 September Hendrix jams at Ronnie Scott's Jazz Club in London with Eric Burdon and War, on 'Mother Earth' and 'Tobacco Road' – bootlegged as 'Can You Please Crawl Out Your Window'.

## 18 Sepetmber 1970
Hendrix's body is found in an emptied room with the door open at the Samarkand Hotel on Landsdowne Crescent, west London; he is pronounced dead on arrival at St Mary Abbot's Hospital, Kensington.

# REFERENCES

## INTRODUCTION: EXTRATERRESTRIAL BLUES

1   Cited by Roy Hollingworth, *Melody Maker* (5 September 1970), in Steven
    Roby, ed., *Hendrix on Hendrix: Interviews and Encounters* (Chicago, IL, 2012),
    pp. 285–6.
2   William Gibson, 'The Science in Science Fiction', *Talk of the Nation*,
    National Public Radio, www.npr.org, 30 November 1999.
3   Mark Reynolds, 'Jimi Hendrix, the Patron Saint of Alt-Blackness', *Pop
    Matters*, www.popmatters.com, 11 November 2010.
4   Bob L. Eagle and Eric S. Leblanc, *Blues: A Regional Exploration* (Santa
    Barbara, CA, 2013), p. 33.
5   Mikhail Bakhtin, 'Forms of Time and of the Chronotope in the Novel'
    (1937), in *The Dialogic Imagination: Four Essays*, trans. Michael Holquist
    (Austin, TX, 1981).
6   Fernand Braudel, 'Histoire et sciences sociales: La longue durée', *Annales:
    Histoire, Sciences Sociales*, XIII/4 (October–December 1958), pp. 725–53.
7   Paul Scheerbart, *Glasarchitectktur* (Berlin, 1914), cited in Ulrich Conrads, *Programs
    and Manifestoes on 20th Century Architecture* (Cambridge, MA, 1964), p. 92.
8   Paul Grein, 'Week Ending March 14, 2010: Hendrix Tops Elvis',
    www.sodahead.com, 20 March 2010.
9   Quoted in Michael Lydon, *Flashbacks: Eyewitness Accounts of the Rock
    Revolution, 1964–1974* (New York, 2003), p. 70.
10  Quoted in 'Address to Publishers and Authors' Luncheon', Shoreham
    Hotel, New York, 7 December 1966. Bonus 36-min. audio track in Kevin
    McMahon and David Sobelman, dir., *McLuhan's Wake* (2002), 16 min.
11  R. Murray Schafer, lecture at University of Waterloo, Conrad Grebel
    College, 5 June 2014, in R. Murray Schafer, *Ear Cleaning: Notes for an
    Experimental Music Course* (Toronto, 1967), p. 20.

12    Marshall McLuhan, 'The Playboy Interview: Marshall McLuhan', *Playboy* (March 1969), available at www.nextnature.net, accessed 16 October 2015.

13    Marshall McLuhan and Quentin Fiore, *The Medium is the Massage: An Inventory of Effects* (New York, 1967), p. 100.

## 1 WEST: VANCOUVER, SEATTLE, MONTEREY, SAN FRANCISCO, LOS ANGELES

1    R. Murray Schafer, *The Tuning of the World* (Toronto, 1977), p. 6. On the World Soundscapes project, see www.sfu.ca.

2    Germano Celant, ed., *Piero Manzoni: Paintings, Reliefs and Objects*, exh. cat., Tate Gallery, London (1974), p. 83.

3    Schafer, *The Tuning of the World*, p. 5.

4    Ibid., p. 8.

5    Ibid.

6    Ibid., pp. 9–10.

7    Ibid., p. 10.

8    Daniel Vrabec, 'FAAIP DE OIAD: Architecture and Aurality', Masters thesis, University of Waterloo, Ontario (2003), p. 197.

9    Matthew Griffin, Susanne Herrmann and Friedrich A. Kittler, 'Technologies of Writing: Interview with Friedrich A. Kittler', *New Literary History*, XXVII/4 (Autumn 1996), pp. 731–42: 'That media influenced bodies through emergence and immersion . . . However, I don't believe in the old thesis that thus the media are prostheses of the body, which amounts to saying, in the beginning was the body, then came the glasses, then suddenly television, and from television, the computer', p. 738.

10    Jimi Hendrix, 'Power to Love' (also titled 'Power of Soul'), *Jimi Hendrix Anthology* (New York, 1975), p. 145.

11    Kristine Lofgren, '*Forest Symphony* Allows Humans to Hear Photosynthesis', www.inhabitat.com, 15 January 2014.

12    Emily Carr, *Growing Pains* (Toronto, 1946), pp. 238, 262. On Carr's resolve to paint totem poles, see p. 211. A Tlingit totem pole has stood in Pioneer Square, Seattle, since 1899.

13    Georges Bataille, 'La Notion de dépense', *La Critique Sociale*, VII (1933); published in English as 'The Notion of Expenditure' in Allan Stoekl et al., eds, *Visions of Excess: Selected Writings, 1927–1939* (Minneapolis, MN, 1985), pp. 116–29. Georges Bataille, 'Theory of Potlatch', in *La Part maudite* (Paris, 1949); published in English as *The Accursed Share: An Essay on General Economy*,

vol. 1: *Consumption*, trans. Robert Hurley (New York, 1988). See also Marcel Mauss, 'Essai sur le don', in *L'année sociologique*, 1923–4, and 'The Gift' (1924), in Marcel Mauss, *The Gift: Forms and Functions of Exchange in Archaic Societies*, trans. Ian Cunnison (London, 1966), p. 4.

14    Carr, *Growing Pains*, p. 261.

15    Peter Blecha, 'Alaska-Yukon-Pacific Exposition (1909): Music at the Fair', *The Free Online Encyclopedia of Washington State History*, www.historylink.org, 27 December 2008.

16    Adrian Mack, 'Jimi Hendrix Haunts Vie's Chicken and Steak House', *Georgia Straight*, www.straight.com, 15 July 2009.

17    Jimi Hendrix, interview with Jane de Mendelsohn of the *International Times*, in Steven Roby, ed., *Hendrix on Hendrix: Interviews and Encounters* (Chicago, IL, 2012), p. 165.

18    Jack Webster (interviewer), 'Jimi Hendrix's Grandmother Reviews One of his Concerts', Autumn 1968, www.youtube.com, accessed 3 June 2014.

19    Terry David Mulligan (interviewer), 'Jimi Hendrix Experience, Interview, 7 September 1968', 7 September 1968, www.youtube.com, accessed 3 June 2014.

20    Quoted in Michael Lydon, *Flashbacks: Eyewitness Accounts of the Rock Revolution, 1964–1974* (New York, 2003), p. 71.

21    Quoted in David Henderson, *'Scuse Me While I Kiss the Sky* (New York, 2008), p. 206.

22    The family was living in Savo Island Village, near the intersection of Derby Street and Martin Luther King Way. Steven Roby, *Black Gold: The Lost Archives of Jimi Hendrix* (New York, 2002), p. 257.

23    Charles Cross, *Room Full of Mirrors: A Biography of Jimi Hendrix* (New York, 2005), p. 13; Charles Cross, 'Beyond a Broken Childhood', *Seattle Times*, www.community.seattletimes.nwsource.com, 5 August 2005.

24    Quoted in Greg Tate, *Midnight Lightning: Jimi Hendrix and the Black Experience* (Chicago, IL, 2003), pp. 107, 109.

25    Ray Charles and David Ritz, *Brother Ray: Ray Charles' Own Story* (New York, 1978), pp. 110–11.

26    Interview in Ellen Weissbrod, dir., *Listen Up! The Lives of Quincy Jones* (2009), 2 min.

27    Interview ibid., 20 min.

28    Paul de Barros, 'Garfield's Glittering Star, Quincy Jones Dared to Dream', *Seattle Times*, www.seattletimes.com, 31 August 2008.

29    Interview in Weissbrod, *Listen Up!*, 30 min.

30    Interview ibid., 23 and 30 min.

31    Quoted in de Barros, 'Garfield's Glittering Star'.

32  William J. Bain, a designer of Yesler Terrace, Seattle's first public housing project in a joint venture with J. Lister Holmes, William Aitken, George W. Stoddard and John T. Jacobson, was a founder of the corporate architectural firm NBBJ. 'Yesler Terrace', www.en.wikipedia.org, accessed 3 June 2014.

33  Jimi Hendrix, cited in Steven Vosburgh, dir., *Jimi Hendrix: The Uncut Story* (2004), 16 min.

34  Harry Shapiro and Caesar Glebbeek, *Jimi Hendrix: Electric Gypsy* (London, 1992), p. 24.

35  Leon Hendrix with Adam Mitchell, *Jimi Hendrix: A Brother's Story* (New York, 2012), p. 55.

36  Hendrix attended Meany Junior High School, 301 21st Avenue East, in 1955; Washington Junior High School, 2101 South Jackson Street, and then Meany Junior High School again, in 1956; and Asa Mercer Junior High School, 1600 South Columbian Way, until December 1958. He returned to Washington Junior High School in December 1958.

37  Hendrix and Mitchell, *Jimi Hendrix*, pp. 55, 67, 69.

38  Ibid., pp. 28–9.

39  Ibid., p. 38.

40  Cross, *Room Full of Mirrors*, p. 57, and Vosburgh, *Jimi Hendrix*, 15 min.

41  Quoted in Ray Conolly, 'Jimi Hendrix: Interview', *London Evening Standard*, October 1967, available at www.rayconolly.co.uk.

42  Jimi Hendrix, interview by Thomas 'Meatball Fulton' Lopez for ZBS Radio, 9 December 1967, in Roby, *Hendrix on Hendrix*, p. 83; Steven Roby and Brad Schreiber, *Becoming Jimi Hendrix: From Southern Crossroads to Psychedelic London: The Untold Story of a Musical Genius* (New York, 2010), p. 5.

43  Leon Hendrix, interviewed in Vosburgh, *Jimi Hendrix*, 39 min.

44  Hendrix and Mitchell, *Jimi Hendrix*, pp. 73–5.

45  Gus Gossert, 'Interview with Jimi Hendrix', FM Radio KMPX, San Francisco, 10–12 October 1968, transcription in Roby, *Hendrix on Hendrix*, p. 138.

46  Jimmy Williams, interview in Vosburgh, *Jimi Hendrix*, 40 min.

47  Quoted in John McDermott with Eddie Kramer, *Hendrix: Setting the Record Straight*, ed. Mark Lewisohn (New York, 1992), p. 2.

48  Quoted in Tony Brown, *Jimi Hendrix in his Own Words* (London, 1999), p. 9.

49  Hendrix and Mitchell, *Jimi Hendrix*, p. 83.

50  Ibid.

51  Eisiminger quoted in *Jimi Hendrix: The Complete Story* (2007), 5–6 min.; 'The History of the Danelectro: Danelectro, the Birthplace of Rock 'n' Roll',

www.danguitars.com, 3 June 2014; on 'Betty Jean': Hendrix and Mitchell, *Jimi Hendrix*, p. 86; and Michael Heatley, *Jimi Hendrix Gear: The Guitars, Amps and Effects that Revolutionized Rock 'n' Roll* (Minneapolis, MN, 2009), p. 26.

52   Interview in *The Complete Story*, 6–7 min.

53   Interview ibid., 8–9 and 11 min.

54   Interview in Vosburgh, *Jimi Hendrix*, 45 min.

55   Zola Mumford and B. N. Barleycorn, 'City of Seattle Landmark Application: Washington Hall', www.seattle.gov, October 2008.

56   Hendrix and Mitchell, *Jimi Hendrix*, p. 86.

57   *The Complete Story*, 14 min.; Heatley, *Jimi Hendrix Gear*, pp. 28–9.

58   Shapiro and Glebbeek, *Jimi Hendrix*, p. 649.

59   Quoted in Tate, *Midnight Lightning*, p. 115.

60   Hendrix and Mitchell, *Jimi Hendrix*, p. 35.

61   Mary Elizabeth Cronin, 'Local Jazz Great "Melody" Jones is Dead', www.community.seattletimes.nwsource.com, 16 August 1996.

62   Quoted in Shapiro and Glebbeek, *Jimi Hendrix*, p. 46, and Roby, *Black Gold*, p. 13, nn. 21, 22, quoting Paul de Barros, *Jackson Street After Hours: The Roots of Jazz in Seattle* (Seattle, WA, 1993), p. 148.

63   Cross, *Room Full of Mirrors*, pp. 256–7.

64   Seattle-based friends of Hendrix who went to Vietnam included his cousin Bobby Hendrix, James Williams and Terry Johnson. Jimi Hendrix left Seattle on 30 or 31 May 1961 to serve thirteen months in the army.

65   Jimi Hendrix, introductory words before 'Like a Rolling Stone' at Monterey Pop on 18 June 1967, quoted in D. A. Pennebaker and Chris Hegedus, dir., *Jimi Plays Monterey* (1986), in Janie Hendrix and John McDermott, prod., *The Jimi Hendrix Experience Live at Monterey* (2007), 30 min.

66   Lars Bang Larsen, 'Anti-disciplinary Feedback and the Will to Effect', *Mute*, III/1 (15 June 2011), www.metamute.org; Alex Gibney and Alison Ellwood, dir., *The Magic Trip: Ken Kesey's Search for a Kool Place* (2011).

67   Quoted in '15 June 1967', in Ben Valkhoff, ed., 'Jimi Hendrix Lifelines, 1966–1967', www.jimihendrix-lifelines.net.

68   'Keith Altham Remembers Monterey, Jimi and The Who, 2013', www.crosstowntorrents.org, 20 September 2013.

69   Lou Adler, interview in 'Music and Flowers', bonus film in Hendrix and McDermott, *The Jimi Hendrix Experience Live at Monterey*, 5 min.

70   John Phillips with Jim Jerome, *Papa John: An Autobiography* (New York, 1986), pp. 227–9.

71   Ibid., p. 229.

72    Marshall McLuhan and Quentin Fiore, *The Medium is the Massage: An Inventory of Effects* (New York, 1967), p. 63.

73    A. M. Nolan, *Rock 'n' Roll Road Trip: The Ultimate Guide to the Sites, the Shrines and the Legends across America* (New York, 1992), pp. 227–8.

74    Quoted in Phillips and Jerome, *Papa John*, pp. 227–8.

75    Lou Adler and D. A. Pennebaker interview (Summer 2001), *The Complete Monterey Pop Festival* (2002), DVD, disc 1, 10 min.

76    Quoted in John Perry, *Electric Ladyland* (London, 2004), p. 48.

77    Charles Shaar Murray, commentary, *The Complete Monterey Pop Festival*, DVD, disc 2, 19 min.

78    Quoted in '18 June 1967', in Ben Valkhoff, ed., 'Jimi Hendrix Lifelines, 1966–1967'.

79    Eric Burdon, 'Monterey', www.youtube.com, accessed 3 June 2014.

80    Mike Bloomfield, quoted in Jann S. Wenner, 'The Rolling Stone Interview: Mike Bloomfield Part 2', *Rolling Stone*, IX (27 April 1968), available at www.jannswenner.com.

81    Interview in Peter Piliafan, dir., *Jimi Plays Berkeley* (1971; reissued 2010), 2 min. In contrast, on The Beach Boys' equipment in 1965, Tommy James wrote: 'They had a truck for nothing but their front sound system and monitors.' Tommy James with Martin Fitzpatrick, *Me, the Mob and the Music* (New York, 2010), p. 108.

82    Mitch Mitchell interview in Joe Boyd, John Head and Gary Weis, dir., 'From the Ukelele to the Strat', bonus film in *A Film about Jimi Hendrix* (1973; reissued 2005), 30–32 min.

83    Interview in Pilafian, *Jimi Plays Berkeley*, 6 min.; Abe Jacob cited in Harvey Kubernik, 'Jimi Plays Berkeley', *Record Collector News*, www.recordcollectornews.com, 17 October 2012.

84    Quoted in Tate, *Midnight Lightning*, pp. 121, 125.

85    Quoted in Graham Nash, 'Graham Nash has Wild Tales to Spare', National Public Radio interview, www.npr.org, 15 October 2013.

86    Robert Santelli, Holly George-Warren and Jim Brown, *American Roots Music* (New York, 2001), pp. 218–21. On the Specialty label, see 'Discogs, Specialty', www.discogs.com, accessed 20 June 2014. The Dunbar Hotel address is given in Clora Bryant et al., eds, *Central Avenue Sounds: Jazz in Los Angeles* (Los Angeles, CA, 1999), p. 18.

87    Quoted in Andrew Loog Oldham, *2Stoned* (New York, 2001), p. 141.

88    Stevie Ray Vaughan mentioned as influence a compilation album called *Blues in D Natural*, on the English import label Red Lightnin' (1958–9). Vaughan also

noted Syl Johnson. Jas Obrecht, 'Stevie Ray Vaughan Interview: Jimi Hendrix and the Blues', www.jasobrecht.com, 9 February 1989.

89   Charles and Ritz, *Brother Ray*, pp. 270–72.

90   Anaïs Nin, *The Journals of Anaïs Nin, 1947–1955*, vol. v, ed. Gunter Stuhlman (London, 1976), pp. 256–7, and 'Anaïs Nin on her Feminist Heroes (and LSD)', video interview, www.dangerousminds.net, 25 February 2013.

91   Roby and Schreiber, *Becoming Jimi Hendrix*, p. 236, and Niko Bauer and Doug Bell, eds, 'The Prehistory of Jimi Hendrix: Updates', www.earlyhendrix.com, 3 June 2014.

92   Roby, *Black Gold*, p. 40, and Roby and Schreiber, *Becoming Jimi Hendrix*, pp. 105–8.

93   Quoted in Jerry Hopkins, *Jimi Hendrix Experience* (New York, 1996), pp. 61, 102; Roby, *Black Gold*, p. 40; and Roby and Schreiber, *Becoming Jimi Hendrix*, pp. 105–8.

94   Bauer and Bell, 'The Pre-history of Jimi Hendrix'.

95   Roby and Schreiber, *Becoming Jimi Hendrix*, p. 109.

96   Edward W. Soja, *My Los Angeles: From Urban Restructuring to Regional Urbanization* (Berkeley and Los Angeles, CA, 2014), p. 27, and Velvert Turner, quoted in John McDermott with Eddie Kramer and Billy Cox, *Ultimate Hendrix: An Illustrated Encyclopedia of Live Concerts and Sessions* (Milwaukee, WI, 2009), p. 106.

97   Some, not all, of the GTOs were groupies. Tom O'Dell, dir., *From Straight to Bizarre: Zappa, Beefheart, Alice Cooper and Los Angeles' Lunatic Fringe* (2011), 32 min. Addresses for Mitchell and Zappa are given in Chris Epting, 'All Aboard the Train: Ten Great Crosby, Stills, Nash and Young Landmarks', www.rockcellarmagazine.com, 2 June 2013.

98   Howard Kaylan with Jeff Tamarkin, *Shell Shocked: My Life with the Turtles, Flo & Eddie, and Frank Zappa, etc.* (Milwaukee, WI 2013), p. 125. See also Jon Brewer, dir., *Legends of the Canyon: Classic Artists* (Image Entertainment, 2010).

99   Quoted in Valkhoff, 'Jimi Hendrix Lifelines', 27 June 1967.

100   Quoted ibid.

101   Cameron Crowe, 'Stephen Stills Interview', *Creem Magazine*, September 1974, www.theuncool.com.

102   Buddy Miles, interview in Boyd, Head and Weis, *A Film about Jimi Hendrix*, 13 min.

103   Quoted in '1 July 1967', in Valkhoff, ed., 'Jimi Hendrix Lifelines, 1966–1967'.

104   Telephone interview with Jimi Hendrix of 22 July 1967, *New Musical Express* (29 July 1967), quoted in '29 July 1967', in Valkhoff, ed., 'Jimi Hendrix Lifelines, 1966–1967'.

105   Quoted in Henderson, *'Scuse Me While I Kiss the Sky*, p. 182.

106   'Jimi Hendrix Experience Playing Voodoo Child [*sic*] on Sept. 14, 1968 –

Hollywood Bowl', www.youtube.com, accessed 20 June 2014. For the Hollywood Bowl, see www.angelenoliving.com. Jimi Hendrix quoted in '18 August 1967', in Valkhoff, ed., 'Jimi Hendrix Lifelines, 1966–1967'.

107 Karen 'Gilly' Laney, 'Jimi Hendrix Vehicle Registration Sells for Over Two Grand on Ebay', *Ultimate Classic Rock*, www.ultimateclassicrock.com, 21 December 2012.

108 A decline in creativity accompanied the spread of cocaine addiction among musicians and of decadence in the music industry in general: see the discussion by David Crosby, Henry Diltz and Dallas Taylor in *Legends of the Canyon*, dir. Brewer, at 1:34–39 min.

109 Hendrix and Mitchell, *Jimi Hendrix*, p. 172.

110 McDermott, Kramer and Cox, *Ultimate Hendrix*, pp. 120–21.

111 Quoted ibid., p. 126.

112 'The Queen versus James Marshall Hendrix', *FBI Records: The Vault*, www.vault.fbi.gov, accessed 15 June 2014.

113 Sharon Lawrence, *Jimi Hendrix: The Intimate Story of a Betrayed Musical Legend* (New York, 2005), pp. 147–9.

## 2 SOUTH: NASHVILLE, MEMPHIS, ATLANTA, NEW ORLEANS

1 Interview in Barnaby Thompson and Tom McGuinness, dir. and prod., *The South Bank Show: Jimi Hendrix* (1973), 20 min.

2 Quoted in Andrew Loog Oldham, *2Stoned* (New York, 2001), pp. 280–81.

3 Quoted ibid., p. 283.

4 Quoted in Jeff Hannusch, *I Hear You Knockin': The Sound of New Orleans Rhythm and Blues* (Ville Platte, LA, 1987), p. 177.

5 Robert Palmer, 'Wolf Live in '65', from *Deep Blues: A Musical and Cultural History of the Mississippi Delta* (New York, 1982), in Peter Guralnick, ed., *Martin Scorsese Presents the Blues: A Musical Journey* (New York, 2003), p. 153.

6 Paul Oscher, 'The Gift', in Guralnick, *Martin Scorsese Presents the Blues*, p. 226. B.B. King's tour schedule from 21 November to mid-December 1962 included stops at the Rhythm Club, Baton Rouge, Louisiana, on 21 November; the Stardust Club, Longview, Texas, on 22 November; a school in West Helena, Arkansas, on 23 November; and almost nightly gigs in numerous towns; see Charles Keil, *Urban Blues* [1966] (Chicago, IL, 1991), p. 149.

7 Interview in Joe Boyd, John Head and Gary Weis, dir. and prod., *A Film about Jimi Hendrix* (1973; reissued 2005), 11 min. 'Jimi Hendrix

Wiki Bandography', www.jimihendrix.wikia.com, 3 June 2014.

8 Steven Roby and Brad Schreiber, *Becoming Jimi Hendrix: From Southern Crossroads to Psychedelic London: The Untold Story of a Musical Genius* (New York, 2010), pp. 16–24.

9 Ibid., p. 30, and John McDermott with Eddie Kramer, *Hendrix: Setting the Record Straight*, ed. Mark Lewisohn (New York, 1992), p. 14.

10 Charlie Gillett, *The Sound of the City: The Rise of Rock and Roll* (New York, 1970), p. 133.

11 Roby and Schreiber, *Becoming Jimi Hendrix*, p. 41.

12 Daniel Cooper, 'Scuffling: The Lost History of Nashville Rhythm and Blues', www.nashvillescene.com, 12 December 1996. See also David Moskowitz, *Jimi Hendrix: The Words and Music* (Santa Barbara, CA, 2010), p. 179, n. 7.

13 Nate Rau, 'New Record Label Looks to Bring Music Back to Jefferson Street', *The Tennessean*, 24 October 2013, www.tennessean.com.

14 'Nashville Then: 1962', *The Tennessean*, 17 December 2012, www.tennessean.com. The lunch counter, as artefact, was installed at the Smithsonian Institution; see Owen Edwards, 'Courage at the Greensboro Lunch Counter', *Smithsonian*, February 2010, www.smithsonianmag.com.

15 Quoted in Roby and Schreiber, *Becoming Jimi Hendrix*, p. 38.

16 PBS American Experience, '1964, Photo Gallery: The Year in Pictures', captioned: 'A group of 200 civil rights protesters marched in downtown Nashville on April 27, 1964. A riot broke out after an organizer was beaten and arrested.' See www.pbs.org, accessed 3 June 2014.

17 Alan Levine wrote: 'I cannot remember a performance that rivaled that one for bravery and eloquence', in 'Sound and Fury: Eyewitness Describes Nina Simone Singing "Mississippi Goddam" in Montgomery, Alabama, 1965', www.blackinamerica.com, 27 March 2010. See also 'Nina Simone: Mississippi Goddam', 25 March 1965, www.youtube.com, accessed 24 July 2014.

18 Quoted in Alan Freeman, 'Quite an Experience', *Rave* (June 1967), in Steven Roby, ed., *Hendrix on Hendrix: Interviews and Encounters* (Chicago, IL, 2012), p. 26.

19 Quoted in Bob Smeaton, dir., Janie Hendrix and John McDermott, prod., *West Coast Seattle Boy: Jimi Hendrix – Voodoo Child* (2012), 13 min.

20 Interview with Jimi Hendrix by Bill Kerby and David Thompson, *Los Angeles Free Press*, 25 August 1967, available at www.crosstowntorrents.org, accessed 3 June 2014.

21 Janie Hendrix and John McDermott, *Jimi Hendrix: An Illustrated Experience*

(New York, 2007), p. 15.

22    Roby and Schreiber, *Becoming Jimi Hendrix*, pp. 35, 44.

23    Quoted ibid., p. 36.

24    Quoted ibid., p. 43.

25    Michalis Limnios, 'I Sing Music that You Can Feel: Legendary Excello Singer Marion James Talks about Hendrix', www.blues.gr, 19 March 2012.

26    'The Official Biography of Billy Cox', www.bassistbillycox.com, accessed 3 June 2014.

27    Charles Cross, *Room Full of Mirrors: A Biography of Jimi Hendrix* (New York, 2005), p. 105.

28    Roby and Schreiber, *Becoming Jimi Hendrix*, p. 57; see also Steven Roby, *Black Gold: The Lost Archives of Jimi Hendrix* (New York, 2002), p. 25. In Harry Shapiro and Caesar Glebbeek, *Jimi Hendrix: Electric Gypsy* (London, 1992), the band is called Bob Fisher & the Barnevilles.

29    Roby, *Black Gold*, p. 24.

30    Billy Cox, interviewed with Mitch Mitchell in Nashville, in Andy Aledort, 'Jimi Hendrix: Star Power', *Guitar World*, 9 December 2008, www.guitarworld.com.

31    Quoted in Jude Rogers, 'Bobby Womack: The Soundtrack of My Life', *The Observer*, 25 November 2012, www.theguardian.com.

32    Bob Putignano (interviewer), 'Blues Wax Sittin' in with Bobby Womack', www.soundsofblue.com, 14 October 2009.

33    Interview with Klas Burling (Stockholm, 25 May 1967) in Niko Bauer and Doug Bell, eds, 'The Pre-history of Jimi Hendrix: Timeline', www.earlyhendrix.com, accessed 3 June 2014.

34    Roby and Schreiber, *Becoming Jimi Hendrix*, p. 230.

35    Quoted ibid., p. 89.

36    Postcard to Al Hendrix, 28 September 1964, Port Columbus Airport, Columbus, Ohio, in Bauer and Bell, 'The Pre-history of Jimi Hendrix'.

37    Ibid.

38    Peter Guralnick, *Dream Boogie: The Triumph of Sam Cooke* (New York, 2005), pp. 601–3.

39    Quoted in Bauer and Bell, 'The Pre-history of Jimi Hendrix'.

40    Quoted in Roby and Schreiber, *Becoming Jimi Hendrix*, p. 111.

41    Quoted in Michael Lydon, *Flashbacks: Eyewitness Accounts of the Rock Revolution, 1964–1974* (New York, 2003), p. 70.

42    Quoted in Charles White, *The Life and Times of Little Richard: The Authorized*

*Biography* (London, 2003), p. 3.

43 'Buddy and Stacy, with Jimi Hendrix, Shotgun 1965 – Night Train Television Show', www.youtube.com, accessed 3 June 2014. *Night Train*, hosted by Noble Blackwell, was produced at the television station WLAC Channel 5 in Nashville and aired from 1964 to 1967. The edition with Hendrix included performances by Buddy Travis and Leroy 'Stacy' Johnson Jr, Jimmy Church, the Avons, the Spidels, Tony Clarke, Pamela Releford, James 'Sugar Boy' Crawford, the High Tones and Jackie Shane. 'Night Train Music Program 1965', www.youtube.com, accessed 3 June 2014.

44 Quoted in Tony Brown, *Jimi Hendrix in his Own Words* (London, 1994), p. 18.

45 Ernest C. Withers, 'I am a Man, Sanitation Workers' Strike, Memphis, Tennessee', gelatin silver print, 28 March 1968, www.chrysler.org.

46 'Mystery Train', www.en.wikipedia.org, accessed 3 June 2014.

47 Quoted in 'Rocket 88', www.en.wikipedia.org, accessed 3 June 2014, citing Holger Petersen, *Talking Music* (Toronto, 2011), p. 154.

48 Interview (December 1969, New York), quoted in Brown, *Jimi Hendrix in his Own Words*, p. 38.

49 Brown, *Jimi Hendrix in his Own Words*, p. 33, and 'Live at Clark University', 15 March 1968, backstage pre-concert interview, on *Jimi Hendrix Live*, CD, in Hendrix and McDermott, *Hendrix: An Illustrated Experience*, 11 min.

50 Quoted in an interview by Hans Carl Schmitt, Frankfurt radio broadcast (station unknown), 17 May 1967, in Roby, *Hendrix on Hendrix*, pp. 32–3, and Brown, *Jimi Hendrix in his Own Words*, pp. 75–6.

### 3 EAST: HARLEM, NEW YORK, NEW JERSEY

1 Harry Shapiro and Caesar Glebbeek, *Jimi Hendrix: Electric Gypsy* (London, 1992), p. 73, and Steven Roby and Brad Schreiber, *Becoming Jimi Hendrix: From Southern Crossroads to Psychedelic London: The Untold Story of a Musical Genius* (New York, 2010), p. 63.

2 Niko Bauer and Doug Bell, eds, 'The Pre-history of Jimi Hendrix', www.earlyhendrix.com, accessed 3 June 2014, and Lonnie Youngblood, 'Go Go Shoes and Go Go Place', www.youtube.com, accessed 3 June 2014.

3 'Apollo Theater', www.apollotheater.org, accessed 2 June 2014.

4 Roby and Schreiber, *Becoming Jimi Hendrix*, p. 67.

5 Minton's Playhouse at 210 West 118th Street, on the ground floor of the Cecil Hotel, founded in 1938 by the tenor saxophonist Henry Minton, was the base

for bebop and jazz innovators, including the house pianist Thelonious Monk and Dizzy Gillespie, Charlie Parker and Charlie Christian in the 1940s. A hotel fire ended Minton's in 1974. The building was renovated and reopened in 2006, but closed again; the club was revived as a gentrified Minton's in about 2012. 'Minton's Playhouse', www.en.wikipedia.org, accessed 30 August 2014.

6    Interview with Faye Pridgon, *Gallery*, September 1982, available at www.theisleofhendrix.gobot.com, accessed 3 June 2014.

7    Roby and Schreiber, *Becoming Jimi Hendrix*, p. 73.

8    David Henderson, *'Scuse Me While I Kiss the Sky* (New York, 2008), p. 66.

9    Jimmy Norman, 'Jimmy Norman, Meet Jimmy Hendrix', www.crosstowntorrents.org, 8 September 2011.

10    Quoted in Roby and Schreiber, *Becoming Jimi Hendrix*, p. 75.

11    Interview in Steven Vosburgh, dir., *Jimi Hendrix: The Uncut Story* (2004), 10–11 min.

12    Quoted in Jim Beckerman, 'Isley Brother Reflects on Jimi Hendrix's Englewood Days', *The Record*, www.northjersey.com, 2 November 2010.

13    Quoted ibid.

14    Quoted ibid.

15    Quoted in Shapiro and Glebbeek, *Jimi Hendrix*, p. 80.

16    Roby and Schreiber, *Becoming Jimi Hendrix*, p. 227.

17    Bauer and Bell, 'The Pre-history of Jimi Hendrix'.

18    'American Experience, Timeline: Headlines for 1964', www.pbs.org, accessed 3 June 2014, and 'Harlem Riot of 1964', www.en.wikipedia.org, accessed 3 June 2014.

19    Graham Nash, *Wild Tales: A Rock and Roll Life* (New York, 2013), p. 69.

20    *New York Times*, 17 April 1965, in Bauer and Bell, 'The Pre-history of Jimi Hendrix'.

21    Nash, *Wild Tales*, p. 70. On the Brooklyn Paramount rock booking and the New York City Paramount, Tommy James (signed to Roulette and under contract to Morris Levy) mentioned Levy's use of the Paramount in an account of his pop career: 'The Brooklyn Paramount was one of Morris's old stomping grounds, where he first had his rock and roll shows with Alan Freed in the fifties. Morris was still doing shows there in the early sixties when he had a famous screaming match with Little Richard, which ended when he pulled Richard's wig off in the elevator.' Tommy James with Martin Fitzpatrick, *Me, the Mob and the Music* (New York, 2010), p. 202. Roulette Records moved from 1631 Broadway to 17 West 60th Street in 1968.

22  Quoted in Roby and Schreiber, *Becoming Jimi Hendrix*, p. 115.

23  Ibid., p. 118.

24  Quoted in Randy Albright, 'Jimmy Plays Indiana 1965', *Univibes*, XLIII (December 2002), www.univibes.com.

25  Quoted in Keith Altham, 'New to the Charts' and 'Wild Jimi Hendrix', *New Musical Express*, 14 January 1967, p. 16, available at www.crosstowntorrents.org, accessed 3 June 2014.

26  Roby and Schreiber, *Becoming Jimi Hendrix*, p. 244.

27  Ibid., photographs inserted between pp. 146 and 147.

28  Miles Davis with Quincy Troupe, *Miles: The Autobiography* (New York, 1989), pp. 67, 98.

29  Ibid., pp. 71–2.

30  Lead Belly (Huddie William Ledbetter) recorded the song 'In New Orleans' in February 1944, and 'The House of the Rising Sun' in October 1948. Dave Van Ronk performed the song with his own chord progression, appropriated by Bob Dylan on his debut album in 1961, as documented in Van Ronk's memoir, *The Mayor of Macdougal Street* (Cambridge, MA, 2005; new edn Boston, MA, 2013), and in Martin Scorsese's documentary on Bob Dylan, *No Direction Home* (2005). The Animals recorded the song on 18 May 1964, while on a tour stopover, using a Vox Continental organ. Van Ronk complained in his memoir: 'Sometime in 1964, Eric Burdon and the Animals made a number-one chart hit out of the . . . same arrangement. I would have loved to sue for royalties, but I found that it is impossible to defend the copyright on an arrangement.' Van Ronk and Wald, *The Mayor of Macdougal Street*, pp. 176–7.

31  Van Ronk and Wald, *The Mayor of Macdougal Street*, p. 178.

32  A. M. Nolan, *Rock 'n' Roll Road Trip: The Ultimate Guide to the Sites, the Shrines and the Legends Across America* (New York, 1992), pp. 17–33.

33  'Joni Mitchell Live at the Couriers Folk Club, Leicester, England', [September 1967], www.youtube.com, accessed 7 June 2014.

34  Interview in Laura Archibald, dir., *Greenwich Village: Music that Defined a Generation* (2013), DVD, 8:30–8:56 min.

35  Quoted ibid., 22 min.

36  Quoted ibid., 9:20 min.

37  Quoted ibid., 22 min.

38  Knight wrote: 'In the lobby of this hotel there was a small recording studio, and I stopped by there one day on an impulse.' Curtis Knight, *Jimi: An Intimate Biography of Jimi Hendrix* (London, 1974), p. 28.

39    Quoted in Roby and Schreiber, *Becoming Jimi Hendrix*, p. 147.

40    Steven Roby, *Black Gold: The Lost Archives of Jimi Hendrix* (New York, 2002), pp. 48–9.

41    Roby and Schreiber, *Becoming Jimi Hendrix*, p. 121. The contracts were moot, as no recordings were made: '1965, 27 July, New York City. Jimi signed an Exclusive Recording Artist Contract with Sue Records, Inc. and Henry "Juggy" Murray Jr at the Sue Records office on 265 West Fifty-fourth Street. Except for a demo recording that according to Jimi he recorded himself and brought to Juggy Murray, there did not appear to be any recordings made for Sue. The demo has never surfaced.' Bauer and Bell, 'Timeline', www.earlyhendrix.com, accessed 3 June 2014.

42    Alastair Gordon, *Spaced Out: Radical Environments of the Psychedelic Sixties* (New York, 2008), p. 46.

43    Quoted in Roby and Schreiber, *Becoming Jimi Hendrix*, pp. 143–5.

44    Quoted ibid., p. 143.

45    Quoted in John Ridley, 'Send My Love to Linda: An Untold Jimi Hendrix Story', National Public Radio, www.npr.org, 15 September 2010.

46    Quoted in Bob Smeaton, dir., Janie Hendrix and John McDermott, prod., *West Coast Seattle Boy: Jimi Hendrix – Voodoo Child* (2012), 17:20 min.

47    Interview in Joe Boyd, John Head and Gary Weis, dir., 'From the Ukelele to the Strat', bonus film in *A Film about Jimi Hendrix* (1973; reissued 2005), 18 min.

48    Lithofayne Pridgon, interview, *Gallery*, September 1982, available at www.theisleofhendrix.gobot.com, and Roby and Schreiber, *Becoming Jimi Hendrix*, p. 151.

49    Quoted in Roby and Schreiber, *Becoming Jimi Hendrix*, p. 153.

50    Quoted ibid., p. 148.

51    'Randy California and Jimi Hendrix', interview by Steven Roby in *Straight Ahead*, October–November 1994, available at www.rockpalastarchiv.de.

52    Interview in Boyd, Head and Weis, 'From the Ukelele to the Strat', 19 min.

53    Cross, *Room Full of Mirrors*, p. 149.

54    'John Hammond Jr. Remembers Jimi, 1975', *Guitar Player Magazine*, September 1975, available at www.crosstowntorrents.org, accessed 20 July 2014.

55    'Robbie Robertson on why he Still Calls Jimi Hendrix "Jimmy James"', www.youtube.com, accessed 3 June 2014.

56    The Albert Hotel, 23 East 10th Street, was built in 1882 by Henry J. Hardenbergh, architect of the Dakota and the Plaza, with additions in 1904 and 1924. Anthony W. Robins, 'The Hotel Albert, 23 East 10th Street, NYC, A History', p. 66, www.leedigitalarts.leeschools.net, 2011; Samuel R. Delany,

*Flight from Nevèrÿon* (Hanover, NH, 1994), pp. 239–40.

57 Roby and Schreiber, *Becoming Jimi Hendrix*, p. 161.

58 Sharon Lawrence, *Jimi Hendrix: The Intimate Story of a Betrayed Musical Legend* (New York, 2005), p. 32.

59 Quoted in Ed Vulliamy, 'Jimi Hendrix: "You Never Told Me He Was that Good"', *The Observer*, 8 August 2010, www.theguardian.com.

60 Andy Warhol and Pat Hackett, *Popism: The Warhol '60s* (New York, 1980), p. 163.

61 Ibid., pp. 156–7.

62 Ibid., p. 162.

63 Quoted in 'Andy Warhol Chronology: Andy Warhol at the Dom', www.warholstars.org, accessed 3 June 2014.

64 'April 1966: The Exploding Plastic Inevitable Premières at the "Open Stage"', www.warholstars.org, accessed 3 June 2014.


## 4 LONDON: A PSYCHEDELIC SCENE

1 Interview with Steve Barker for *West One*, the London Polytechnic student newspaper, February 1967, in Harry Shapiro and Caesar Glebbeek, *Jimi Hendrix: Electric Gypsy* (London, 1992), p. 134, n. 36.

2 Interview in Joe Boyd, John Head and Gary Weis, dir., 'From the Ukelele to the Strat', bonus film in *A Film about Jimi Hendrix* (1973; reissued 2005), 22 min.

3 Chris Ingham in *Going Underground: Paul McCartney, The Beatles and the UK Counter-culture*, Tom O'Dell, dir. (2013), 1:21 min.

4 Eric Clapton, *Clapton: The Autobiography* (New York, 2007), p. 80.

5 Interview in Boyd, Head and Weis, 'From the Ukelele to the Strat', 22 min.

6 Interview ibid., 23 and 32 min.

7 Ibid.

8 Dixon's estate funded the Blues Heaven Foundation in 1984, in the former Chess Records offices and recording studios at 2120 South Michigan Avenue in Chicago. Dead Man, 'Led Zeppelin: Plagiarism? Whole Lotta Love', www.turnmeondeadman.com, 10 July 2013. Steve Hochman, 'Willie Dixon's Daughter Makes Sure Legacy Lives On', *Los Angeles Times*, 8 October 1994, www.articles.latimes.com.

9 Clive Richardson, liner notes for Irma Thomas, 'Time is on my Side', Kent Records, July 1966.

10 Quoted in Bob Putignano, 'BluesWax Sittin' in with Bobby Womack', www.soundsofblue.com, accessed 10 June 2014.

11   Dave Davies, *Kink* (New York, 1996), pp. 1–2.

12   Matthew Frye Jacobson, 'Conversations with Scholars of American Popular Culture', *Americana: The Journal of American Popular Culture, 1900 to Present* (Autumn 2011), www.americanpopularculture.com.

13   Interview in Boyd, Head and Weis, 'From the Ukelele to the Strat', 32 min.

14   Eric Clapton, interview ibid., 21 and 40 min.

15   Roby and Schreiber, *Becoming Jimi Hendrix*, p. 177.

16   Interview in Boyd, Head and Weis, 'From the Ukelele to the Strat', 37 min.

17   'The Vic Briggs Interview', www.hendrix.guide.pagesperso-orange.fr, January 2013.

18   Quoted in Norman Jopling, 'Man, Myth or Magic? Jimi Hendrix is Back, and Happy . . .', *Music Now* (12 September 1970), in Steven Roby, ed., *Hendrix on Hendrix: Interviews and Encounters* (Chicago, IL, 2012), p. 291.

19   Interview in Boyd, Head and Weis, 'From the Ukelele to the Strat', 6 min.

20   Simon Frith, Will Straw and John Street, eds, *The Cambridge Companion to Pop and Rock* (Cambridge, 2001), p. 81.

21   Hendrix signed and contracted with the Bahamas-based Yameta in December 1966, rather than with his manager, Jeffery. See Shapiro and Glebbeek, *Jimi Hendrix*, pp. 484–5, and Charles Cross, *Room Full of Mirrors: A Biography of Jimi Hendrix* (New York, 2005), p. 163.

22   '10 March 1967', in Ben Valkhoff, ed., 'Jimi Hendrix Lifelines, 1966–1967', www.jimihendrix-lifelines.net; 'The Club A Go Go, Newcastle upon Tyne', 10 March 1967, www.hendrixnortheast.pwp.blueyonder.co.uk; 'Michael Jeffery: Manager', www.pages.rediff.com, accessed 3 June 2014; and Andrew Loog Oldham, *2Stoned* (New York, 2001), p. 302.

23   Noel Redding and Carol Appleby, *Are You Experienced? The Inside Story of the Hendrix Experience* (London, 1990), p. 34.

24   Joe Boyd, *White Bicycles: Making Music in the 1960s* (London, 2006), p. 117.

25   'This Much I Know', *The Guardian*, 15 February 2014, www.theguardian.com.

26   Pete Townshend, *Who I Am: A Memoir* (London, 2012), p. 64. The Track offices were on Old Compton Street: John McDermott with Eddie Kramer, *Hendrix: Setting the Record Straight*, ed. Mark Lewisohn (New York, 1992), p. 280.

27   Interview in Boyd, Head and Weis, 'From the Ukulele to the Strat', 24 min.

28   Interview ibid., 25 min.

29   Interview ibid., 26–27 min.

30   Ibid.

31   Townshend, *Who I Am*, p. 69.

32   Jim Marshall quoted in Edward B. Driscoll Jr, 'Part One: The Birth of the

Marshall', *Vintage Guitar*, September–October 2003, www.vintageguitar.com.

33　Ibid.

34　Townshend, *Who I Am*, p. 103.

35　Quoted in Ed Vulliamy, 'Jimi Hendrix: "You Never Told Me He Was that Good"', *The Observer*, 8 August 2010, www.theguardian.com.

36　Quoted in Bill Kerby and David Thompson, 'Spanish Galleons off Jersey Coast or "We Live off Excess Volume"', *Los Angeles Free Press*, 25 August 1967, in Roby, *Hendrix on Hendrix*, p. 57.

37　Quoted in Ken Sharp, 'The Quiet One Speaks! A Chat with the Ox, The Who's John Entwistle', *Goldmine*, 416 (5 July 1996), available at www.thewho.net.

38　The Paris Olympia opened in 1889 as the Montagnes Russes, and was renamed in 1893. It remains a prestigious venue, also used for broadcast television. 'L'Olympia Bruno Cocatrix', www.en.olympiahall.com, accessed 10 July 2014.

39　John McDermott with Eddie Kramer and Billy Cox, *Ultimate Hendrix: An Illustrated Encyclopedia of Live Concerts and Sessions* (Milwaukee, wi, 2009), p. 61 (rte radio was Radiodiffusion Télévision Française public broadcasting).

40　De Lane Lea Studio, a basement under a branch of the Midland Bank, named after its owner, Major Jacques De Lane Lea, moved to 75 Dean Street in Soho. 'A History of British Recording Studios from the 50s to the 80s: Kingsway Studios', www.philsbook.com, accessed 3 June 2014.

41　'23 October 1966', in Valkhoff, ed., 'Jimi Hendrix Lifelines, 1966–1967'.

42　In Bob Smeaton, dir., Janie Hendrix and John McDermott, prod., *West Coast Seattle Boy: Jimi Hendrix – Voodoo Child* (2012), 26–7 min.

43　Redding and Appleby, *Are You Experienced?*, p. 50.

44　Interview in Janie Hendrix and John McDermott, prod., *The Jimi Hendrix Experience Live at Monterey* (2007), 7 min.

45　Marc Spitz, *Bowie: A Biography* (New York, 2009), p. 81.

46　Jimi Hendrix, quoted by Mike Ledgerwood, *Disc & Music Echo* (28 January 1967), p. 10, available at www.crosstowntorrents.org; 'Jimi Hendrix in his Own Words', *The Observer*, 8 December 2013, www.theguardian.com. John Lennon and Yoko Ono later lived in the Montagu Square flat, where they held the *Two Virgins* photo shoot. A blue plaque was placed there in autumn 2010 to commemorate their tenancy.

47　Interview in Steven Vosburgh, dir., *Jimi Hendrix: The Uncut Story* (2004), 37–8 min.

48    Quoted ibid., 37 min.

49    Quoted ibid., 38 min.

50    On recording at CBS on 13 December 1966, the engineer Mike Ross said of
      the Experience's Marshall stacks: 'It was so loud you couldn't stand in the
      studio . . . I'd never heard anything like it in my life.' Ross asked Hendrix
      about a microphone position, and Hendrix responded: 'Put a mic about
      twelve feet away on the other side of the studio. It'll sound great.' Ross used
      a 'Neumann U-87 tube mic'. Sean Egan, *Jimi Hendrix and the Making of Are You
      Experienced, Updated and Expanded* (Chicago, IL, 2013), p. 104, quoted in 'Are
      You Experienced', www.en.wikipedia.org, accessed 15 December 2014.

51    'Olympic Studios, Cinema and Café, 117–123 Church Road, Barnes',
      www.olympiccinema.co.uk, accessed 7 June 2014.

52    Mitch Mitchell interview in Boyd, Head and Weis, 'From the Ukelele to the
      Strat', 29–30 min.

53    Interview with Keith Altham, *New Musical Express* (14 January 1967), p. 16,
      available at www.crosstowntorrents.org, accessed 20 July 2014.

54    Thomas 'Meatball Fulton' Lopez, 'Interview with Jimi Hendrix',
      9 December 1967, in Roby, *Hendrix on Hendrix*, p. 81.

55    Perry, *Electric Ladyland*, p. 121.

56    EMP interview, 'Chris Squire of Yes, Meeting Jimi Hendrix',
      www.youtube.com, accessed 3 June 2014.

57    Quoted in '25 February 1967', in Valkhoff, ed., 'Jimi Hendrix Lifelines,
      1966–1967'.

58    Interview in Hendrix and McDermott, *The Jimi Hendrix Experience Live at
      Monterey*, 7 min.

59    Quoted in '9 January 1967', in Valkhoff, ed., 'Jimi Hendrix Lifelines, 1966–1967'.

60    Marianne Faithfull with David Dalton, *Faithfull: An Autobiography* (London,
      1994), pp. 120–21.

61    '9 and 27 January 1967', in Valkhoff, ed., 'Jimi Hendrix Lifelines, 1966–1967'.

62    The Roundhouse was built in 1847 by Branson & Gwyther, to designs
      by the architects Robert B. Dockray and Robert Stephenson. Renamed
      Centre 42, it was renovated for performance in 1964–6 and became a
      counterculture arts venue. It was listed Grade II by English Heritage in 2010,
      and John McAslan & Partners and Buro Happold renovated it in 2006; it
      now has a capacity of 3,300 people standing or 1,700 seated. 'Roundhouse',
      www.roundhouse.org.uk, accessed 7 June 2014, and 'Roundhouse',
      www.en.wikipedia.org, accessed 7 June 2014.

63    The Who, 'Glittering Girl – 1967', www.youtube.com, accessed 15 June 2014.

64   'The Jimi Hendrix Experience, The Who, Small Faces, Manfred Mann, Beat
     Club', www.youtube.com, accessed 15 June 2014.
65   The BBC Playhouse Theatre, on Northumberland Avenue near Trafalgar
     Square, was built by F. H. Fowler and Hill. The theatre, originally with
     1,200 seats and now seating 786, was rebuilt in 1907, retaining the original
     sub-stage machinery. 'Playhouse Theatre', www.playhousetheatrelondon.com,
     accessed 9 June 2014.
66   McDermott et al., *Ultimate Hendrix*, p. 38.
67   Ibid., p. 445.
68   The latter survives because it was re-broadcast in 1970. Valkhoff, 'Jimi
     Hendrix Lifelines', 17 April 1967; 'Late Night Line-up Psychedelic
     Happening', 17 May 1967, www.youtube.com, accessed 9 July 2014.
69   Quoted in '12 May 1967', in Valkhoff, ed., 'Jimi Hendrix Lifelines, 1966–1967'.
70   Michael Heatley, *Jimi Hendrix Gear: The Guitars, Amps and Effects that
     Revolutionized Rock 'n' Roll* (Minneapolis, MN, 2009), p. 129.
71   Quoted in Keith Keller, 'Come to a Soul Revival with Jimi Hendrix, a Rebel
     from Mars via Cuba', BT, 15 May 1967, in Roby, *Hendrix on Hendrix*, p. 30.
72   The original Finsbury Astoria interiors were by Tommy Somerford,
     decorated by Marc-Henri Hunt and G. Laverdet. The Beatles performed 30
     sold-out Christmas shows there from 24 December 1963 to 11 January 1964.
     They played again on 1 November 1964 and 11 December 1965. The renamed
     Rainbow Theatre continued as a rock venue; it is now a church.
73   Roby and Schreiber, *Becoming Jimi Hendrix*, p. 97.
74   Bonhams, 'Jimi Hendrix Experience: A Concert Poster for the Liverpool
     Empire', www.bonhams.com, 18 December 2013.
75   Interview in Boyd, Head and Weis, 'From the Ukelele to the Strat', 39 min.
76   Interview in *Going Underground*, 1:39 min.
77   R. Murray Schafer, *The Tuning of the World* (Toronto, 1977), p. 78.
78   'The Beatles and Drugs', www.beatlesbible.com, p. 3, accessed 10 June 2014.
79   Ibid., pp. 5, 4.
80   Chris Ingham, interview in *Going Underground*, 1:28 min.
81   Joe Massot, 'The Story of Wonderwall' booklet, p. 22, in Joe Massot, dir.,
     *Wonderwall* (1968; reissued 2014).
82   Quoted in William Saunders, *Jimi Hendrix London* (Berkeley, CA 2010), p. 94.
83   *Syd Barrett Under Review: An Independent Critical Analysis* (2005), 23 min.
84   Townshend, *Who I Am*, pp. 106–7.
85   Valkhoff, 'Jimi Hendrix Lifelines', 28 April 1967.
86   *Syd Barrett Under Review*, 13 min.

87   A newspaper cutting on the Million Volt Light and Sound Rave called
     it 'psychedelic son et lumiere': 'A Million Volt Light and Sound Rave',
     www.wiki.delia-derbyshire.net, accessed 7 June 2014.
88   Alexandra Palace was built in 1863, and rebuilt twice after fires in 1875 and 1980.
     Set in 79 ha (196 acres) of park between Muswell Hill and Wood Green on a hill
     with a panoramic view, it remains a popular music venue for mounting spatially
     ambitious performances, such as Björk's in-the-round *Biophilia* concert, filmed
     in 2013; www.alexandrapalace.com, accessed 10 August 2014.
89   'Games for May: Space Age Relaxation for the Climax of Spring', 12
     May 1967, available at www.pinkfloydhyperbase.dk; Toby Manning, *The
     Underground* (London, 2006), p. 38.
90   The Star Club closed on 31 December 1969 and fire destroyed the
     building it had occupied in 1987. Beatles-Platz remains at the intersection
     of Grosse Freiheit and Reeperbahn. '50th Anniversary of the Star Club',
     www.liverpoolbeat, 13 May 2012.
91   Dave Jennings, 'Jimi Hendrix: Interviews and Reviews, 1967–71, Book
     Review', www.louderthanwar.com, 11 December 2012.
92   '22 May 1967', in Valkhoff, ed., 'Jimi Hendrix Lifelines, 1966–1967'.
93   David Moskowitz, *The Words and Music of Jimi Hendrix* (Santa Barbara, CA,
     2010), p. 15.
94   Quoted (as Otto Donner) in Shapiro and Glebbeek, *Jimi Hendrix*, p. 162.
95   Moskowitz, *The Words and Music*, p. 21. On 'Are You Experienced': 'Jimi
     played the piano part and it created a chiming effect in the overall texture
     of the song. Another interesting addition to this song was the use of guitar,
     bass, and drum overdubs that were played backward . . . various parts hung
     together to create an interesting product.'
96   Howard Sounes, *Amy, 27: Amy Winehouse and the 27 Club* (London, 2013), p. 92.
97   Germaine Greer, 'Hey Jimi Where You Gonna Go to Now?', *Oz*, x (1970),
     reprinted in *The Madwoman's Underclothes: Essays and Occasional Writings,
     1968–1985* (London, 1986), pp. 41–4.
98   Quoted in Valkhoff, 'Jimi Hendrix Lifelines', 2 June 1967.
99   Interview in Boyd, Head and Weis, 'From the Ukulele to the Strat',
     40 min.
100  Ibid., 39–41 min.
101  Quoted in Barry Miles, *Many Years from Now*, in 'McCartney and
     Harrison Watch Jimi Hendrix in London', 4 June 1967, available at
     www.beatlesbible.com.

## 5 THE NEW YORK–LONDON AXIS: A SERIES OF RETURNS

1   Interview in Joe Boyd, John Head and Gary Weis, dir., *A Film about Jimi Hendrix* (1973; reissued 2005), 47 min.

2   Rick Marino, 'The Jacksonville Veterans Memorial Coliseum: Another Landmark where Elvis Presley Performed is Coming Down', www.ladyluckmusic.com, accessed 5 May 2014.

3   Noel Redding and Carol Appleby, *Are You Experienced? The Inside Story of the Hendrix Experience* (London, 1990), p. 57.

4   Interview in *New Musical Express*, 29 July 1967, available at www.jimihendrix.com and www.experiencehendrix.com; '12 July 1967', in Ben Valkhoff, ed., 'Jimi Hendrix Lifelines, 1966–1967', available at www.jimihendrix-lifelines.net.

5   Quoted in '12 July 1967', in Valkhoff, ed., 'Jimi Hendrix Lifelines, 1966–1967'.

6   Interview in *New Musical Express*, 29 July 1967.

7   David Gross, 'Clubs in NY', www.talkinaboutmygeneration.com, 25 January 2010. Frank Zappa recalled: 'He came over and sat in with us at the Garrick Theatre that night', *Guitar Player*, January 1977, in Valkhoff, ed., 'Jimi Hendrix Lifelines' (7 July 1967).

8   Interview in Joe Boyd, John Head and Gary Weis, dir., 'From the Ukelele to the Strat', bonus film in *A Film about Jimi Hendrix*, 12 min.; '5 July 1967', in Valkhoff, ed., 'Jimi Hendrix Lifelines, 1966–1967'.

9   Kees de Lange, 'Zappa Story No. 8, Part Two: Frank Zappa and Jimi Hendrix', available at www.crosstowntorrents.org, accessed 1 June 2014.

10   Redding and Appleby, *Are You Experienced?*, p. 58.

11   'Frank Zappa: We're Only in It for the Money Cover Shooting Session', www.crosstowntorrents.org, accessed 3 June 2014.

12   Quoted in 'Zappa's Inferno', *Guitar World*, April 1987, available at 'Zappa and Hendrix', http://wiki.killuglyradio.com, accessed 16 July 2015.

13   Quoted in Michael Buffalo Smith, 'John Hammond', in 'January 2007', in Valkhoff, ed., 'Jimi Hendrix Lifelines'.

14   Quoted in Valkhoff, ed., 'Jimi Hendrix Lifelines', accessed 3 June 2014.

15   Paul Zullo, 'Twin Shadows', ibid.

16   The Salvation Club was the location of the Café Society Club, the first integrated club in the United States. It operated until 1950. Later the Ridiculous Theatrical Company, led by Charles Ludlam, operated at the address. Axis Company NYC, 'The Theatre at 1 Sheridan Square', www.axiscompany.org, accessed 7 June 2014.

17   David Henderson, *'Scuse Me While I Kiss the Sky* (New York, 2008), p. 181.

18    Jack Newfield, 'Hippies & New Frontier On "Desolation Row"', *Village Voice*, XII/38 (6 July 1967), www.blogs.villagevoice.com: 'The scene was the opening of the Electric Circus, the latest total environment, McLuhanist discotheque. Its owners spent $300,000 for the flashing strobes, films, music, astrodome-style turf, and circus acts – but neglected to include air conditioning . . . the whole gala event was like a mixed-media happening on the BMT [Brooklyn–Manhattan Transit] rush hour . . . 3,000 people filed past the sign in the lobby announcing that "Occupancy by more than 740 people is illegal." The sponsors admitted to mailing out 5,000 invitations. By 10 pm . . . there was a line of people on St Mark's Place a half-block long . . . Four costumed karate experts slowly shepherded the customers – $15 a head . . . There was . . . the Fugs's Tuli Kupferberg . . . Out of the gigantic loudspeakers pranced the music . . . There were circus acts by a perfumed trapeze performer and an escape artist; the jugglers, however, couldn't make it because of the blinding strobes.'

19    'An Inevitable Circus Begs a Question of Temperature', www.streetsyoucrossed.blogspot.ca, 29 June 2005, and Alastair Gordon, 'What a Long Strange Trip It's Been: How the Psychedelic Aesthetic Morphed from Mind-blowing to Money-making', *Interior Design*, LXXVIII/3 (March 2007), p. 354.

20    Quoted in Frank Mastropolo, 'A Look Back at the Electric Circus, the Greatest Show on St Marks Place', www.bedfordandbowery.com, 17 September 2013.

21    Andrew Loog Oldham, *2Stoned* (New York, 2001), p. 116.

22    '17 July 1967', in Valkhoff, ed., 'Jimi Hendrix Lifelines, 1966–1967'.

23    Interview by Thomas 'Meatball Fulton' Lopez, 9 December 1967, for ZBS Radio, in Steven Roby, ed., *Hendrix on Hendrix: Interviews and Encounters* (Chicago, IL, 2012), p. 79.

24    Quoted in 'Lot 190: Jimi Hendrix's Epiphone FT79 guitar', www.bonhams.com, 15 December 2010; see also Kathy Etchingham with Andrew Crofts, *Through Gypsy Eyes: My Life, the 60s, and Jimi Hendrix* (London, 1998), pp. 99–100.

25    Etchingham and Crofts, *Through Gypsy Eyes*, pp. 99–100.

26    Ibid.

27    Quoted in 'All Along the Watchtower', www.en.wikipedia.org, accessed 20 July 2014.

28    Quoted in John Dolen, 'A Midnight Chat with Bob Dylan', *Fort Lauderdale Sun-Sentinel*, 29 September 1995, www.interferenza.net/bcs/interw/florida.htm.

29    Arthur Brown, and Tony Bramwell, quoted in Valkhoff, 'Jimi Hendrix Lifelines, 1966–1967', 27 August 1967.

30    Interview in Barnaby Thompson and Tom McGuinness, dir. and prod., *The*

*South Bank Show: Jimi Hendrix Documentary* (1989), 36 min.

31 Ibid., 38 min.

32 'About the Hall', www.royalalberthall.com, accessed 7 June 2014.

33 'Graham Nash Gets High with Jimi Hendrix and Brian Jones at a Frank Zappa Concert', www.youtube.com, accessed 7 June 2014.

34 Chris Grace, 'Uncle Meat Louie Louie (at the Royal Albert Hall in London)', www.arf.ru, accessed 15 July 2014. From a *Melody Maker* report on the Albert Hall concert: '"There is the mighty and majestic Royal Albert Hall Pipe Organ," said Zappa coolly as the audience fell about. Mother Don leapt from the stage and, like a mischievous ape, clambered up the balconies high above[,] settling into the organ nook. He fumbled about in the darkness and got a rousing ovation when he found the light switch. Zappa hitched his breeches and drawled into the mic, "Play something for the kids, Don, play something that'll really sock it to 'em – like 'Louie Louie.'" . . . when Zappa noticed Jimi entering the venue, he immediately went into a parody of "Hey Joe",' in Kees de Lange, 'Zappa Story #8 Part Two', *The Big Note*, www.thebignote.killuglyradio.com, accessed 15 July 2014.

35 De Lange, 'Zappa Story #8 Part Two'. Don Preston's performance on the Royal Albert Hall organ was recorded on Frank Zappa and the Mothers of Invention's album *Uncle Meat* (April 1969). '*Uncle Meat* (the album)', www.en.wikipedia.org, accessed 10 June 2014.

36 Quoted in 'Mick Taylor on Hendrix', www.crosstowntorrents.org, accessed 3 July 2014.

37 Mitch Mitchell and John Platt, *The Hendrix Experience* (London, 1998), p. 76.

38 Interview in Steven Vosburgh, dir., *Jimi Hendrix: The Uncut Story* (2004), 33 min.

39 Interview in Boyd, Head and Weis, 'From the Ukelele to the Strat', 43 min.

40 Michael Heatley, *Jimi Hendrix Gear: The Guitars, Amps and Effects that Revolutionized Rock 'n' Roll* (Minneapolis, MN, 2009), p. 87.

41 Quoted in Andy Doerschuk, 'The Hendrix Experience: Interview by Nicky Gebhart', www.mitchmitchell.de, February 1998.

42 Quoted in Sharon Lawrence, *Jimi Hendrix: The Intimate Story of a Betrayed Musical Legend* (New York, 2005), p. 112.

43 Timothy White, *The Nearest Faraway Place: Brian Wilson, the Beach Boys, and the Southern California Experience* (New York, 1994), p. 183.

44 Glenn Gould, *Variations*, ed. John McGreevy (Toronto, 1983), p. 231.

45 Quoted in William Saunders, *Jimi Hendrix London* (Berkeley, CA, 2010), p. 100.

46 '26 October 1966', in Ben Valkhoff, ed., 'Olympic or not Olympic, That is the Question', www.jimihendrix-lifelines.net.

47    Interviews in Boyd, Head and Weis, 'From the Ukelele to the Strat', 30–32
      min., and in Dick Meadows, 'Sounds Talk-in – Mitch Mitchell', *Sounds*, 11
      (December 1971), available at www.mitchmitchell.de.

48    Eric Burdon, *I Used to Be an Animal, but I'm All Right Now* (London, 1986), p. 84.

49    John Crome, dir., *Supershow* (1969; reissued 2003).

50    Dave Clemo, 'Straining to Be Heard', www.daveclemo-strainingtobeheard.
      blogspot.ca, 1 February 2012.

51    'JHE 2nd UK Tour November–December 1967', www.novdec1967.blogspot.ca,
      5 February 2010; 'Cinema City', www.glasgowfilm.org, accessed 18
      December 2014.

52    Tom Phillips, 'A Genuine Nightmare', *New York Times*, 12 November 1967,
      quoted in Henderson, *'Scuse Me While I Kiss the Sky*, p. 189: 'The Jimi Hendrix
      Experience is . . . three young musicians . . . with a stage act that's . . . enough
      to make a sailor blush. The album cover reinforces the degeneracy theme,
      with the three sneering out from under their bouffant hairdos looking like
      surrealistic hermaphrodites . . . the disc itself is a serious nightmare show,
      with genuine lust and misery . . . blending of simple folk-blues forms with
      advanced electronic sound effects . . . The sound is robust and hellish.'

53    'Jimi Hendrix – Sergeant Peppers', www.youtube.com, accessed 5 June 2014,
      and Ian Macintosh, 'A Hippy Remembers', *The Madcap Pages*,
      www.madcaplaughs.narod.ru, accessed 5 June 2014.

54    'The Apple Boutique Closes Down', www.beatlesbible.com, accessed
      5 June 2014.

55    Steven Roby, *Black Gold: The Lost Archives of Jimi Hendrix* (New York, 2002), p. 226.

56    David Pearcy, 'I was just Drunk', in 'King Jimi, He was There: Procol
      and Hendrix', www.procolharum.com, accessed 1 August 2014, and
      'Danish Newspaper Reports on Jimi Hendrix, 1967–1970', available at
      www.alrunen.melipona.org, August 1994/July 2001.

57    'HEN0082 Jimi Hendrix Autographed 1968 Swedish Court Documents, 1968',
      sale of Jimi Hendrix signature on court documents, www.tracks.co.uk,
      accessed 15 August 2014.

58    McDermott, *Hendrix: Setting the Record Straight*, p. 135.

59    John Perry, *Electric Ladyland* (London, 2004), note on p. 14.

60    Harry Shapiro and Caesar Glebbeek, *Jimi Hendrix: Electric Gypsy* (London,
      1992), pp. 676–82.

61    Interview with Noel Redding in Bob Smeaton, dir., *Jimi Hendrix: Hear my
      Train a Comin'* (2013), 55 min.

62    Interview with the concert promoter Larry Vaughn, in ibid., 53 min.

63   Interview ibid., 53–4 min.

64   Quoted in John McDermott with Eddie Kramer and Billy Cox, *Ultimate Hendrix: An Illustrated Encyclopedia of Live Concerts and Sessions* (Milwaukee, WI 2009), p. 94; quoted in 'Jimi Hendrix Custom Recording and Mixing Console', 20 October 2003, www.sites.google.com/site/hendrixconsole/home.

65   'The Dirty Tape', www.earlyhendrix.com, accessed 3 June 2014.

66   Quoted in Edwin Poncey, 'Alan Douglas, the Man who Sold the Underworld', *The Wire*, 161 (July 1997), p. 28.

67   Interview in 'Dreamer', Talk of the Town, *New Yorker* (31 December 1991), quoted in Chris Potash, *The Jimi Hendrix Companion: Three Decades of Commentary* (New York, 1996), p. 186.

68   A spectator posted a video of the Mark Boyle and Joan Hills light show on YouTube, with the following comment: 'Saw this kind of light show projected on a big movie screen behind Soft Machine when they opened for Hendrix at the Capitol Theater in Ottawa, Canada in March 1968.' 'Psychedelic Light Show UFO 1967: Soft Machine', www.youtube.com, accessed 10 June 2014.

69   Quoted in Karen O'Brien, *Joni Mitchell: Shadows and Light* (London, 2005), p. 82. Joni Mitchell's address in New York is given on p. 78.

70   Quoted ibid., p. 82. Hendrix's cursive writing in his diary on that date is reproduced in Janie Hendrix and John McDermott, *Jimi Hendrix: An Illustrated Experience* (New York, 2007), pp. 32–3.

71   Mitchell and Platt, *The Hendrix Experience*, p. 132.

72   Quoted in Sylvie Simmons, *I'm Your Man: The Life of Leonard Cohen* (Toronto, 2012), p. 161.

73   McDermott, Kramer and Cox, *The Ultimate Hendrix*, p. 98.

74   Eddie Kramer and Richard Buskin, 'Eddie Kramer Interview, Classic Tracks: Jimi Hendrix Experience, All Along The Watchtower', *Sound On Sound*, November 2005, www.soundonsound.com.

75   'Jack Casady: The Interview', www.epiphone.com, 29 March 2006.

76   Quoted in Johnny Black, *Jimi Hendrix: The Ultimate Experience* (New York, 1999), p. 147.

77   Interview with Andy Doerschuk, 'The Hendrix Experience: Interview by Nicky Gebhart', February 1998, available at www.mitchmitchell.de.

78   A. M. Nolan, *Rock 'n' Roll Road Trip: The Ultimate Guide to the Sites, the Shrines and the Legends Across America* (New York, 1992), p. 24.

79   'Carlos Santana on Jimi Hendrix', *Univibes: International Jimi Hendrix Magazine*, 17 (February 1995), in the Douglas J. Noble Guitar Archive, www.djnoble.demon.co.uk, accessed 10 February 2013.

80　Janis Ian, *Society's Child: My Autobiography* (New York, 2008), p. 87: 'I went down to the Village to see B. B. King . . . he was still playing some dive clubs. Jimi had introduced me to his music, and we made it a point to go see him together whenever possible. I loved that B. B. had named his guitar "Lucille." . . . B. B. was opening at the Generation Club for Big Brother & the Holding Company . . . Jimi finished his own gig early, and came to watch B. B.'s set with me. He was pretty pleased, because he'd bought the club just a little while earlier, intending to turn it into a studio. The two of us stood at the back of the club, slouched against a wall. The place was only half full, but somehow B. B.'s music always sounded better if you stood up . . . a man walked onstage and handed B. B. a note. B. B. read it, looked down at the floor for a while, then announced that Martin Luther King Jr. was now officially dead. We stood in silence against the wall, watching as B. B. clutched Lucille in his arms. Time stopped . . . I stayed at the club with Jimi until early morning.'

81　Chris Bishop, 'Jimi Hendrix Experience and the Soft Machine at the Virginia Beach Dome, 3 April 1968', *Garage Hangover*, 1 December 2007, www.garagehangover.com. (The other banned band was MC5, who incited attendees to riot during their show in a Hampton club.)

82　On a jam on 7 April 1968, see Ben Valkhoff, ed., with Kees de Lange and Johan van Wieren, 'The Jimi Hendrix/Roy Buchanan jam . . . True or False?', 'Jimi Hendrix Lifelines', accessed 5 June 2014.

83　Interview in Thompson and McGuinness, *The South Bank Show*, 35–7 min.

84　Michael Herr, *Dispatches* (New York, 1977), p. 158.

85　Interview with Bob Merlis, Warner Brothers Records executive, in Smeaton, *Hear my Train a Comin'*, 1:08 min.

86　Quoted in McDermott, Kramer and Cox, *Ultimate Hendrix*, p. 105.

## 6 HEAVY TOURING

1　Interview with Dick Meadows, 'Sounds Talk-in – Mitch Mitchell', *Sounds*, 11 (December 1971), available at www.mitchmitchell.de.

2　'Interview with John Burks', 4 February 1970, in Steven Roby, ed., *Hendrix on Hendrix: Interviews and Encounters* (Chicago, IL, 2012), p. 265.

3　Paul Rosano, 'Concerts Vol. 13: Jimi Hendrix', www.thetrickismusic.com, February 2011.

4　Comment posted by 'simmons51', 'Jimi Hendrix: An Electronic Thanksgiving at Philharmonic Hall, 28 November 1968', www.classic-rock-concerts.com, 4 April 2011.

5 Ioana Satescu, quoted in 'Carnegie Won't Experience', *Danneville Virginia Register*, 17 November 1969, p. 34, available at www.crosstowntorrents.org, accessed 7 August 2014.

6 Quoted in feature interview with Bob Dawbarn, *Melody Maker*, 1 March 1969, in Steven Roby, *Black Gold: The Lost Archives of Jimi Hendrix* (New York, 2002), p. 237, n. 21; see also *Univibes*, 42 (August 2002).

7 Michael Heatley, *Jimi Hendrix Gear: The Guitars, Amps and Effects that Revolutionized Rock 'n' Roll* (Minneapolis, MN, 2009), p. 92.

8 Quoted in John McDermott with Eddie Kramer and Billy Cox, *Ultimate Hendrix: An Illustrated Encyclopedia of Live Concerts and Sessions* (Milwaukee, WI, 2009), p. 103.

9 Quoted in 'Lot 190: Jimi Hendrix's Epiphone FT79 guitar', www.bonhams.com, 15 December 2010.

10 Kathy Etchingham with Andrew Crofts, *Through Gypsy Eyes: My Life, the 60s, and Jimi Hendrix* (London, 1998), p. 134.

11 Jane de Mendelssohn, interview with Jimi Hendrix, in Roby, *Hendrix on Hendrix*, pp. 165–77.

12 'Experience Jimi Hendrix', CBC Digital Archives, 23 February 1969, available at www.cbc.ca.

13 'The Woburn Music Festival, 6–7 July 1968', www.ukrockfestivals.com, accessed January 2015.

14 A natural amphitheatre, Denver Red Rocks was designed by the architect Burnham Hoyt in 1928. 'History and Geology, Red Rocks Park and Amphitheater', www.redrocksonline.com, accessed 10 August 2014.

15 Tony Brown, *Jimi Hendrix in his Own Words* (London, 1999), pp. 33–4.

16 Quoted in John Lombardi, 'The Jimi Hendrix Experience: Slowing Down and Growing Up', in *Distant Drummer* (17–23 April 1969), in Roby, *Hendrix on Hendrix*, pp. 180–81.

17 Interview in Peter Piliafan, dir., *Jimi Plays Berkeley* (1971; reissued 2010), 5 min.

18 Quoted in William Saunders, *Jimi Hendrix London* (Berkeley, CA, 2010), p. 94.

19 Quoted in J.L.L. Locher, 'Mark Boyle's Journey to the Surface of the Earth', www.boylefamily.co.uk, accessed 5 June 2014.

20 Jimi Hendrix, *Cherokee Mist: The Lost Writings*, ed. Bill Nitopi (New York, 1993), p. 32.

21 'Welcome to Cerebrum, Do You Have a Reservation?', www.theboweryboys.blogspot.ca, 4 December 2009, and Bart Friedman, 'Cerebrum, Soho, 1968', www.youtube.com, 26 February 2009.

22  'Welcome to Cerebrum', and Bart Friedman, 'Cerebrum was an Influence', www.bartfriedman.blogspot.ca, 6 May 2009.

23  Both quoted in Alastair Gordon, 'What a Long Strange Trip It's Been: How the Psychedelic Aesthetic Morphed from Mind-blowing to Money-making', *Interior Design*, LXXVIII/3 (March 2007), p. 354.

24  Harry Shapiro and Caesar Glebbeek, *Jimi Hendrix: Electric Gypsy* (London, 1992), pp. 288–9.

25  There is 8 mm film from the Zurich Monster concert; see Roby, *Black Gold*, p. 232.

26  William W. Jablon, 'Hendrix Experience was Tame Show', *St Petersburg Times*, 20 August 1968, in Jay Cridlin, 'Jimi Hendrix Delivers "Bad Trip", "Tame Show" at Tampa's Curtis Hixon Hall in 1968', www.tampabay.com, 27 November 2012.

27  Quoted in Kay Donahue, 'The "Experience" Offers Bad Trip', *Evening Independent*, 25 November 1968, in Cridlin, 'Jimi Hendrix Delivers "Bad Trip"'.

28  Interview with Terry D. Mulligan for *Good Rockin' Tonight*, 7 September 1968, quoted in Bob Smeaton, dir., *Jimi Hendrix: Hear my Train a Comin'* (2013), 1:27 min.; also Terry David Mulligan, 'Jimi Hendrix: B/W Interview Vancouver BC 7/7/68', 7 July 1968, www.youtube.com, accessed 3 June 2014.

29  Quoted in Janie Hendrix and John McDermott, *Jimi Hendrix: An Illustrated Experience* (New York, 2007), p. 43.

30  Ibid.

31  Mitch Mitchell and Billy Cox interview, *Guitar World*, www.jimihendrix.forumactif.org, October 2005.

32  Toronto Airport was then called Malton Airport (also called Aeroquay One); it was designed by John B. Parkin and Associates and built in 1957–64. 'Toronto Pearson International Airport', www.en.wikipedia.org, accessed 10 June 2014.

33  Mary Ishimoto Morris, review of Sharon Lawrence, *Jimi Hendrix: The Man, The Magic, The Truth*, www.washingtonpost.com, 15 May 2005.

34  Quoted in Ritchie Yorke, 'The Gypsy Sun Jimi Hendrix', *Hit Parader* (January 1969); quoted in Ray Brack, interview with the Experience (10 May 1969), *Charleston Gazette*, 17 May 1969, in Shapiro and Glebbeek, *Jimi Hendrix*, pp. 362–4 and p. 513, n. 1.

35  Ibid.

36  Roby, *Black Gold*, p. 123.

37  'City Realty Top Ten Residential Buildings Designed by Emery Roth', www.cityrealty.com, accessed 10 June 2014.

38  Roby, *Black Gold*, p. 127.

39  Quoted in Steven Roby, 'Melinda Merryweather: Interview', *Straight*

*Ahead*, LXXIX–LXXX (October–November 1995), available at www.newyorkhendrix.gobot.com; Steven Roby, *Black Gold*, p. 128.

40  Kirk Silsbee and Linda Grasso, 'Festival Forgotten', *Our Ventura Boulevard*, www.ourventurablvd.com, February–March 2013; 'Jimi Hendrix – Devonshire Downs Pop Festival', parts 1, 2 and 3, www.youtube.com, 9 August 2010.

41  'Jimi Hendrix Experience, Live at the Denver Pop Festival, Denver 6/29/1969 – Part 1, Part 2', www.jimihendrix.com, accessed 3 January 2014.

42  Shapiro and Glebbeek, *Jimi Hendrix*, p. 690.

43  Quoted in Joe Boyd, John Head and Gary Weis, dir., 'From the Ukelele to the Strat', bonus film in *A Film about Jimi Hendrix* (1973; reissued 2005), 35 min.

44  The video recording of *The Tonight Show* hosted by Flip Wilson on 10 July 1969 is lost. Audio and transcripts remain; they are published online and in 'The Tonight Show Interview', in Roby, *Hendrix on Hendrix*, pp. 207–11.

45  'The Dick Cavett Show Interview', 9 September 1969, in Roby, *Hendrix on Hendrix*, pp. 219–25.

46  'Walk on the Wild Side Tour', New York City, www.maps.google.com, accessed 9 August 2014.

47  Quoted in Roby, *Hendrix on Hendrix*, pp. 215–16. For another account of the Harlem Block Association concert, see Chris Hodenfield, 'Experience Break-up: Noel Splits and Jimi Moves Uptown', *Circus* (November 1969), available at www.jimihendrix.forumactif.org, accessed 5 September 2014.

48  Ungano's, 210 West 70th Street, between Amsterdam and West End Avenues. Hendrix jammed with Elvin Bishop and Buddy Miles on 1 January 1970. See www.jimihendrix.com, accessed 5 September 2014.

49  Quoted in Edwin Pouncey, 'Alan Douglas: The Man Who Sold the Underworld', *The Wire*, 161 (July 1997), p. 29, available at www.alandouglas.com; 'Doriella du Fontaine', www.youtube.com, accessed 15 July 2014.

50  Jack Chambers, *Milestones II: The Music and Times of Miles Davis since 1960* (Toronto, 1985), p. 215.

51  Miles Davis with Quincy Troupe, *Miles: The Autobiography* (New York, 1989), p. 300.

52  Chambers, *Milestones II*, p. 219.

53  Quoted in 'The Queen versus James Marshall Hendrix' [8–9 December 1969], *FBI Records: The Vault*, www.vault.fbi.gov, accessed 15 June 2014.

54  Quoted ibid.

55  Interview in Boyd, Head and Weis, 'From the Ukelele to the Strat', 56 min.

56  Interview in Bob Smeaton, dir., *Band of Gypsys* (2011), 44 sec. and 116 min.

57  Interview in Boyd, Head and Weis, 'From the Ukulele to the Strat', 14 min.

58 Interview in Smeaton, *Band of Gypsys*, 30 min.

59 Quoted in McDermott, Kramer and Cox, *Ultimate Hendrix*, p. 193.

60 Ibid., p. 197.

61 Warner Bros executive, quoted in Smeaton, *Hear My Train a Comin'*, 1:44 min.

62 Interview ibid., 1:42 min.

63 Ballin' Jack supported on 25 April, Forum, Los Angeles (with Buddy Miles Express); 5 June, Dallas Memorial Auditorium; 6 June, Sam Houston Coliseum, Houston; 7 June, Assembly Center Arena, Tulsa; 13 June, Civic Center, Baltimore (with Cactus); 21 June, County Fairgrounds, Ventura, California (with Grin); 22 June, Mammoth Gardens, Denver (with Grin). There was no opening act on 9 June, at Mid-South Coliseum, Memphis, or 10 June, Roberts Municipal Stadium, Evansville, Indiana. Shapiro and Glebbeek, *Jimi Hendrix*, p. 693.

64 Charles Cross, *Room Full of Mirrors: A Biography of Jimi Hendrix* (New York, 2005), p. 291.

65 Gary Comenas, 'Andy Warhol's My Hustler', 2003 (revd 2015), www.warholstars.org.

66 Quoted in Roby, 'Melinda Merryweather'.

67 Matthew Griffin, Susanne Herrmann and Friedrich A. Kittler, 'Technologies of Writing: Interview with Friedrich A. Kittler', *New Literary History*, XXVII/4 (Autumn 1996), pp. 731–42.

68 Quoted in Roby, 'Melinda Merryweather'.

69 Mel Stuart, dir., *Wattstax* (1973); Sidney J. Furie, dir., *Lady Sings the Blues* (1972).

70 Roby, *Black Gold*, p. 202.

71 Interview in Piliafan, *Jimi Plays Berkeley*, 12 min.; see also and Harvey Kubernik, 'Jimi Plays Berkeley', www.recordcollectornews.com, October 2012.

72 'Johanincr', '1970-07-17 NY Pop – "The Day The Music Died" DVD', www.crosstowntorrents.org, accessed 3 September 2014.

73 Tom Tannahil, 'Houston Rocks', www.ruf.rice.edu, accessed 5 July 2014.

74 Françoise Choay, 'De la demolition', in *Les Métamorphoses Parisiennes* (Paris, 1996); available in English as 'On Demolition', www.architectureinphilosophy.wikispaces.com, accessed 15 August 2014.

75 Alex Ross, 'Searching for Silence: John Cage's Art of Noise', *New Yorker*, 4 October 2010, p. 52.

76 Quoted in Hendrix and McDermott, *Hendrix: An Illustrated Experience*, p. 45.

77 Juma Sultan interviewed in Paul Smart, 'Are You Experienced?', Parts I and II, *Woodstock Times*, www.woodstock.ulsterpublishing.com, 1 September 2011.

78   Velez quoted in John McDermott, with Eddie Kramer and Billy Cox, *Jimi Hendrix Sessions* (New York, 1995), p. 111; Sultan interviewed in Boyd, Head and Weis, 'From the Ukelele to the Strat', 55 min.
79   Quoted in Shapiro and Glebbeek, *Jimi Hendrix*, p. 389. Jeffery's address is given in Hendrix and Nitopi, *Cherokee Mist*, p. 123.
80   Mitchell and Platt, *The Hendrix Experience*, p. 142; Mitchell, quoted in Andy Aledort, 'Jimi Hendrix: Star Power', *Guitar World* (October 2005), available at www.guitarworld.com, p. 2.
81   Sherman Alexie, 'Because my Father Always Said he was the Only Indian who Saw Jimi Hendrix Play "The Star-Spangled Banner" at Woodstock', in *The Lone Ranger and Tonto Fistfight in Heaven* (New York, 1993), p. 26.
82   Harlem United Block Association press conference, Frank's Restaurant, 125th Street, 5 September 1969, transcription in Roby, *Hendrix on Hendrix*, p. 217.
83   Quoted in Jeff Tamarkin, *Got a Revolution: The Turbulent Flight of Jefferson Airplane* (New York, 2003), p. 206.
84   Jon Brewer, dir., *Legends of the Canyon: Classic Artists* (Image Entertainment, 2010), DVD.
85   David Fricke, *Rolling Stone* journalist, in Smeaton, *Hear My Train a Comin'*, 1:36–1:37 min.
86   Murray Lerner, dir., *Message to Love: The Isle of Wight Music Festival, 1970* (1997), 37–38 min (Yogi Joe), 56 min (Joni Mitchell).
87   Quoted in John Lewis, 'Gilberto Gil and Caetano Veloso in London', *The Guardian*, www.theguardian.com, 15 July 2010.
88   Interview with Chris Romberg and Sergeant Keith Roberts in the dressing room prior to the performance on 4 September 1970, at Superconcert 70, Deutschlandhalle, Berlin, broadcast on Armed Forces Network in Germany in late September 1970; in Roby, *Hendrix on Hendrix*, p. 311.
89   'September 6th, 1970', www.fehmarnfestival1970.com, accessed 5 August 2014.
90   Quoted in 'Eyewitnesses', www.fehmarnfestival1970.com, accessed 5 August 2014.
91   Quoted ibid.
92   'September 5th, 1970', www.fehmarnfestival1970.com, accessed 5 August 2014.
93   'Aftermath', www.fehmarnfestival1970.com, accessed 5 August 2014.
94   Michael Herr, *Dispatches* (New York, 1977), p. 215.
95   Ibid., p. 180.
96   Ibid., pp. 8, 235.
97   Quoted in Tony Brown, *Jimi Hendrix in his Own Words* (London, 1999), p. 38.
98   Shapiro and Glebbeek, *Jimi Hendrix*, p. 390.
99   Quoted in McDermott, Kramer and Cox, *Ultimate Hendrix*, p. 138.

100   Shapiro and Glebbeek, *Jimi Hendrix*, p. 391.

101   Interview in Smeaton, *Hear My Train a Comin'*, 1:43–1:44 min.

102   Tony Barrow, *John, Paul, George, Ringo and Me: The Real Beatles Story* (London, 2005), pp. 234–48.

103   Quoted in Vanessa Thorpe, 'Sadie Frost's Psychedelic Artist Father Gets his Due – With a Little Help from Ray Davies', *The Observer*, 11 May 2014, www.theguardian.com.

104   Kiesler, who struggled through the Depression, eventually found a steady source of income teaching stage design at the Juilliard School in Manhattan. He designed the Art of this Century Gallery on the seventh floor of 30 West 57th Street for Peggy Guggenheim; it opened on 20 October 1942 and lasted until 1947.

## CONCLUSION

1   Quoted in Steven Roby and Brad Schreiber, *Becoming Jimi Hendrix: From Southern Crossroads to Psychedelic London: The Untold Story of a Musical Genius* (New York, 2010), p. 145.

2   Interview (28 August 1970) in Roy Hollingworth, 'Hendrix Today', *Melody Maker*, 5 September 1970, in Steven Roby, ed., *Hendrix on Hendrix: Interviews and Encounters* (Chicago, IL, 2012), p. 285.

3   Jacques Attali, *Bruits* (Paris, 1977), p. 9.

4   Quoted in Keith Altham, 'Hendrix: "I'd Like a Hit Single . . ."', *Melody Maker*, 9 May 1970, in Roby, *Hendrix on Hendrix*, p. 271.

5   Mitch Mitchell and Billy Cox interview, *Guitar World*, October 2005, available at www.jimihendrix.forumactif.org, accessed 9 August 2014.

6   Interview (25 May 1967) with Klas Burling for Swedish Radio, Pop 67 Special, broadcast 28 May 1967; transcription in Roby, *Hendrix on Hendrix*, p. 40.

7   Interview with Mike Bloomfield, *Guitar Player* (September 1975), available at www.montereyhendrix.gobot.com.

8   Marshall McLuhan and Quentin Fiore, *The Medium is the Massage: An Inventory of Effects* (New York, 1967), p. 44.

9   Interviewed by Buck Walmsley of *Chicago Daily News*, 24 February 1968, in Harry Shapiro and Caesar Glebbeek, *Jimi Hendrix: Electric Gypsy* (London, 1992), p. 264.

# SELECT BIBLIOGRAPHY

**BOOKS**

Attali, Jacques, *Bruits* (Paris, 1977)

Black, Johnny, *Jimi Hendrix: The Ultimate Experience* (New York, 1999)

Blecha, Peter, *Rock & Roll Archeologist* (Seattle, WA, 2005)

Bockris, Victor, *Transformer: The Complete Lou Reed Story* (London, 2014)

Bowman, Rob, *Soulsville: The Story of Stax Records* (New York, 1997)

Boyd, Joe, *White Bicycles: Making Music in the 1960s* (London, 2006)

Brown, Tony, *Jimi Hendrix Concert Files* (London, 1999)

——, *Jimi Hendrix: The Final Days* (London, 1997)

——, *Jimi Hendrix in his Own Words* (London, 1994)

Burdon, Eric, *I Used to Be an Animal, but I'm All Right Now* (London, 1986)

Charles, Ray, and David Ritz, *Brother Ray: Ray Charles' Own Story*
    (New York, 1978)

Clapton, Eric, *Clapton: The Autobiography* (New York, 2007)

Cross, Charles, *Room Full of Mirrors: A Biography of Jimi Hendrix* (New York, 2005)

Davies, Dave, *Kink* (New York, 1996)

Davies, Ray, *X-Ray* (London, 1994)

Davis, Angela, *Blues Legacies and Black Feminism: Gertrude 'Ma' Rainey, Bessie
    Smith, and Billie Holiday* (New York, 1998)

Davis, Miles, with Quincy Troupe, *Miles: The Autobiography* (New York, 1989)

De Barros, Paul, *Jackson Street After Hours: The Roots of Jazz in Seattle* (Seattle,
    WA, 1993)

Dixon, Willie, with Don Snowden, *The Willie Dixon Story* (New York, 1989)

Etchingham, Kathy, with Andrew Crofts, *Through Gypsy Eyes: My Life, the 60s,
    and Jimi Hendrix* (London, 1998)

Frith, Simon, Will Straw and John Street, eds, *The Cambridge Companion to Pop
    and Rock* (Cambridge, 2001)

Geldeart, Gary, and Steve Rodham, *Jimi Hendrix from the Benjamin Franklin Studios: The Complete Guide to the Recorded Works of Jimi Hendrix* (Cheshire, 2008)

Gillette, Charlie, *The Sound of the City: The Rise of Rock and Roll* [1970] (New York, 1996)

Gordon, Alastair, *Spaced Out: Radical Environments of the Psychedelic Sixties* (New York, 2008)

Guralnick, Peter, *Dream Boogie: The Triumph of Sam Cooke* (New York, 2005)

——, *Sweet Soul Music: Rhythm and Blues and the Southern Dream of Freedom* (New York, 1986)

Heatley, Michael, *Jimi Hendrix Gear: The Guitars, Amps and Effects that Revolutionized Rock 'n' Roll* (Minneapolis, MN, 2009)

Henderson, David, *'Scuse Me While I Kiss the Sky* (New York, 2008)

Hendrix, James A., *My Son Jimi* (Seattle, WA, 1999)

Hendrix, Janie L., and John McDermott, *Jimi Hendrix: An Illustrated Experience* (New York, 2007)

Hendrix, Jimi, *Cherokee Mist: The Lost Writings*, ed. Bill Nitopi (New York, 1993)

Hendrix, Leon, with Adam Mitchell, *Jimi Hendrix: A Brother's Story* (New York, 2012)

Herr, Michael, *Dispatches* (New York, 1977)

Hopkins, Jerry, *Jimi Hendrix Experience* [1983] (New York, 1996)

Hoskyns, Barry, *Across the Great Divide: The Band and America* (London, 1993, 1994)

James, Tommy, with Martin Fitzpatrick, *Me, the Mob and the Music* (New York, 2010)

Johnson, John, and Joel Selvin, with Dick Cami, *Peppermint Twist: The Mob, the Music, and the Most Famous Dance Club of the '60s* (New York, 2012)

Knight, Curtis, *Jimi: An Intimate Biography of Jimi Hendrix* (London, 1974)

Lawrence, Sharon, *Jimi Hendrix: The Intimate Story of a Betrayed Musical Legend* (New York, 2005)

Lydon, Michael, *Flashbacks: Eyewitness Accounts of the Rock Revolution, 1964–1974* (New York, 2003)

McDermott, John, with Eddie Kramer, *Hendrix: Setting the Record Straight*, ed. Mark Lewisohn (New York, 1992)

——, with Eddie Kramer and Billy Cox, *Ultimate Hendrix: An Illustrated Encyclopedia of Live Concerts and Sessions* (Milwaukee, WI, 2009)

——, with Eddie Kramer and Billy Cox, *Jimi Hendrix Sessions* (New York, 1995)

McLuhan, Marshall, and Quentin Fiore, *The Medium is the Massage: An Inventory of Effects* (New York, 1967)

Mitchell, Mitch, and John Platt, *The Hendrix Experience* (London, 1990)

Moskowitz, David, *Jimi Hendrix: The Words and Music* (Santa Barbara, CA, 2010)

Murray, Charles Shaar, *Crosstown Traffic: Jimi Hendrix and Post-war Pop* [1989] (London, 2001)

Nash, Graham, *Wild Tales: A Rock and Roll Life* (New York, 2013)

Nolan, A. M., *Rock 'n' Roll Road Trip: The Ultimate Guide to the Sites, the Shrines and the Legends Across America* (New York, 1992)

O'Brien, Karen, *Joni Mitchell: Shadows and Light* (London, 2005)

Oldham, Andrew Loog, *Stoned: A Memoir of London in the 1960s* (New York, 1998)

——, *2Stoned* (New York, 2001)

Perry, John, *Electric Ladyland* (London, 2004)

Potash, Chris, *The Jimi Hendrix Companion: Three Decades of Commentary* (New York, 1996)

Redding, Noel, and Carol Appleby, *Are You Experienced? The Inside Story of the Hendrix Experience* (London, 1990)

Richards, Keith, with James Fox, *Life* (New York, 2010)

Roby, Steven, *Black Gold: The Lost Archives of Jimi Hendrix* (New York, 2002)

——, ed., *Hendrix on Hendrix: Interviews and Encounters* (Chicago, IL, 2012)

——, and Brad Schreiber, *Becoming Jimi Hendrix: From Southern Crossroads to Psychedelic London: The Untold Story of a Musical Genius* (New York, 2010)

Saunders, William, *Jimi Hendrix London* (Berkeley, CA, 2010)

Schafer, R. Murray, *The Tuning of the World* (Toronto, 1977)

Selvin, Joel, *Here Comes the Night: The Dark Soul of Bert Berns and the Dirty Business of Rhythm and Blues* (Berkeley, CA, 2014)

Shadwick, Keith, *Jimi Hendrix Musician* (London, 2003)

Shapiro, Harry, and Caesar Glebbeek, *Jimi Hendrix: Electric Gypsy* (London, 1990)

Stubbs, David, *Jimi Hendrix: The Stories Behind Every Song* (London, 2002, 2010)

Tate, Greg, *Midnight Lightning: Jimi Hendrix and the Black Experience* (Chicago, IL, 2003)

Townshend, Pete, *Who I Am: A Memoir* (London, 2012)

White, Charles, *The Life and Times of Little Richard: The Authorized Biography* (London, 2003)

Willix, Mary, *Voices from Home* (Seattle, WA, 1995)

Zappa, Frank, with Peter Occiogrosso, *The Real Frank Zappa* (New York, 1989)

## ARTICLES AND ESSAYS

Adams, Marcus K., 'The Racialization of Jimi Hendrix', Senior Honours thesis, Eastern Michigan University, Ypsilanti (2007)

'Jimi Hendrix, Speaking for Himself', *Rolling Stone* (9 March 1968), in *The Rolling Stone Rock 'n' Roll Reader* (New York, 1974), pp. 289–94

McClure, Daniel R., '"Have You Understood Anything I've Said?": The Dick Cavett Show, Jimi Hendrix, and the Framing of the Black Counterculture in 1969', *The Sixties: A Journal of History, Politics and Culture*, v / 1 (2012), pp. 23–46

Zak III, Albin J., 'Bob Dylan and Jimi Hendrix: Juxtaposition and Transformation "All along the Watchtower"', *Journal of the American Musicological Society*, LVII / 3 (Autumn 2004), pp. 599–644

## DVDS

Archibald, Laura, dir., *Greenwich Village: Music that Defined a Generation* (2013)

Boyd, Joe, John Head and Gary Weis, dir., *A Film about Jimi Hendrix* (including bonus film, 'From the Ukulele to the Strat') (1973; reissued 2005)

Brewer, Jon, dir., *Legends of the Canyon: Classic Artists* (Image Entertainment, 2010)

Hendrix, Janie, and John McDermott, prod. *Live at Woodstock* (2010)

*Jimi Hendrix: The Complete Story* (2007)

Lerner, Murray, dir., *Message to Love: The Isle of Wight Festival, the Movie* (1970; reissued 1995)

——, dir., *Jimi Hendrix: Blue Wild Angel Live at the Isle of Wight* (2011)

McMahon, Kevin, and David Sobelman, dir., *McLuhan's Wake* (2002)

O'Dell, Tom, dir., *From Straight to Bizarre: Zappa, Beefheart, Alice Cooper and LA's Lunatic Fringe* (2011)

——, *Going Underground: Paul McCartney, The Beatles and the UK Counter-culture* (2013)

Pennebaker, D. A., and Chris Hegedus, dir., *Jimi Plays Monterey* (1986), in *The Complete Monterey Pop Festival* (1997; reissued 2002)

Pilafian, Peter, dir., *Jimi Hendrix: Jimi Plays Berkeley* (1971)

Smeaton, Bob, dir., *Jimi Hendrix: Band of Gypsys* (2011)

——, dir., *Jimi Hendrix Hear My Train a Comin'* (2013)

——, dir., *West Coast Seattle Boy: Jimi Hendrix: Voodoo Child* (2010)

*Syd Barrett Under Review: An Independent Critical Analysis* (2005)

Thompson, Barnaby, and Tom McGuinness, dir. and prod., *Jimi Hendrix Documentary* (1973)

Vosburgh, Steven, dir., *Jimi Hendrix: The Uncut Story* (2004)
Wein, Chuck, dir., *Jimi Hendrix: Rainbow Bridge* (1971)
Weissbrod, Ellen, dir., *Listen Up! The Lives of Quincy Jones* (2009)


## WEBSITES

www.crosstowntorrents.org
www.earlyhendrix.com
www.hendrix-in-deutschland.blogspot.ca
www.theisleofhendrix.gobot.com
www.jimihendrix.com
www.jimihendrix.forumactif.org
www.jimihendrix-lifelines.net
www.jimpress.co.uk
www.novdec1967.blogspot.ca
www.picturesofjimi.com
www.soul-patrol.com

# DISCOGRAPHY

The Jimi Hendrix Experience, *Are You Experienced*, Reprise / Track Records, 1967
The Jimi Hendrix Experience, *Axis: Bold as Love*, Reprise / Track Records, 1968
The Jimi Hendrix Experience, *Electric Ladyland*, Reprise / Track Records, 1968
The Jimi Hendrix Experience, *Smash Hits*, Reprise / Track Records, 1969, 1968
Band of Gypsys, *Band of Gypsys*, Capitol / Track Records, 1970
The Jimi Hendrix Experience, *Stages* (four-cassette box set), Warner Bros, 1991
Jimi Hendrix, *Stages*, Reprise, 1991
Jimi Hendrix, *First Rays of the New Rising Sun*, Experience Hendrix LLC, MCA, 1997
Jimi Hendrix, *South Saturn Delta*, Experience Hendrix LLC, MCA, 1997
The Jimi Hendrix Experience, *The Jimi Hendrix Experience* ('The Purple Box')
      (four-CD box set), Experience Hendrix LLC, MCA, 2000
Jimi Hendrix, *Blues*, Experience Hendrix LLC, MCA, 1994; Sony, 2010
Jimi Hendrix, *Valleys of Neptune*, Sony (Legacy Recordings), 2010
The Jimi Hendrix Experience, *Winterland Experience*, Sony (Legacy Recordings), 2011
Jimi Hendrix, *People, Hell and Angels*, Sony (Legacy Recordings), 2013
The Jimi Hendrix Experience, *Miami Pop Festival*, Sony (Legacy Recordings), 2013

# ACKNOWLEDGEMENTS

I would like to acknowledge the influence of the contemporary sounds of 'Quand le Jazz est là', by Stanley Péan, on Radio-Canada, which is transmitted daily and nightly five days a week. Several used and new book and record stores proved to be good places to acquire vinyl, books, DVDs and CDs, including Select Sounds of Bedford Nova Scotia, Drawn and Quarterly and Archambault in Montreal, Soundscapes and Bay Street Video in Toronto, KW Bookstore in Kitchener and Word Bookstore in Waterloo.

Places of research included the libraries of Dalhousie University and NSCAD University in Halifax, Nova Scotia, the Marvin Duchow Music Library of McGill University, the Université du Québec à Montréal Music Library in Montreal, the Toronto Reference Library, the Music Library of the University of Toronto, as well as the Dana Porter Library at the University of Waterloo.

Jared Leon of the POP Montréal Symposium invited me to participate in discussion on 18 September 2014, led by Will Straw, that brought together musicians, club owners and the public for an interesting dialogue. The Center for American Architecture and Design at the University of Texas at Austin hosted the Music in Architecture – Architecture in Music Symposium in October 2011, and published an award-winning book of conference proceedings, CENTER 18: Music in Architecture – Architecture in Music, in 2014, including my contribution on the urban geography of a musical trajectory, 'The London Flat and Manhattan Studio of Jimi Hendrix'.

I would like to thank Aimee Selby, Michael Leaman and John Scanlan at Reaktion Books for their professional expertise. The musical erudition of Ron Foley Macdonald and of the Lévesque, Almon and Macdonald families has been an ongoing inspiration. A very early influence was the 1970s Halifax Arrow's Club, founded by William 'Billy' Downey, who scouted at Montreal clubs, including the Esquire and the Rockhead, for his Brunswick Street nightclub, booking such acts as Ike & Tina Turner and Sam & Dave before it closed in 1979.

# PHOTO ACKNOWLEDGEMENTS

The author and the publishers wish to express their thanks to the below sources of illustrative material and/or permission to reproduce it.

Robert Altman: p. 48; Robert J. Boser, Editor asc, www.airlinesafety.com/ editorials/AboutTheEditor.htm (CC): p. 193; Michael Bowen: p. 38; Environmental Design Archives, University of California Berkeley: p. 47; Iconic Images Ltd: p. 239; Islington Local History Centre: pp. 130, 131; John McAslan + Partners: p. 125 (photographer Guy Montagu-Pollock); Joe Mabel: p. 34; courtesy B. Macdonald Collection: pp. 140, 141, 165; Marie-Paule Macdonald: pp. 58, 103, 188, 190, 203, 233; courtesy of Roger Mayer: p. 214; Museum of the City of New York: p. 102; Seattle Municipal Archives: p. 30; John Stamets: p. 24; courtesy John Storyk, WSDG: p. 234; U.S. Geological Survey: p. 60; A. Vente: p. 146.

# INDEX